The Institute of British Geographers
Special Publications Series

24 Teaching Geography in Higher Education

The Institute of British Geographers
Special Publications Series

EDITOR: Dr N. J. Thrift
University of Bristol

For a complete list see pp. 261-262

Teaching Geography in Higher Education

A Manual of Good Practice

John R. Gold, Alan Jenkins, Roger Lee, Janice Monk,
Judith Riley, Ifan Shepherd and David Unwin

Basil Blackwell

Copyright © The Institute of British Geographers, 1991

First published 1991

Basil Blackwell Ltd
108 Cowley Road, Oxford OX4 1JF, UK

Basil Blackwell, Inc.
3 Cambridge Center
Cambridge, Massachusetts 02142, USA

British Library Cataloging in Publication Data

A CIP catalogue record for this book is available from the British Libary.

Library of Congress Cataloging in Publication Data

Teaching geography in higher education: a manual of good practice/
John R. Gold . . . [et al.]
  p.   cm.—(Institute of British Geographers special
publications series; 24)
  Includes bibliographical references and index.
  ISBN 0-631-15726-3
  1. Geography—Study and teaching (Higher)   I. Gold, John Robert.
II. Series: Special publications series (Institute of British Geographers); no. 24.
G73.T422 1991
910'.71'141——dc20   90-1038
                                                      CIP

Typeset in 11 on 13 point Plantin
by Dobbie Typesetting Limited, Tavistock, Devon
Printed in Great Britain by The Alden Press Ltd, Oxford

Contents

Preface

For a book written jointly by seven individuals, this volume has a comparatively straightforward history. The authors have long worked together as part of the editorial group that produces the *Journal of Geography in Higher Education* (*JGHE*), a publication founded in 1976 on the belief that teaching has been consistently undervalued in geographical higher education. Several years ago, a good friend in academic publishing suggested that what we were saying in the *JGHE* was important and merited a book that would present its ideas to the wider geographical audience.

The result is the book that you see before you. It is concerned primarily with the practicalities of teaching geography in higher education and is written for anyone with a current, or prospective, interest in such teaching. Responsibility for producing the first drafts of the various chapters was assigned to particular individuals, but the drafts were subsequently discussed at a series of seminars and rewritten – often by another author. The final outcome is a genuinely collective product of both teaching and learning.

In the process of writing, we have been assisted by a large number of good-natured and long-suffering friends. These include Lee Andresen, Alan Backler, Jacquelyn Beyer, Tim Burt, John Cowan, John Fien, Dee Fink, Colin Flood Page, Pip Forer, Vincent Gardiner, Rod Gerber, Graham Gibbs, Margaret Gold, Peter Gould, Norman Graves, Martin Haigh, Graham Humphrys, Nick Isbister, David Jaques, Alan Jones, Sally Marston, Joe Powell, Derek Rowntree, Iain Stephenson, Paul Tranter, David Walker and Tom Wilkinson. As ever, we bear the sole responsibility for our own follies. Above all, we thank our colleagues on the editorial board of the *JGHE*, past and present, who have all contributed to making this book a reality.

Finally, we would also like to record our formal gratitude for permission to reproduce copyright material here to the Johnson Foundation of Racine, Wisconsin, Martin Secker and Warburg, the National Council for Educational Technology and the editorial board of the *JGHE*.

1

Introduction

1.1 WHAT THIS BOOK IS ABOUT

In the film *The Magnificent Seven*, the character played by Steve McQueen tells a story about a man who jumped out of a building several storeys high. As he passed each floor, the man called out 'so far, so good' to the startled onlookers. From our point of view, the story provides an apt analogy for the state of geography teaching in higher education: heading for an inevitable outcome but hoping that gravity and mass can be defied, or at least suspended, for the duration of the fall.

Geography teaching, like other areas of teaching in higher education, faces severe pressures from inadequate funding, but these are compounded by the fact that teachers in higher education are obliged to divert ever-greater amounts of their time and energy into such non-teaching activities as entrepreneurship, making grant applications and administering scarce resources. In saying this, we recognize that teaching at this level has always been a part-time occupation in the sense that, besides teaching, its practitioners are also required to undertake administration and research as part of their job specification. Our experience, however, suggests that these pressures have intensified to the point at which the priority and *value* placed on teaching are under attack and, in turn, the quality of education offered to students is being diminished.

The book that follows is a direct response to these new circumstances. It is based on three interlinked premises: first, that teaching is important rather than merely inescapable; second, that failure to pause and think about what we are doing actually makes the task of teaching far more difficult and; third, that improved teaching and learning makes life easier and more fun for all concerned. Above all, this book challenges all those who teach geography in higher education to think more clearly about how and why they do so.

Having said this, we stress that we make no direct connections between advocacy of good teaching and any particular standpoint on the purpose of education. Good teaching is vital whatever the objective: whether it be inculcating a critical stance toward the *status quo*, or providing the basis of a liberal education, or supplying the labour market with skilled workers. In addition, we have tried throughout to avoid preaching. While our own experiences as teachers in higher education have convinced us that there are better and more effective ways to teach than those traditionally used, we do not ask you, the reader, to take this on trust. Equally, while we make reference to educational theory and practice when relevant and enlightening, we have tried to avoid doing so merely to lend legitimacy to our efforts.

Overall, the book has two general objectives. First, we hope that it will help to defend teaching as an important aspect of work in higher education. We do so not only because we believe that good teaching is the key to successful higher education, but also because a response that downgrades teaching is not even a rational reaction to the challenge of constrained circumstances. Pressures of the type outlined above make it imperative that *more* rather than less time be invested in devising strategies that make best use of constrained time and resources. Indeed, we would argue that the intellectual demands that this task makes can be every bit as great as those involved in producing effective research.

Our second objective is to supply a guide to good practice – to good *educational* practice and good *geographical* practice. Although, as authors of this book, we share a general interest in educational theory, our starting point lay in our own practical experiences of teaching in higher education in Britain, Australia and North America. A glance at the contents page reveals a set of chapters defined by immediately recognizable teaching tasks, making it perfectly possible to dip into the book for discussion of issues about which we have to take decisions throughout the year. These issues might be concerned with a specific aspect of teaching – such as lectures, fieldwork, assessment or course evaluation – or with more general questions, such as the need to reform the curriculum, the wish to make teaching more cost- or time-effective, or even just how to revitalize an area of teaching which has become jaded. Throughout, we have tried to produce the sort of text that we would want to turn to ourselves when faced with these and kindred problems – pragmatically based but versed in appropriate educational theory. At the same time, we stress that this is avowedly a geography book, concerned first and foremost with the problems and issues involved in geography teaching, and is written to meet the needs of anyone with a current, or prospective, interest in teaching geography in higher education. In other words, the book was written not just because we believe that teaching matters, but also because we believe that teaching *geography* matters.

1.2 TEACHING AND LEARNING

Given the essentially practical concerns of this book and its emphasis on *teaching* rather than learning, we have forgone an extensive formal discussion of the nature of the learning process (for more information, see the 'Key Reading' section at the end of this chapter). Nevertheless, we feel that it is important at the outset to summarize our views on the matter, which revolve around three interrelated points.

1 *Student-centred learning* The teaching methods advocated in the following pages challenge students to take responsibility for their own learning and, in so doing, alter radically the role of the teacher from authority figure, through interpreter and demonstrator, to adviser and colleague. Such 'student-centred learning' has many dimensions, which are themselves varyingly emphasized by different teaching methods. Nevertheless, the four key dimensions with which we are concerned are as follows: *control* over the aims, objectives, content, method, level, pace, assessment and evaluation of the work; *workload*, in the balance of work between teacher and student; *activity*, from passive (listening to a lecture) to active (doing things); learning *autonomously* rather than being taught.

2 *Active learning* Reinforcing this last point, we believe that successful teaching is that which facilitates active learning. Students contribute to, or participate in, the learning process in three main ways: as passive receivers of knowledge, as explorers of existing knowledge or as creators of their own knowledge. As one moves from the first type of response to the second and third, the student's role changes from passive to active learning. The progression involved here might be illustrated by the differences between students silently listening to a lecture, through the type of work involved in undertaking projects as part of a research-based field course, to the creation and production of an undergraduate dissertation. In short, we see a move from receiving structures of existing knowledge through to the student's involvement in creating new ones.

3 *Learning as an open-ended process* Active learning motivates student and teacher alike to reflect critically on knowledge and to seek actively to find out more. Each becomes more of a geographer, rather than merely learning or teaching geography. This, we argue, contributes to the personal development and growth of both parties since education is an open-ended process in which knowledge is a product of its own learning.

By being geographers, we do not merely find out more and more geography but extend and transform what geography is. In other words, those who study geography as an academic discipline are, at the same time, inescapably involved in the development of geographies of the world in which they live.

1.3 THE SOCIAL CONTEXT

This last point has broader implications. Higher education has an undeniable, perhaps unenviable, image of individualism. Teachers are hired as specialists in their particular fields. They work in departments which often resemble confederations of academic fiefdoms, in which talented individuals have complete control over the teaching and planning of courses in their areas of expertise and demur fully to the opinions of subject specialists in other areas. Similarly, learning is also seen as a process in which students participate as individuals. Traditionally, they sit in lectures making notes which they will use to guide their subsequent *private* reading in the library and, later, their examination revision.

Much can be gained, however, from viewing teaching and learning in a social context. First, geographical knowledge is itself rooted in that context. Sensitive teaching can help students to make connections between geographical knowledge and problems of social significance. Second, teaching takes place in a social context. To be effective, it should not be a one-way transmission of information, but rather a process which encourages the free flow of communication between all parties involved. Good teaching benefits from recognizing barriers to communication that sometimes exist in the classroom and in opening up dialogue between teacher and learner. Finally, effective learning can often take place in a social context. As will be seen at various points in this book, it can be profitable to break down the isolated nature of learning by creating conditions in which students are required to act collaboratively and are assessed jointly.

1.4 STRUCTURE

This text contains eleven chapters, which initially examine specific teaching methods before turning to consider broader issues. Following this introduction, chapters 2-4 deal in turn with the traditional staples of the geography programme – the lecture, fieldwork and practical and project work. In each case, we consider the conventional use of these teaching methods before suggesting alternative ways that they might be employed. Chapter 5 tackles teaching geography through discussion, particularly through students working in groups. Some elements in this chapter (seminars and personal tutorials) may also be familiar; others (simulations and various forms of group tutorial) may be less so. The next two chapters (chapters 6 and 7) examine and try to codify principles of good practice in two areas which are generating considerable interest in the changing world of higher education, namely resource-based learning and computer-assisted teaching and learning.

At this stage, we turn to examine wider issues. Chapter 8 explores issues involved in assessing students, with chapter 9 examining how courses can be evaluated and improved. In many ways, the concerns of all these chapters come together in the penultimate chapter (chapter 10), which explores principles for designing the geography curriculum. In designing a curriculum, one reflects on a host of questions besides the specific content of individual courses – questions which might well include the following.

- What is geography in higher education supposed to achieve?
- Is there a single objective or should a diverse range of objectives inform curriculum design and teaching practice?
- Are we concerned with a core curriculum or with a curriculum designed to meet individual wants and needs?
- What are to be the aims and objectives and how are they translated into the curriculum?
- How are individual courses designed?
- How can we design courses that will allow creative teaching in circumstances in which, as noted above, professional geographers are likely to be under growing institutional and external pressures to give priority to activities other than teaching?

The final chapter (chapter 11) rounds off the discussion by sketching out ten guiding principles that underpin much of our discussion and adds some final thoughts on the nature of good teaching. However, in a sense, it is questions like the ones posed above that are the real outcome. We do not supply systematic, let alone definitive, answers to any of these questions, but at least seek to present the issues squarely for debate. We would all be truly delighted if the practical suggestions that we make for tackling these questions are quickly superseded by other geographers addressing themselves to the same problems.

KEY READING

There are many general books on teaching in higher education. We particularly recommend the frequently revised and reprinted American text *Teaching Tips*

(McKeachie, 1988) and its most recent British counterpart (Brown and Atkins, 1988). The relationship between teaching and learning is one of the most significant and difficult areas of educational research. Studies that start from a view of how students learn and then outline ways to teach effectively include Rogers (1969), Entwistle and Hounsell (1975), Knowles and Associates (1984), Boud (1985, 1988) and Gibbs (1988). The question of the competing demands on the geographer's time and the pressures imposed by the external environment are addressed at various stages in Martin Kenzer's stimulating collection of essays entitled *On Becoming a Professional Geographer* (Kenzer, 1989).

2

The Lecture

Behold I do not give lectures or a little charity,
When I give I give myself.

Walt Whitman, *Song of Myself*

2.1 INTRODUCTION

An apocryphal story is told about a senior academic who was much in demand as a consultant and on the conference circuit. Recognizing that he would rarely be available to give lectures in his own college, he prepared a series of tape recordings and arranged to have the appropriate tape switched on at each weekly session. Unexpectedly finding himself in the department on one such occasion, he decided to go along to see how the class was faring. On reaching the room, he found his disembodied voice booming out loud and clear and his lecture being steadily absorbed by tape recorders arranged in serried ranks in the classroom.

The frequency and enthusiasm with which this story is told and re-told reflects the acuity of its observations about the lecture at its worst, in which surrogate means of giving and receiving the information could just as easily suffice. The lecture, defined by the *Oxford English Dictionary* as 'a discourse given before an audience on a given subject, usually for the purpose of instruction', has been the heart of higher education since the days of Antiquity – to the extent that lecturing and teaching are often regarded as synonymous terms. Indeed, so ubiquitous is the traditional lecture that many of its practitioners rarely reflect on its nature and characteristics.

In this chapter, we analyse the lecture as a teaching device. We consider its various forms and its advantages, before offering a critique of current practices. Thereafter, suggestions are offered about how to develop more effective lectures, concentrating on ways to improve student involvement in the process.

2.2 LECTURING AS TEACHING

Used to teach classes of widely diverging numbers, the typical lecture is a one-way transmission of information which takes place at regular (probably weekly) intervals, and lasts 50–55 minutes. Indeed, the regular slots of lecture times often create the outline framework for both the teacher's and the student's weekly timetable.

Wherever they are delivered, lectures have various common characteristics. They require that teachers prepare and structure presentations for oral transmission to their student audience on a particular subject. Of course, the subject material varies widely. Amongst other things, the lecturer may be seeking to provide insight into specific theoretical or empirical aspects of geographical knowledge, grounding that knowledge in its wider philosophical, economic, social or cultural context, outlining what students should study, informing them about emerging developments in knowledge too recent to be in textbooks or advising them on how to approach independent reading. In delivering their lectures, teachers may use audiovisual and other aids, but they retain control over the material presented and the pace of presentation. Occasionally, a lecturer may choose to segment the lecture session, perhaps periodically pausing to ask students to carry out lecture-related tasks (e.g. working their way through distributed worksheets) and then reporting back on their findings. Such procedures, however, are uncommon. During the typical lecture, the audience remains passive. Little is required of them other than to attend or else, as suggested above, to find a surrogate means of obtaining a record of the lecture's content.

Lectures do have certain advantages. First, teachers and students can organize their time effectively, knowing that their commitments are straightforward and regular. A series of lectures is an efficient solution, for example, if a course on 'World Regional Geography' needs to be taught to 300 students for an hour on a Tuesday morning; indeed, it may seem the only way of teaching a group of this size. Second, lecturers have the comfort of knowing that the teaching experience is almost entirely under their own control, that the course can be planned in detail in advance, that the content can be divided into convenient pigeon-holes and that the syllabus is fully covered. Such characteristics can help assuage the fear that many feel when confronted with teaching large groups of people. Third, the lecture is an efficient use of the lecturer's time. Although preparation of lectures may be time consuming in the first instance, once written a lecture can be quickly updated, used and re-used. Finally, good lecturing is an art that *can* be very satisfying for everyone involved: for the lecturer the satisfaction of a job well done; for the audience the stimulus and sense of occasion of a lecture well and enthusiastically delivered.

These are real advantages but, when not in the hands of truly gifted practitioners, the benefits mainly centre on the tactical or time-saving aspects of lecturing. Viewed in terms of their effectiveness as a method of teaching, lectures are much less satisfactory (Bligh, 1972; Gibbs, 1982). Consider, for example, this assessment of lecturing in a study undertaken in Britain by Her Majesty's Inspectorate of around a hundred degree courses across a range of subjects:

> By and large teaching was in the traditional mode of formal lectures and seminars. Lectures were usually factual and descriptive, consisting of a review of areas of organised knowledge and including only a limited amount of analysis. The majority of lectures in all subjects had been carefully prepared and were competently delivered, though they were rarely exciting. A considerable amount of note-taking was observed during lectures . . . Much (and occasionally extreme) reliance was placed on lecture notes as a preparation for . . . examinations . . . With so much regard given to the imparting of information, it was unusual to come across the exposition of opposing viewpoints, the evaluation of evidence and an attempt to balance and assess it. (DES, 1983: 15)

Similarly, the Carnegie Foundation's study of undergraduate experience in the USA observed that:

> the lecture method is preferred by most professors. With few exceptions, when we visited classes, the teacher stood in front of rows of chairs and talked most of the 45 minutes. Information was presented that often students only passively received. There was little opportunity for positions to be clarified or ideas challenged. (Boyer, 1987: 149)

Taken together, these statements highlight concern about the efficacy of lecturing. Despite evident conscientiousness on the part of lecturers, the results were 'rarely exciting', the audience were uninvolved and deeper reflection on information was lacking. These comments are supported by the available research, from which we can draw three important criticisms of lecturing as a teaching method. In the first place, lecturing draws on a view that people learn by acquiring, storing and organizing information in an internal filing system which exists to be fed with knowledge. Although not necessarily wrong, this is only one way in which learning takes place (Brown and Atkins, 1988). Other ways, especially those that stem from experience, discussion and reflection, are poorly served by lecturing.

Second, even if information transfer is the most important mechanism of learning, the available research (e.g. Bligh, 1972) suggests that the information is often neither fully nor accurately transferred from the lecturer to the audience. No matter how good the lecturers or how much they try to retain students' interest, the standard length of a lecture is usually far longer than the audience's attention span. In general terms, attention rises to a peak about 5 minutes into a lecture, but falls away markedly after 20 minutes, rising again slightly towards the end.

Third, the evidence shows that the lecture is an inadequate means of tackling what will later be termed higher-level objectives (e.g. see chapters 4 and 8). In other words, whereas lectures may be a way of encouraging basic cognitive skills such as memorizing factual knowledge and may be a way of promoting comprehension of key concepts and principles, they are a less effective means of encouraging skills of critical analysis and synthesis. As Bligh suggests:

> comparisons of the effectiveness of the lecture method with other teaching methods . . . suggest that it may be used appropriately to convey information, but it cannot be used effectively on its own to promote thought or change and develop attitudes without variations in the usual lecture technique. (Bligh, 1972: 13)

Reflection on these points suggests that the effectiveness of lecturing as a form of teaching has to be evaluated critically. The response depends in part upon *context*: the need to respond to the limitations of lecturing is more insistent if the lecture is the primary form of teaching rather than one form of teaching among many. Our view is that, whatever the context, there is much that can be done to improve the lecture and to find better alternatives for purposes for which it is ill suited. The rest of this chapter concentrates on the former; much of the rest of the book attends to the latter.

2.3 DEVELOPING EFFECTIVE LECTURES

To develop effective lectures, we have to recognize and respond to both the advantages and limitations of lecturing. The following suggestions may be helpful in tackling this objective

Lectures as performances

All lectures are partly theatrical performances. Lecturers have to project their voices and, to some extent, their personalities to strike up a relationship with the audience. The various aspects of non-verbal behaviour (e.g. body language, eye contact, movement about the room, smiling), along with verbal communication, are used to present a persona to the audience. As academics, we may play down these aspects of teaching as being trivial, but this suggests that we do not take the techniques of professional communicators seriously. Effective communication helps to increase the accessibility of the lecture and to stimulate the students' interest in the topic.

One way to improve performance in this respect is to have a lecture video-recorded and then scrutinized, if possible in company with a sympathetic colleague or consultant. Distracting mannerisms or unhelpful idiosyncrasies can then be identified. The immediate effect of this exercise can be to increase the insecurity which all such performances induce, but self-awareness of lecturing style may be further exploited to enhance the timing and pace of the performance as a whole.

Limiting content

One of the authors of this book once attended a lecture that is now part of the folklore of British higher education. A distinguished historical geographer was due to be absent from a class and had given his lecture notes on the changing English landscape to a colleague who agreed to run the session for him. During the first half of the lecture, the substitute lecturer noticed that no one took any notes, but after 30 minutes pens were grabbed and note-taking proceeded apace. The answer to his bemusement came later when he realized that he had actually given two lectures, one from the previous week and the one intended for the current week. His colleague's lectures were delivered at half the pace of his own and were distinguished by a high level of performance involving gestures, vocal dexterity, pregnant pauses and unscripted personal anecdotes.

The message here is that lecturers frequently attempt to impart too much information. Most people absorb information more readily when reading than when listening, and large amounts of information are best given as recommended reading or in the form of a handout. Lectures are better employed for conveying broad outlines and the key ideas associated with a topic. Pauses and recapitulations are necessary and, again, practice may help in appreciating how long different types of lectures should take.

Structure

An audience's attention soon wanders when it is difficult to follow the flow of a lecture and one of the most common reasons for this is inadequate structuring. All too often, this occurs either because the structure is too complex to be readily understood at one hearing or because the lecturer believes, incorrectly, that the structure is self-apparent. Various techniques are available to improve matters.

One such method is the *progress report*. At particular times in the course, it is well worth displaying, on a handout or an overhead transparency, the key themes of the course so far and how the main ideas presented in the current session fit into this accumulated knowledge. At times when the course is about to change direction into a new area in which the students have little previous knowledge or grounds for anticipating a lecture's contents, *advance organizers* can be useful. An advanced organizer is a skeletal outline, usually presented at the start of a lecture, which conveys the major elements of the lecture and perhaps the key questions to be asked. During lectures, simple *sequencing* techniques can be employed. These are ways of giving clues about the flow of information and where a particular point fits into the argument, which need be no more than listing of items ('first, second . . .', 'there are three main points' and then listing them), or by establishing contrasts and comparisons ('in contrast with this view', 'an alternative view . . .'). *Explicit structuring* devices may also be useful, whereby students are given formal frameworks within which to locate the material that they receive. This can be done in various ways. Brown and Atkins (1988), for example, indicate that lectures can be structured by *signposts* offering direction to the structure and content of a lecture, *frames* which delimit the beginning and end of sections of the lecture, *foci* that signify important points and *links* between different sections.

Very different lecture structures result depending on which type of framework is selected. Take, for instance, a lecture on regional economic performance. This might be set out according to the 'classic method' (Brown, 1978, 64) in which it is subdivided into broad sections and subsections, each of which contains a key point, examples, qualifications and a brief summary. Table 2.1 indicates how the first part of a lecture on regional economic performance might appear if this method is applied. While not particularly exciting, it does convey information in an organized manner, for which reason it may be very suitable for a lecture with a large empirical content.

Another, and very different, structure for presenting the same empirical content could be accomplished by using film clips of jobless workers marching from

Table 2.1 Structuring a lecture through the 'classic method'

Introduction
    Contemporary variations in regional economic performance
    Statistical indicators
Measuring regional economic performance
    Employment data
    Output figures
A problem region
    Northeast England/Appalachia

Jarrow (in North-East England) in 1936 and again in 1987 to draw attention to the area's problems. The lecture could then focus on the nature of the region's economic performance, drawing in the empirical data and, in the process, drawing connections with the social and political significance of the Jarrow march. The rest of the lecture could use this basis as a platform for discussing the ideologically divergent interpretations of the regional problem.

Student involvement

An advantage of well-delivered lectures is that students receive a useful set of notes but, unless care is taken, note-taking may preclude thought and reflection. There are a variety of ways of alleviating this problem (see e.g. Howe and Godfrey, 1978; Kiewra, 1985), which include the following.

- *Limiting the need for note-taking* One can limit the need for frenetic note-taking by providing students with outline notes, a task undertaken by commercial organizations at some North American colleges. Outline notes can prove more effective than full notes, especially where students are encouraged to work on them during and *after* the lecture (e.g. annotate them, highlight points of difficulty and re-work them on the basis of further reading). Empty spaces deliberately left in the handouts given to students can invite critical and reflective note-taking in response to points being raised.
- *Limiting the period of passive learning* As indicated earlier, attention falls away after about 20 minutes of passive listening. The answer to this problem is to restrict the amount of time spent in this way. For example, a lecture session might start with an introductory talk ('mini-lecture') followed by a handout with quotations from a number of authors. Students can then be invited to identify the position of the authors by using the categories outlined in the lecture. Alternatively, a short film may be used to generate discussion among students working in groups of three or four, followed by brief reports to the rest of the class.
- *Encouraging reflection on new knowledge* Various techniques are available to encourage students to reflect on the knowledge with which they are being presented. These can include classroom tests and questionnaires (see chapter 8), completing outline handouts which ask students, say, to fill in the key elements in a systems diagram, or informal discussion groups. A demonstration of these techniques in practice is presented by Gibbs and Jenkins (1984), who applied them to a lecture on central place theory (figure 2.1).

14   *The Lecture*

		Time
Stage 1:	Revision OHP displayed	10.00 am
Stage 2:	Revision talk on last lectures	10.05 am
Stage 3:	Task: discuss in pairs	10.14 am
Stage 4:	Talk	10.19 am
Stage 5:	Task: discuss in pairs	10.26 am
Stage 6:	A.J. summarizes student answers 10.33 starts lecturing again	10.30 am
Stage 7:	Task: specific questions on a map: discuss in pairs	10.36 am
Stage 8:	A.J. answers first two questions	10.42 am
Stage 9:	Continued discussion in pairs	10.43 am
Stage 10:	Talk: A.J. gives answers and lectures (using OHPs)	10.45 am
Stage 11:	30 second task: in pairs	10.48 am
Stage 12:	A.J. refers to handout not covered in lecture	10.54 am
Stage 13:	Students summarize lecture for themselves	10.56 am
		End

Total lecturer (A.J.) talk	31 min
Total student work	25 min
Longest lecturer talk	9 min
Longest student task	6 min
Number of 'segments' of lecture	13

Figure 2.1 Time and motion analysis of one lecture
Source: Gibbs and Jenkins (1984: 31)

This lecture was given in a first-year undergraduate human geography course (enrolment of around 110) which attempts to introduce students to the varying approaches used in contemporary human geography. In this session, Christaller's central place theory was used to exemplify the aims and methodology of spatial analysis. Previous lectures had set out Christaller's aims, how the model works, some tests of that model and discussion of modifications that other researchers made to the original version of central place theory. This lecture's aim was to show the power and flexibility of the model by extending it to the provision of retail facilities within towns, the provision of public service and leisure facilities, and Third World periodic markets.

To ensure that students began with a common starting point, the early part of the session recapitulates the themes of previous weeks. What is involved in the first part of this session is not merely a re-run or summary of earlier content but an attempt to stimulate questioning of that knowledge or its integration into what is already known. Through reflection, the learner moves beyond mere knowledge absorption and lays the basis and motivation for further learning.

The next stage in the session shown in figure 2.1 concerns improving student involvement in the lecture by question-and-answer sessions whereby, with help from the lecturer, the students bring out the main points themselves. Students are presented with a set of circumstances and asked to discuss them. In stage 3, for instance, the lecturer posed the following question on an overhead transparency: 'What aspects of central place theory can be used to analyse the number and location of shopping facilities in towns?'. Students were asked to discuss the question in groups of two or three. After allowing time for this to be accomplished, the lecturer then worked through the questions posed taking answers from the audience. These are then fed into the ensuing discussion of the underlying concept. This simple procedure has the merit of involving the student audience in the discussion and has been found to offer some success in improving the absorption of abstract concepts.

The visual imagination

Sight is of prime importance in human sensory perception (Gold, 1980) and therefore it is good policy for lecturers to do everything possible to harness their audience's visual imagination. Although novelty for its own sake should be avoided, effective use of visual aids can enliven lectures, serve to confirm and reinforce the main points of lectures and improve the audience's knowledge of space and place. Moreover, thoughtful use of illustration can provide powerful reinforcement of abstract ideas, since ideas which are linked to and by visual symbols are also likely to be retained in the long-term memory (Brown and Atkins, 1988). Experience, however, suggests that teachers are poorly trained in using visual aids (Flood Page, 1976; Beard et al., 1978), a point that most veterans of professional geography conferences would readily support.

There is not space here to give detailed treatment of the wide range of visual aids that are available: a list that includes television, film, videotapes, overhead projector transparencies, computer-linked displays, slides, blackboards and whiteboards, wall maps and hardware models. However, some general principles may be helpful when using them (see also chapter 7).

- Effective use of visual media need not involve mastering complicated or technologically sophisticated media. Although more glamorous aids are available, the most valuable visual media for most teachers continue to be blackboards, slides and overhead transparencies (McKeachie, 1986).
- Visual materials should be simple, brief, properly prepared, easily seen from all parts of the room and presented in the correct order. It is important to think carefully about the lighting requirements necessary in the case of slide or overhead projectors, where the need for black-out facilities can create stuffy rooms that adversely affect the audience's concentration.
- The content of visual materials should be fully integrated into the lecture and not turned into something that competes for the student's attention. Overhead projectors are frequently misused in this respect, with lecturers showing transparencies that contain too much writing or detail to be read, talking to the projector or the screen rather than to the audience, and assuming that the audience will have absorbed something simply because it has been shown on the screen. If the illustrations are important, students will need time to interpret and, if necessary, copy them. Lecturers should not feel obliged to talk at such moments. It is usually much better to indicate the key features and then remain silent for a few moments.

Student note-taking

Taking notes is an activity that is rarely analysed rigorously, yet is worthy of close scrutiny. Good note-taking helps to alleviate some of the difficulties of lecturing as a teaching method; indeed, a systematic and consistent method of note-taking can help to structure the process of listening to a lecture. It may be that the college offers study skills courses which cover note-taking. If so, students can profitably attend them. We have also suggested above the possibility of introducing lecture outlines as a way of helping students to structure their notes. While there is no single format for taking notes that is ideal for each student, there are tips that can be given to students to help them in this task.

Very occasionally, for example, it is instructive to remind students that not all the content of lectures is of equal significance. Brown and Atkins (1988), for instance, dissect the structure of lectures and, in doing so, produce the mnemonic POKE EARS (which stands for preamble, orientation, key points, extensions, examples, asides, reservations and summaries). By making students aware of these dimensions and positively encouraging them to recognize their appearance within lectures, one can help students to take a more active role in shaping their own learning. In addition, it is worth encouraging students to review periodically their notes and any handouts associated with the lectures, even to the point of setting aside time at the start of the lecture for this purpose. Quite apart from improving retention of information, a review helps students to understand the structure of the course and follow the direction in which it is going.

2.4 CONCLUSION

Lectures are the staple of higher education teaching, being particularly helpful, first, in introducing a topic and providing a platform from which informed learning can take place and, second, in synthesizing material within a course. When used for these purposes, in connection with the teaching methods described in the following chapters, lectures retain a valuable place in the teaching of geography in higher education. Nevertheless, as currently practised, they suffer from various deficiencies, not least of which is that they are often a poor form of communication. In this respect, it is perhaps most useful to close this chapter by listing our suggestions of what makes for good and bad lecturing practice (based on Eble, 1976; Lowman, 1984). These suggestions provide not only a checklist for good and bad practice but also a basis for the evaluation of our own lectures.

Twenty suggestions for bad lecturing . . .

1 Begin a course with no introduction to the subject or to your own bias. Simply start with the first topic that you wish to present – preferably without any justification for doing so.
2 Make no reference to the broader context of the topic under consideration.
3 Do not acknowledge the students' own interests, previous knowledge or experience.
4 Become preoccupied with the historical background to the topic or with your own categorizations of it. Leave little time for the central theme of the lecture course.

5 Give excessive attention to particular details of the subject or to those parts that most interest you. Do not explain this focus to your audience.

6 Dwell excessively on your private quarrels with other authorities. This is particularly effective if it leads to a quite unbalanced view of the subject matter as a whole.

7 Set out an extensive range of qualifications and reservations at the outset that will bore and confuse the listeners.

8 Insert long quotations without fitting them into the context and fail to give any information about where these quotations may be found.

9 Justify conclusions by reference to authority and tradition without explaining the derivation of such traditions.

10 Use arcane terms without explanation.

11 Do not look at your audience, stand stock-still and gaze fixedly at your notes, the ceiling, the floor, the walls or, best of all, at what is happening out of the window.

12 Speak in a monotonous voice without emphasis or enthusiasm and hesitate frequently in the middle of sentences.

13 Allow the content of the course and the timetable to get out of phase. Begin and end lectures in the middle of major points.

14 Do not provide handouts of any kind.

15 If photographic slides are used, ensure that they are out of order, out of focus and occasionally upside-down.

16 If overhead projectors or blackboards are used, ensure that all writing is of a size legible only to yourself. Take every opportunity to use your body to obscure the material that is being displayed and always remove the transparency or wipe the board before the audience has written down more than 60 per cent of what was there.

17 If video-recordings are to be shown, ensure that the equipment arrives at least 15 minutes into the lecture, creating the maximum disruption. Thereafter ensure that the monitor is placed where some students cannot see, that the videocassette has not been wound to the correct place and that a missing connecting wire prevents any sound coming from the monitor.

18 If reading lists are provided, make them as long as possible. Exclude all annotation and amend the list as often as possible during the lectures. Make sure that inadequate bibliographic detail is offered for these modifications.

19 Constantly modify the structure of the course and insert extra sections or omit others without indicating this to students.

20 Combine sudden modifications to course structure with modifications to reading by introducing a previously unreferenced item as a central contribution to the course.

. . . and thirteen suggestions for good lecturing

1 Begin each course by relating the material to be covered to the students' own experience (of the previous course content, other courses, day-to-day interests) and by expressing and explaining your own enthusiasm for the subject.

2 Outline the objectives of the course of lectures and explain the structure being adopted.

3 Fit the material to the time available. Remember that too little material is better than too much.

4 Seek concise ways to present content. Express concepts in the simplest terms and define technical terms and jargon, but do not oversimplify.

5 Follow a prepared outline but include improvised material and appear spontaneous – especially if the material can be illustrated with current events.

6 Use a wide range of voices, gestures and physical movements, but be yourself. Develop a varied and interesting style consistent with your own values and personality.

7 Break up the monotony of lectures by varying methods of presentation.

8 If using audiovisual equipment, check that it is in working order before the students arrive. Videotapes should be primed at the correct place for showing. Slides should be in the correct order. Overhead projector transparencies should be clearly legible from all parts of the room. Remember that good illustrations can be a potent and effective source of communication; equally they can ruin a lecture if you use them badly.

9 Minimize passive learning by incorporating alternative teaching strategies within the lecture.

10 Give students regular points to catch their breath and ask questions.

11 Be responsive to students during a lecture: observe their reactions and respond to them.

12 End each lecture with a conclusion connecting the material to that which is to be discussed at the next meeting.

13 Remember that teaching and learning are always highly personal. Both activities can only be enhanced by personalizing your lecturing and acknowledging the social relationships involved in teaching and learning.

KEY READING

Donald Bligh's *What's the Use of Lectures?* (1972) is justifiably the classic source. Its blend of research evidence and practical advice still makes it essential reading.

Valuable summaries of subsequent research into effective teaching are supplied by Brown (1978), Eble (1988) and Brown and Atkins (1988). Graham Gibbs has written copiously on the problems and drawbacks of lecturing (e.g. Gibbs, 1982), and is also co-author of a practical guide which contains a wealth of practical and self-contained ways of improving lectures (Gibbs et al., 1984). North American and Australian experience of teaching large introductory courses to students who are making the transition from school to college has much to offer those faced with the problem of teaching larger classes. Three particularly useful sources in this respect are Weimer (1987), Andresen (1988) and Brown (1989).

3

Fieldwork

There is nothing immoral about taking students to see strange and wonderful places, and no teacher needs feel guilty about enjoying the Golden Gate Bridge or cobras at the zoo. One should not, however, confuse a field trip in geography with picnics, outings or senior class excursions.

P. F. Lewis, *Field Training in Geography*

It is arguable that in geography, biology and related subjects field work is as intrinsic to the discipline as clinical practice is to medicine. Indeed educational visits are used in the teaching of many subjects, yet I know of no controlled study of their effectiveness.

D. A. Bligh, *Teaching Students*

3.1 INTRODUCTION

Geographers have long regarded fieldwork as being central to their teaching and research and as something intrinsic to the very nature of being a geographer. Carl Sauer (1956: 296), for example, in his presidential address to the Association of American Geographers, declared that 'the principal training of the geographer should come, wherever possible by doing fieldwork'. Many others, from all levels of geographical education, have strongly articulated similar views (including Wooldridge, 1955; Hutchings, 1962; Association of American Geographers, 1969; Board, 1965; Brown, 1969; Everson, 1973; Friberg, 1975; Mikesell, 1978; Spencer and Hebden, 1982; Brunsden, 1987; Tranter, 1988). Much of this literature, however, consists either of general philosophical treatises on the assumed value of fieldwork or specifically relates to individual field exercises. The educational aims and objectives of fieldwork are rarely examined and there is very little evaluation of outcomes. In the words of Lonergan and Andresen (1988: 63), 'this means that we have virtually nothing in the public domain that could be recommended to a new lecturer needing guidance on how to justify and design a field-based course or course component'.

In this chapter, we examine the origins of field teaching, look at the wide variety of fieldwork practices and then consider the various objectives that fieldwork is thought to serve. After that, we discuss the objections to fieldwork as currently undertaken and suggestions as to how to organize it more effectively. In particular, we argue that much of the educational value of the conventional field course arises from its being a form of concentrated study, which could be achieved in the classroom by reorganizing the timetable so that a week or a month is devoted to a specific limited topic.

3.2 ORIGINS AND CHARACTERISTICS

Fieldwork was intrinsic to several traditions that played an important part in the development of geography itself which, in turn, have contributed to the emphasis commonly placed on fieldwork in the geography curriculum. These traditions include the following:

- *The exploration tradition* The desire to examine things in the field, just to 'go and see new places' (Smith, 1987: 209), remains a powerful part of the geographer's background, recalling the emergence of the discipline from the exploration tradition. This tradition has been nurtured by many long-established voluntary organizations that have popularized geographical study (see Stoddart, 1986; Brunsden, 1987). In this context, there is no way that one could ever measure the impact on future geography students of attending meetings at the local Sierra Club or the children's Christmas Lectures at the Royal Geographical Society in London, or even from simply reading *The National Geographic*. Nevertheless, it is fair to say that these agencies have helped to shape a particular image of geography. Whether or not we like it, students entering higher education frequently expect that fieldwork will be an integral part of their geographical studies.
- *The regional tradition* As academic geography developed, it emphasized the interrelationship of physical and human phenomena in regional associations. As late as 1945, Wooldridge defined the geographer's aim as being 'to examine rocks, landforms, soils, plants as well as human phenomena in their natural contexts in area, one to another and all together' (Wooldridge, 1945: reprinted as Wooldridge, 1969: 9). Later, he considered that 'the improvement of our status as a subject lies in . . . the careful, indeed minute study of limited areas' (Wooldridge, 1955: 80). How detailed and careful that observation could be is demonstrated in Jones and Sauer's (1915: 522) outline for the inexperienced fieldworker on 'how to stimulate observation from all geographical points of view'. If fieldwork is the major research method, then it should also be intrinsic to the curriculum.

● *Observation and empiricism* Educational philosophies stressing observation and empiricism also gave support to field study. Brunsden (1987: 196), for example, showed how the principles of 'look, see, observe, describe and learn' stems from educational philosophers who stress the role of education through nature. Teaching practices, especially in British schools, were heavily influenced by Fairgrieve's (1926) insistence on the primacy of the inductive method – of starting from observable facts and then working towards generalizations. These, in turn, also contributed to an emphasis on active learning through fieldwork (Graves, 1980).

The evidence shows that the attachment to formal fieldwork remains a prominent feature of undergraduate geography. An analysis of British degree courses listed in the publication *Matter of Degree* (Geo Books, 1986), for example, reveals that most students undertake compulsory fieldwork before graduating. Typically, British geography students attend one such a course in each of their three college years, usually of a week's duration, with at least one trip being based abroad. In addition, students may well take field courses related to specific options within the curriculum. In the USA, the annual field course is a less integral feature of the college curriculum, but courses on field skills remain popular options. A 1978 survey, for instance, shows that about 75 per cent of US departments offered courses in field methods and techniques (Thomas, 1978). In addition, many institutions have an optional overseas field-based tour in their programmes (Panton and Dilsaver, 1989).

Care is necessary when interpreting statistics, however, because definitions of 'fieldwork' differ markedly, with the term covering a wide variety of educational methods and experiences. A review of North American practice in the late 1960s indicated 'that a surprising amount of effort has been devoted to attempts to stretch the definition of "fieldwork" to cover a ludicrous range and variety of activities' (AAG, 1969: 1), while Dando and Weidel's (1971) analysis of the relevant geographic literature reveals that fieldwork included field teaching, field trips, field research and field camps. In other disciplines, the term is used to describe field or job internship programmes, visits to bars, factories and offices – indeed anything that takes the student into 'a world or perspective beyond the traditional classroom' (Hursch and Borzack, 1979: 63).

To ensure consistency, therefore, it is important to pick a single clear definition. The one used here, taken from Lonergan and Andresen (1988: 1), meets this criterion admirably, taking field work to cover 'any arena or zone within a subject where, outside the constraints of the four-walls classroom setting, supervised learning can take place via first hand experience'. It is still possible to subsume many different teaching and learning processes within this definition, but five types of variation can be identified.

● *Teaching method*   There is a strong contrast between the teacher-centred 'look–see' approach, (often referred to as the 'Cook's Tour' after the pioneering English holiday travel agent) and more student-centred project-based approaches. Educationally, the Cook's Tour is similar to the lecture (chapter 2), whereas the project method is basically the same as the methods discussed in chapter 4.

● *Venue*   Field course venues vary considerably. At a systematic level, they might be categorized in terms of the environment under study (for example, whether urban or rural, familiar or unfamiliar, unique or broadly representative). At a more practical level, a distinction can be drawn between local fieldwork, fieldwork carried out in distant locations of the same country and fieldwork carried out in another country or even another continent (as in the 'study tours' organized by American geography departments to Europe and elsewhere).

● *Duration*   While the week-long course is an established feature of most British departments, fieldwork can be as short as a single day's excursion or as long as a 6-week study tour or field camp.

● *Relationship to the rest of the curriculum*   Field courses can be compulsory or optional, linked to specific courses or completely independent of the rest of the curriculum, focused on particular aspects of geography or attempting a synoptic overview.

● *Academic or social emphasis*   Literature on fieldwork often emphasizes its role in developing various personal skills. Field courses which are intended to develop these skills will be different from those in which the primary emphasis is development of student proficiency in research techniques or in acquisition of knowledge. Equally, such field courses will also be different from induction courses, held early in a degree programme, in which the prime purpose is to help students to get to know one another and staff.

Table 3.1   Types of field-based activity

1	Limited travel plus limited time, e.g. short field excursion
2	Limited activity plus extended travel, e.g. Cook's Tour
3	Extended travel and time, e.g. typical UK residential course
4	Multilocation activity, e.g. study tours
5	Learner–practitioner and participant observation, e.g. project work

Source: After Lonergan and Andresen, 1988

Putting these sources of variety together generates a typology of fieldwork with a very large number of possibilities but, in practice, the five major types listed and described in table 3.1 are the most common.

3.3 THE ROLE AND VALUE OF FIELDWORK

The literature (e.g. Lonergan and Andresen, 1988; Tranter, 1988) suggests that geographical fieldwork can be used to address many educational objectives and, indeed, field education is often justified by appeals to these multifarious objectives.

- *Developing observation skills*   To geographers steeped in the morphological and landscape traditions of the subject, the objective of field teaching might well be 'to develop an eye for country – i.e. to build up the power to read a piece of country' (Wooldridge, 1955: 78). Indeed, to Fraser Hart (1969: 29), 'a true field experience is a Socratic seminar in the open air, centring around observations, whether with or without the aid and guidance of an instructor'. Although these observational skills can be developed in the lecture theatre, ultimately 'the field is the only place where students can be shown what was only talked about in the classroom' (Lewis, 1969: 53).
- *Facilitating experiential learning*   This focus on the field as 'reality' is reinforced by those who emphasize that learning is best developed through concrete experience. According to this view, one should start in the field and then go to the classroom, not *vice versa* (see Hall, 1976: 247).
- *Encouraging students to take responsibility for their own learning*   One of the major North American writers on fieldwork emphasizes that 'what is different about field study is the emphasis on the *process of learning itself* . . . . Students in field study are *more responsible for their own learning* than they are when material is presented in the typical classroom' (Borzack, 1981: 10, emphasis added).
- *Developing analytical skills*   An emphasis on fieldwork as a way of developing analytical skills is common in courses which emphasize instruction in research methods, techniques and technical skills (Lounsbury and Aldrich, 1979; Stoddard, 1982). Such techniques-based field courses may be designed to serve a variety of geographic specialisms or they may be linked to specific subject options.
- *Experiencing 'real' research*   Techniques-based courses often attempt to encourage students 'to appreciate the problems and difficulties of collecting data in the field . . . . Fieldwork should breed a healthy scepticism of all published data' (Hart, 1979). For example, a field trip to France by Dutch students has

been described by its designers (Ashworth, 1983: 141) as 'a contribution to the development of a critical faculty for evaluating the research findings of others which can remove the awe with which students regard the idea of research itself ... [This objective] is achieved by students undertaking simple data collection exercises in the learning by doing mode'. Others argue that a major field work objective is 'to enable the student to experience the thrill of personal discovery' (Hart, 1969: 29). At a more focused level, this 'discovery' might well be structured around the systematic collection of data to test well-known models. Burt (1988), for example, describes fieldwork conducted in such a manner, with students collecting data to test the variable source area model in hydrology.

● *Developing a respect for the environment*   Some geographers see fieldwork as playing a key role in developing students' wonder and concern for the environment. In the United Kingdom, for example, the Geographical Association recently argued that:

> Awareness and understanding of, and concern and eventual responsibility for 'real places' can only be achieved through direct contact. There is not and there cannot be any substitute for the immediacy of field experience.'
> (Pearce, 1987: 35)

In a similar vein, Peter Keene, a coastal geomorphologist who has edited a series of geographical trails aimed at students and the general public, argues that a key aim of fieldwork 'is to encourage an increased awareness of, and empathy for, the environment in the belief that this . . . [is] sociably desirable in developing a body of opinion aware of the needs of conservation' (Keene, 1987: 1).

● *Developing personal skills*   Proponents of field-based instruction stress that a field course can bring a particular quality and depth to student learning. Just as with boarding schools, outdoor pursuits courses and the children's summer camp (Smith, 1987), residential field courses are often held to enhance the student's sense of their individual worth and contribute to the development of such social skills as group work, leadership and responsibility for others.

● *Breaking down barriers*   It is often claimed that residential field courses break down barriers between students and staff (Salisbury, 1969), and that this can significantly affect classroom relationships on return to college. As students learn to trust each other, and overcome the social distance between themselves and staff, it is argued that they will more readily take part in other learning experiences and so learn more effectively (Dando and Weidel, 1971).

Collectively, these reasons suggest that fieldwork can have enormous educational potential but, equally, can be completely sterile if not planned and executed sensibly. The advantages should not be assumed to accrue irrespective of how fieldwork is conducted. It has limitations like any other form of instruction, and the teacher's job is to find out which of these goals are best achieved in the field and how they can be realized. We see the following as key problems in the way that fieldwork is employed.

● *Effectiveness* The fundamental educational question to be asked is whether or not fieldwork achieves any of its stated objectives and, in all honesty, we must recognize that we do not know. The literature on fieldwork in geography, as noted earlier, is largely about assumed benefits, descriptions of particular field courses and specific field techniques. What is missing is evidence on whether or not the effort and expenditure are effective.

The evidence that is available allows no more than initial inferences in this respect. Fink's (1977) survey of students' reactions to three courses suggests that fieldwork did have a positive effect on attitudes to the course and on what students remembered a year or so after leaving. Ashworth (1983) analysed the accuracy of data gathered by his students in a field course designed to teach research methods, which were tested against equivalent commercially available data to give some objective measure of the course's success in developing students' data-gathering skills. Similarly, Harrison and Luithlen (1983) report their experience over a 7-year period of running field courses, evaluating the changing character of these courses against an educational model which shows the extent to which students are involved in active learning, group problem-solving and analysing values. Finally, Maizels et al. (1984) analyse a 2-day field project on stream measurement which aimed to develop proficiency in a specific field technique and in research design. They detail the preparation, the field work itself and the follow up, intercalating staff and student views on what the exercise was trying to develop and what progress was made. The comments of the six student participants give some indication of the value of this exercise and, more tentatively, of what field courses can achieve: 'We felt we were finding out something for ourselves . . . . It was also rewarding . . . to find that new ideas emerged as we were actually carrying out the field work' (Maizels et al., 1984: 149).

Yet, whatever the value of these and other evaluations of particular field courses (including Dando and Weidel, 1971; Cloke et al., 1981; Wheeler, 1985), they provide us with no clear evidence on the general value of fieldwork. This would require far more thorough and extensive investigation and could well benefit from the insights and methodology developed through research on fieldwork in other disciplines (Novak, 1976; Falk and Balling, 1979; Mason, 1980; Disinger, 1985; Kern and Carpenter, 1986; Lopushinsky and Besaw, 1986; McKenzie et al., 1986).

● *Centrality* Although fieldwork may have been vital to geographers of Wooldridge's and Sauer's generation, contemporary geographers ask rather different questions and employ different research methods. The old concerns for the areal study of linked physical and human phenomena and of visible landscape have declined relative to interest in theory and process (e.g. see Burt, 1988). It follows that the traditional rationale for the field course is also harder to maintain (Corey, 1969; Gibson, 1972; Sauer, 1976). As Hart (1979: ix) wistfully observed: 'dirty boots have largely gone out of fashion in Geography since World War II. The focus of the discipline has shifted . . . from the empirical and the concrete to the abstract and theoretical'.

● *Cost* The heavy time and financial costs of fieldwork have long been recognized as a factor weakening the position of geography in most undergraduate and graduate programmes in the USA (Gibson, 1972, p. 58). In Britain, fieldwork has come under increasing attack from central and local governments and college administrators seeking to cut costs. Pressures on fieldwork, especially for longer trips, are bound to persist while resources remain limited.

● *Alternatives* As we shall show in chapter 4, project work need not be fieldbased. As project work spreads across the geography curriculum and use of independent study grows, it may well be that many of the stated objectives for fieldwork will be met elsewhere in the curriculum. In such circumstances, fieldwork may not receive the same protected status that it has in the past.

3.4 ORGANIZING EFFECTIVE FIELDWORK

Whatever is concluded about the value of fieldwork, most teachers in geographical higher education are called on, at some time or other, to design and execute a field course of at least several days' duration. In this section, we suggest some general guidelines, drawn from both the available literature and our own experience to help in this process.

Similarities in course design   There should be clear aims and objectives and the form of teaching and assessment should be directed towards them. Pay particular attention to the sequencing of activities. A field course designed to develop student's wonder and concern for the environment will be very different from one designed to develop competence in research techniques.

Differences in course design   Field courses also present problems and opportunities in course design that are different from conventional taught courses. In particular, they offer educational opportunities for students to experience discovery, autonomy in learning and powers of leadership. The students are also required to attend for a relatively long continuous period. In all these respects designing an effective field course is different from designing other areas of the curriculum.

The wider curriculum   It is perfectly acceptable for fieldwork to be something special since, if well designed, it supplies an intensity and range of experiences that classroom studies cannot match. Yet, equally, it should not be rigidly separated from other parts of the curriculum. In Britain the annual field course often seems a required, and perhaps relict, part of a degree course rather than being integral to it. Field courses linked to particular options may offer easier ways of integrating what is learnt in the field with what is developed through classroom and private study, but they will be effective only if these links are made.

Choose an appropriate location   The choice of location for a geography field course is often the most important decision to be made, yet too often it is chosen without much reference to educational criteria. Some of the issues to consider are outlined in table 3.2.

Table 3.2   Issues in the choice of fieldwork location

Special	————	Everyday
Urban	————	Rural
Foreign	————	Local
Central	————	Dispersed
Familiar	————	New

To elaborate, it is very common to choose field course venues that are somehow 'special' at the expense of more 'everyday' landscapes. To give a British example, we suspect that many more courses go to seaside resorts than to heavy industrial centres. There may be practical reasons for choosing the seaside resort, not least of which is the attraction of cheap accommodation out of the tourist season, but it might be more educationally desirable that students experience the everyday environment of an industrial town. An exotic location may lift morale, give an academic intensity to the course and even help recruit students into the geography programme, but it is important to ensure that the excitement of the special location is not achieved at the expense of the academic programme.

'Foreign' fieldwork, with its opportunities to visit exotic places and cultures, presents particular problems in this respect. Here the temptation to visit numerous locations, Cooks Tour style, can be irresistible, but students and staff then spend long hours in buses. Some geography can be learned like this, but our experience is that interest soon declines and much time is wasted. Although there are practical things that can be done to overcome the boredom and fatigue that seemingly endless coach tours generate, such as moving students around so that each spends time in a window seat and ensuring that they know exactly where they are on a map at all times, the educational benefits might be far greater by simply choosing a domestic location that is outside the student's normal ambit.

Some departments repeatedly return to the same locations for their fieldwork. This helps develop staff expertise, builds up contacts, allows the college library to build up necessary resources and enables students to build on the work of previous visits. In this respect, it may be possible for collaborative staff–student research projects to be developed in the manner of some American anthropology departments (Kemper, 1981). However, repeated use of the same venue risks staff becoming bored by the same old routine and becoming too obviously authorities on the area concerned rather than facilitators of student learning. More practically, contacts may be overused and sites damaged.

Preparation   Like other forms of teaching, fieldwork is most effective when well prepared. Since fieldwork is often expensive, as noted above, it behoves teaching staff to ensure that its rewards are maximized. It is sensible to spend preparatory time in the classroom explaining and developing the field-course theme or themes.

Specifying themes   Developing the last point further, a field course benefits from having a clear theme. It should have an intellectual rationale, which translates into clearly identified goals. Students need to see how one day's work links into the rest of the programme and how the work of the various student groups link into each other. Gibson (1972) describes how the geography programme at the University of Arizona developed a field seminar in just such a manner.

Balancing student autonomy and staff supervision   This balance is a problem in all forms of teaching, but it becomes particularly important in field teaching where students often work independently. For many, this is the joy of learning in the field – of learning by seeing and, in particular, the thrill of the unexpected and the unplanned. To make the most of this opportunity, however, staff and students need to define topics that, first, are intellectually demanding and operationally feasible in the time available and, second, give the feeling of personal discovery while still linking into the general course theme.

Developing personal skills   We have already emphasized that, in addition to specifically geographic objectives, field courses provide major opportunities to develop a wide range of skills – in presentation, communication, group work and so on. However, development of these skills is not an automatic consequence of undertaking field work, but has to be planned, ensuring that a range of learning situations is offered to the students.

Attend to detail   The level of detailed preparation required in field work is far higher than the inexperienced teacher could ever imagine. Among other things, the present authors have seen otherwise carefully planned data-gathering exercises in climatology fail for the want of a screwdriver, a video project fail because a student left the battery charger in college, a library-based project fail because the archives were closed for stock-taking and a project on glacial landscapes abandoned because the coach became wedged between two drystone walls on a narrow country lane. If working abroad, remember that some quite familiar items at home may be unobtainable. There are a number of practical handbooks which, although directed at school level, should be consulted (e.g. McKay and Parson, 1986; Hindson and Savin 1988).

Attend to safety   Legal responsibility for taking students on field courses, especially when residential, is a complex matter which varies from country to country (according to such matters as the age of majority, insurance regulations and the legality or otherwise of waivers of responsibility). It is not possible to give specific advice here, other than recommending that safety be taken seriously. Most colleges have a safety officer who can be consulted. It cannot be stressed too strongly that accidents have happened on field courses; never assume that they will not happen to you or your students and always have contingency plans available in case they do.

Encourage proper data analysis   Data, once collected, deserve proper analysis. Gardiner and Unwin (1986) show how the portable computer now enables data from field exercises to be analysed immediately on a field course and then used to inform further work in the same course. Similarly, qualitative data should be properly collated and made ready for further analysis. Students must be given a feeling of having completed work that they are asked to undertake.

Follow-up sessions   It is all too easy for research-oriented field courses to be preoccupied with gathering data and lose sight of the necessity to analyse and reflect on these data. Equally, field courses centred on the student's encounters with people and landscape can remain at the level of the personal and anecdotal. Follow-up sessions at college, especially after a short while has elapsed, are a cheap and effective means of encouraging proper analysis and mature reflection. Harrison and Luithlen (1983), for example, describe a fieldwork programme in which students progressed through a series of stages culminating in a role-playing simulation.

3.5 ALTERNATIVES TO TRADITIONAL FIELD COURSES

There are a variety of reasons why it might be necessary to limit or even abolish fieldwork. The college may decide that it is too dangerous or, more probably, too expensive, the necessary block of time may be needed for something else seen as more important or students might decide to avoid any courses based around it. In this section we argue that there are alternatives that can meet many of its objectives.

Wooldridge argued that geographers should develop 'the art of seeing' using accessible local ground as a laboratory for teaching (Wooldridge, 1955: 80) and was a brilliant exponent of the intensive day-long field excursion (usually taken slowly and on foot). This local tradition remains alive in many North American geography departments which use the local environment for short field trips (Wheeler, 1985; McNee, 1987) and seminar- or project-based work (e.g. Kakela, 1979). Elsewhere, we suspect that far too few geography departments use that which is immediately accessible. Certainly one of the probable benefits of re-directing fieldwork towards the local environment is that, by using such an approach, fieldwork becomes better linked into the student's everyday experience.

In a similar manner, the advantages of student-centred work, which fieldwork offers, can be obtained by incorporating linked project work into the curriculum. As argued in chapter 5, almost any individual course, even a whole degree programme, can be taught in this way. For example, Kakela (1979) describes a course at Michigan State University in which student groups followed a legislative bill designed to enforce deposits on soft drink and beer containers. The evident success of the course stemmed from the students' interest in the issue, but the way it was taught, in a manner that had most of what one normally sees in a residential field course but at far less cost, was also important.

It is clear that a course like that described by Kakela can address many of the objectives that we consider to be important. Unfortunately, it may not so readily achieve the intellectual and social intensity that many see as central to a successful residential field course. One way for such courses to develop intellectual intensity and at the same time avoid this second danger is to revise the timetable to enable students and staff to concentrate on a single theme for a single concentrated block of time. The usual timetable structure in higher education makes this difficult to achieve. As Hewton (1977: 79) observes, 'the large majority of undergraduate courses have in common a dedication to a particular form of timing which, for want of a better term might be called dispersed'. He goes on to note that, even in single-subject degree programmes, students usually take a variety of courses each term, with each course meeting a number of times each week: 'this pattern is, now, so well established . . . that it is seldom questioned'.

There are various examples from other disciplines in which concentrated study schemes have been attempted in higher education. At the Massachusetts Institute of Technology, for example, the physics department revised the timetable to allow staff and students to immerse themselves in a set of related topics for a month. The type of teaching varied but the topics under study remained the same. This organization of the timetable is predicated on the ideas, first, that having a variety of topics under study distracts from effective learning and, second, that concentration on a single theme using a variety of learning activities enables the student to reach higher levels of synthesis. The study concluded that there 'was an overwhelming consensus that they felt they had learned far more physics than in the previous courses they had taken, and their knowledge was richer, more diverse, more interesting, more interconnected and unified' (Parlett and King, 1971; cited by Hewton, 1977: 83). It also indicated that, although students' views differed as to the amount of work done, all agreed that this procedure greatly affected the quality of relationships in the classroom and the amount they participated in discussions. In research into similar concentrated study programmes for the Nuffield Foundation in Britain, field courses in geography, biology and archaeology were seen simply as particular examples of concentrated study programmes (Squires, 1976).

It seems to us, therefore, that a possible alternative to the traditional field course is available by changing the departmental timetable to create particular periods of the year when classes can concentrate on a specific theme. The literature on concentrated study programmes convinces us that they offer many of the advantages of the residential field courses and minimize some of the difficulties.

3.6 CONCLUSION

Fieldwork is an expensive form of teaching but many argue that it is also one of the most effective and enjoyable. The historic legacy of fieldwork as a desirable part of the training of geographers clearly still exists and departments have struggled hard to maintain their programmes against a background of substantial cuts in resources. In the United Kingdom, these courses are mostly compulsory. Elsewhere in the world, as a result of different degree structures and funding mechanisms, fieldwork is less commonly a compulsory part of the curriculum, often appearing as an option. Yet, whether compulsory or not, every year many thousands of geography students participate in residential field courses away from their institutions, and these courses consume a great deal of staff time and nervous energy both in their planning and execution.

Given all this activity and the assumed importance of fieldwork, it is surprising that virtually no studies have attempted to evaluate its effectiveness. In the absence of such studies, we prefer to remain sceptical about its true value. It may well be that fieldwork as currently practised is effective simply because it is one of the few times that most of us engage in explicitly student-centred work. We have no doubt that the vast majority of our own students enjoy their fieldwork and that they can learn a great deal from it, but we feel that similar benefits might accrue from the same, or even fewer, resources being invested in other forms of teaching such as concentrated study blocks, practicals and projects. The next chapter deals with some alternative options. Before closing, however, we offer some suggestions about further action that flow from the current chapter.

- *Look hard at existing use of fieldwork*   Too often field courses and shorter field trips habitually return to the same locations and follow the same patterns because that is the way that things are done. Yet, given the expenditure of time and money on such events, it is worth sitting down and discussing whether or not another type of teaching might yield better results.
- *Look hard at the educational purpose of field courses*   As these are usually annual events, there is plenty of time between field courses to plan them from an educational point of view, paying attention to sequencing of the activities and to student development over the course's duration. In addition, if the timetable is within your department's control, consider if it could or should be changed to facilitate concentrated study on a particular topic, possibly using fieldwork as one teaching method.
- *Provide adequate briefing*   Field courses benefit from allowing sufficient time for both briefing and de-briefing sessions. If the students collect any data during the course, it is vital that they receive enough time to analyse their information properly.
- *Encourage students to be active*   Even on 'look–see' types of excursion, students learn more by being required to complete worksheets or similar response sheets.
- *Assess the students' work*   Students work better when they see that fieldwork is assessed as seriously as other parts of the curriculum and that, in the process, they receive full recognition and reward for the work that they do.
- *Carry out student evaluations*   These can usefully include asking students for suggestions about how their projects might be developed on later field courses. If handled effectively, it is possible not just to build on their experiences but also to show students something of the process by which research programmes develop over time.

KEY READING

Apart from the somewhat dated Association of American Geographers' manual on field training in geography (AAG, 1969), there is very little published literature on fieldwork in geography and most standard texts on teaching methods ignore it completely. However, the book on *Teaching in Laboratories* by Boud et al. (1986) contains a great deal of useful advice that can readily be incorporated into the practice of geography field courses, particularly in respect of defining aims and objectives, sequencing and organizing. Recently, Australian writers have gone some way towards remedying this overall deficiency, and the works by Lonergan and Andresen (1988) and Tranter (1988) are strongly recommended. Examples of useful projects and case studies are to be found in many issues of the *Journal of Geography in Higher Education* (e.g. see Finlayson, 1979; Keene, 1982; Ashworth, 1983; Harrison and Luithlen, 1983; Maizels et al., 1984; Gardiner and Unwin, 1986; Burt, 1988; Cosgrove and Daniels, 1989).

4

Practicals and Projects

Tell me, I forget
Show me, I remember
Involve me, I understand

4.1 INTRODUCTION

This Chinese proverb provides justification for those teaching methods which encourage what we termed 'student-centred learning' in chapter 1, namely, methods that challenge students to take responsibility for their own learning and, in so doing, to alter radically the role of the teacher. Student-centred work in geographical higher education can take various forms but has traditionally been confined to fieldwork courses (chapter 3) or classes concerned with techniques of geographical analysis. In the United Kingdom, the latter are usually called 'practicals' (the generic term that we use here) whereas readers based elsewhere will probably recognise them as 'laboratories'. In this chapter we examine the use of practicals, along with project work, in teaching geography.

Before proceeding with our analysis, it is worth noting that most of the literature takes the view that practical work is necessarily skills based, with very few published studies giving examples of its use in substantive teaching (the major exceptions reported in geography seem to be experiments using games and simulations; see chapters 5 and 7). In fact, there are numerous ways that practicals and project-based teaching can be employed besides simply teaching about techniques. Moreover, there are three reasons for arguing that the conventional techniques-based practical is actually *bad* teaching strategy. First, by making active learning a feature of just one or two courses, we seriously neglect one of the most effective routes to student learning in other courses. Second, divorcing technique from substance tends to isolate them both, so that only the best students are able to link them when called on to do so. Almost invariably, students end up thinking that they know a great deal about techniques yet are incapable of suggesting appropriate ones for specific research problems. Third, when there are legitimate reasons for teaching about methods of investigation, such as geographical information systems and remote sensing, there is a false assumption that this must always be by means of the practical. Geography is not alone in this conflation of 'practical' with 'teaching about techniques'; the same error is made in one of the best known general texts on teaching in higher education (Beard, 1976).

The separation within academic geography between teaching about techniques and teaching about substance has occurred fairly recently. The traditional style of practical teaching followed a pattern first introduced into higher education during the nineteenth century in physics and chemistry courses (Brown and Atkins, 1988). The aim was that students should repeat many of the classical experiments of science and, by looking over the shoulders of the great scientists, acquire relevant technical skills, understand methods of scientific enquiry, develop skills in problem solving and acquire professional attitudes. The earliest geographical courses were concerned with land survey, which, by the early 1950s, had broadened out to become essentially cartographic courses – incorporating material on land survey, map projections, map appreciation, map interpretation and usually some draftsmanship. This early diet of skills had several useful characteristics. By and large, it was self-contained with very little interaction with the rest of the curriculum. It also avoided duplication of skills teaching elsewhere. What was taught was effectively substantive geography; it just happened that the practical method was an appropriate and obvious way to teach it. Although some maps, hardware models and relatively cheap survey instruments might be used, this approach did not make heavy demands on departmental resources and it was assumed that it could be implemented by almost any member of the teaching staff.

Over the years, however, changes occurred in the content, character and perceived importance of practical teaching. Statistics, remote sensing, computing and geographical information systems were progressively taken on board. As courses expanded to include these new topics, much of the older material was discarded, but this placed pressure on the design of the practical class since important new sets of knowledge and skills were required. For example, students needed a working knowledge of mathematics, keyboard skills, and some familiarity with basic laboratory procedures – knowledge and skills that might be better provided in ancillary courses rather than on an *ad hoc* basis in the practical itself.

In saying this, we do not argue that the old-style practical-based techniques course is completely outmoded. There are some basic and general skills, such as statistical analysis to the level of correlation and regression, cartography and map appreciation, computer use and, possibly, remote sensing, that are necessary background to other courses. The styles of work to be introduced are pertinent to teaching the use of techniques, but 'learning by doing' itself can be used over the entire curriculum.

4.2 ADVANTAGES OF PRACTICAL AND PROJECT WORK

Practicals and project-based teaching have various advantages over other teaching methods. One such advantage, as Monk and Alexander (1973) illustrate in their design of a laboratory class in introductory physical geography, is that this style of teaching can be designed to address almost all educational objectives or combinations of objectives. Following Boud et al. (1986; after Carter and Lee, 1981), it is useful to distinguish three basic styles of work:

- *controlled exercises*, which are wholly devised by the teacher for completion in one or two supervised classes and which usually yield a well-known result;
- *experimental investigations*, which offer choices of procedure and may extend over several formal classes with limited supervision;
- *research projects*, which are significant pieces of work in which an original problem is assigned to, or selected by, the student who then pursues it over an extended period of time with minimal supervision.

A similar, but more extended, typology is presented by Brown and Atkins (1988: 97–100). Table 4.1 shows how these styles of work can be used to address different educational objectives. Each style of work can be used to address any, or all, of the listed objectives but, as the Table shows, some are more easily used to address a specified objective and are more effective at achieving that objective.

Table 4.1   Educational objectives and style of student-centred work

Objective	Style of work		
	Controlled exercise	Experimental investigation	Research project
Memorization of knowledge	Good	Moderate	Moderate
Comprehension and understanding	Excellent	Good	Good
Ability to think critically	Good	Excellent	Excellent
Creativity and problem solving	Moderate	Excellent	Excellent
Practical skill	Excellent	Good	Good

Source: Based on Brown and Atkins, 1988: 97–100

A second advantage of these methods is that they enable teachers to change radically their relationship with the students to the benefit of both. Each method allows some measure of responsibility to be devolved from the lecturer to the student and, in the case of a research project, the relationship can turn into that of the teacher acting as adviser to a colleague, with the expectation of high student commitment.

A third advantage is that these methods provide different learning opportunities. Considerable research evidence shows that students learn in different ways and there are no *a priori* grounds for favouring one over the other in the teaching methods adopted. A number of models of how students learn have been proposed, of which one of the most useful classifications is that produced by Kolb (1976) in which four learning modes are recognized: concrete experience, reflective observation, abstract conceptualization and active experimentation. Traditional teaching methods may offer few opportunities for students who learn well through concrete experience or active experimentation. Controlled experiments and experimental investigations should allow more opportunity for these modes of learning, as should most research projects.

The overall principle that students can learn effectively by undertaking practical tasks should be qualified in two ways. First, it is essential that any practical or project is relevant to the student's needs and is seen as a meaningful experience rather than a daunting hurdle to be climbed. Second, students cannot possibly learn from such work unless constructive feedback is offered.

4.3 USING PRACTICALS AND PROJECTS

It is clear that planning and supervising any practical or project is hard work. It simultaneously involves abilities to explain and present information (as in lecturing) along with the questioning, listening and answering typical of group discussion work. To these are also added the managerial tasks associated with the production of support materials, using graduate assistants and technicians, and organizing student activities. To give a better idea of the operational implications of these points, we shall consider matters further under the three categories of controlled exercises, experimental investigations and research projects.

Controlled Exercises

There are many ways of using controlled exercises in teaching and in this section we give guidelines for lecture-linked assignments, reading lists, practical classes and 'self-paced' schemes.

Lecture-linked assignments   The simplest controlled exercise is a short project, linked to a lecture or seminar, over which the teacher has broad control. Such exercises can be used to break up a single lecture, or as an additional exercise to be completed in the student's own time, or linked to a laboratory class. In North America, short assignments of this type are often used and assessed, but in Britain and elsewhere they are neglected. Assignments can reinforce material introduced in class, test student comprehension, point the way to further work and supply additional factual material. If assessed they provide invaluable and rapid feedback on student performance.

Take, for example, the case of a third year option climatology course. Principles of atmospheric motion are notoriously hard to teach and the lecture is particularly ill suited to the task. Simple assignments, involving practical tasks provide an easy yet incisive way of tackling this problem. Some examples might be as follows.

1   Ask students to solve a simple numerical problem; for example, find the magnitude of the geostrophic wind for given pressure gradients and latitudes.

2   Provide pressure and actual wind data for a synoptic situation and ask students to plot isobars and interpret these data in relationship to the geostrophic model.

3   Use a computer program to calculate the geostrophic vorticity (see Fisher, 1986).

The 'Coriolis' Acceleration

The following experiment is designed to illustrate the Coriolis effect in determining wind direction by setting up a direct physical analogy to the earth's rotation. After completing it you should be able to express rates of rotation in the SI unit (radians/second), state what sense a rotation is in, and understand how the apparent deflection of an object's motion measured relative to a rotating co-ordinate system comes about. Finally, you should appreciate the effects of the speed of the object and the co-ordinate system used on its deflection. The lecture will give a formal treatment of these topics.

Take care as you do this; I will not be responsible for any damage to your hi-fi system!

(a) Cut a piece of card to record shape with a spindle hole and place on your turntable. The plane of the turntable is analogous to the tangent plane to the earth's surface at any latitude as described in the lecture.
(b) Set the turntable rotating at 33 r.p.m. What is the sense (clockwise or anti-clockwise) of this rotation when viewed from both above and below? Remembering that the earth rotates about its polar axis at 7.3×10^{-5} rads/second, what is the rate of rotation about its local vertical of your turntable and how does this compare with earth?
(c) Now, with the turntable still rotating, try to draw a pencil line from the perimeter to the centre spindle. What happens? Is the apparent deflection in the same sense as the turntable rotation or opposite to it? Is it to the right or left of the intended direction of motion?
(d) Repeat at 45 r.p.m., and, if you have a really old player, at 78 r.p.m. What are these rotations in radians per second and how do they influence the apparent deflection?

Figure 4.1   An assignment providing a simple physical analogy to illustrate the Coriolis effect

4 Ask students to take readings of wind speed and direction over a day.

5 Suggest a simple physical analogy that illustrates the Coriolis effect.

There is not space here to elaborate on each of these assignments, but figure 4.1 illustrates how one might proceed in the case of example 5.

In preparing such assignments, however, it is important to be aware of the time that preparation can take. Brown and Atkins (1988), for instance, report that a 10-minute demonstration of a laboratory procedure can take 4 hours to record and a complex demonstration as much as 20 hours. Warnings about time are particularly significant if the decision is made to produce high quality output for handouts, tape–slide presentations and the like. Even when readily accessible media are used, such as desk top publishing systems for producing handouts, the amount of time necessary can be considerable. Therefore it pays to see if appropriate assignments do not already exist. These might be obtained by mutual co-operation with colleagues working in other institutions or from commercial sources (e.g. the practical manuals devised for North American physical geography courses), which might be used directly or suitably modified.

Following on from the last point, it is also important to realize that assignments can rapidly generate an enormous marking and administrative task, especially if used for the assessment of large classes. A solution often adopted is to employ graduate students as markers, but another worth considering is to use computer-managed learning in which the computer generates and marks individual tests using selections from a bank of test items set up by the instructor (see also chapter 7).

The reading list   Much is made of the idea of 'reading' for a degree and, in effect, a traditional reading list is really a type of assignment – even if rarely thought of in this way. Regrettably, many reading lists seem to be designed to impress rather than to guide, defeating the presumed object of the exercise, which is to encourage students to read the original literature for themselves. Frequently, book lists are very long and unannotated. It is possible to justify this by arguing that long reading lists do not bias interpretation by comprehensively covering the pertinent literature in a given field, but this is a counsel of perfection. All too often this strategy leads to inefficient reading by students, biased, ironically, by factors like the immediate availability of the material.

Recognizing that students are unlikely to follow up more than two or three references for each topic, it makes sense to offer short annotated lists clearly indicating the most useful sources for each lecture with possible alternatives, along with a specific question for each topic towards which the reading should be directed. It goes without saying that reading lists should be checked with librarians to ensure that sources are reasonably available; most librarians are only too anxious to help. Reading materials can often be put on reserve under the course title by college librarians to ensure that individual students do not monopolize them, and, subject to whatever copyright laws are in force, it is sometimes possible to make photocopies available.

The practical class   Practical classes, a common feature of many geography programmes, usually consist of a lecture introduction followed by a student exercise using worksheets provided by the teacher. Students are often asked to write up such exercises for assessment. In academic geography, these exercises are usually sequenced with all activities following each other at much the same pace for every student. They are thus relatively easy, if time consuming, to set up and control, and give the instructor a clear impression of what the students actually learn.

The style of working involved has been referred to as a 'closed' practical. It is a way of enlivening an otherwise passive lecture (see chapter 2), letting students 'learn by doing', but overuse as a teaching method in its own right does highlight certain underlying deficiencies (Unwin, 1980). Closed practicals can often resemble rote learning. Apart from the single specified sequence of activities, all other possible sequences have been closed, giving the student no choice in problem selection, data analysis or presentation. Any data provided will usually be very simple, free of errors and small in volume. Similarly, the accompanying worksheet will detail the sequence of activities required, and the success or failure of the exercise is likely to be judged, not by how much the students learn, but by how smoothly the session runs. Throughout this type of exercise, the accent is very much on mechanical performance at the expense of thought and insight: a useful strategy when initially teaching difficult concepts or operational skills, but less useful for teaching conceptual material.

It is sensible to make the worksheets for closed practicals independent of the data, since they can then be varied from class to class or within the same class according to the interests of individual students. It goes without saying that the data used should be real and have some substantive interest. Artificial data selected for ease of computation were very much a feature of pre-computer texts, but nowadays there is no reason why students should not use realistic volumes of data. It can also be valuable to provide students with a bibliography of real applications of the methods covered so that they can see the wider relevance of their work. Any assessment of work from this kind of practical is difficult. It may be important to ensure that the work has been completed, but hard to find criteria by which such work can be assessed properly.

A much neglected skill in practical teaching lies in the effective use of graduate assistants ('demonstrators') and technical staff (see Brown and Atkins, 1988: 96). Both are employed to help students carry out the required activities, and so it is essential that they understand the practical and have some training in posing, as well as answering, questions about the work. It pays for staff to meet their assistants on a regular basis through the course to go through the activity, discuss problems and suggest teaching strategies. Brown and Atkins (1988) recommend the use of a comprehensive practical manual setting out the timetable of work, the individual worksheets and some idea of the expected answers.

Self-paced schemes   Controlled experiments are used extensively in the physical sciences, usually in connection with a theory-based lecture programme (for a more general discussion of such resource-based teaching, see chapter 6). This approach needs careful detailed documentation and considerable supervision from demonstrators or technical staff. It has the advantage of smoothing the demand for instruments and might be adopted with profit for courses in geography that need access to limited computer or laboratory facilities. Against this, however, it must be said that it is difficult to monitor student progress and to evaluate how well the package achieves its aims. Furthermore, the course designer has no mechanism for sequencing experiments according to their difficulty or relationship to theory, both of which become the student's responsibility.

Therefore several variations on this model have been suggested. One extension is self-pacing, in which students have to master one block of work before proceeding to the next. Several such self-paced schemes have been described for introductory courses in human geography (Fox and Wilkinson, 1977; Backler, 1979; Fox et al., 1987), but the method can be adopted for closed practicals. Cho (1982) gives a detailed description of a self-paced course in spatial data analysis, which replaced a traditional course that had run into difficulties arising from differences in student backgrounds. The new course uses a self-paced mastery approach often referred to as a Personalized System of Instruction, or Keller Plan, in which the student works through a number of units, each with an introduction and a list of behavioural objectives, activities and exercises.

The advantages of self-pacing are principally those of flexibility. Students are able to pace themselves as befits their timetables, backgrounds and inclinations. In particular, it is claimed that weaker students are less likely to be overwhelmed by what they see as 'falling behind'. Units can be switched at will and, once the framework has been established, the course is able to evolve organically. If needed, sections of a course can be bought or brought in from outside. However, one should not make too much of this flexibility. Self-pacing offers the possibility of *good* rather than easy teaching, with most of the relevant research (e.g. on Keller Plans), indicating that they do improve student performance. The disadvantages lie, first, in the effort and resources needed, which can lead, in turn, to a reluctance to update and improve course materials, second, in the fact that some students find it difficult to organize their work load properly, tending to spend far more time on self-paced projects than on other, more discretionary, activities such as reading, and, finally, in the difficulty of monitoring self-paced schemes, since students can easily collude in assessed work.

Some of these difficulties are illustrated by a self-paced course developed by a team of physical geographers over a period of 5 years using grant aid (Clarke and Gregory, 1982). It consists of a series of units each designed to illuminate a measurement technique in physical geography and is intended for second year students. The twelve topics addressed range from considerations of erosion rates, through field techniques, to laboratory analysis, modelling and simulation. Each unit was designed to take about 5 hours and is delivered by weekly workbooks and tape–slide presentations, supported by weekly 'clinics' where instructors are available for consultation. Assessment is by compulsory work in each unit, project essays and an examination that probes the student's ability to use the techniques in the design of research projects (see also chapter 8). The labour in setting this up is evident, as are the demands made on students. It is interesting to note that the university's 'alternative' student prospectus describes the course as 'only for the masochistic'!

Experimental investigations

Experimental investigations allow some student choice and initiative and reward these appropriately. Ideally, they consist of experiments in which the outcome, if not exactly unknown, is at least mildly uncertain and depends critically on what the student decides to do. As table 4.1 earlier indicated, they provide opportunities to exercise practical skills, test comprehension and understanding, and display critical abilities. In science teaching, the evidence shows that students can become highly motivated when undertaking experimental investigations (Bliss and Ogborn, 1977). In geography, where the experimental tradition is much weaker and where it is often asserted that the real world is so complex that it precludes the reductivist approach that characterizes the experimental method, similar experiments are harder to devise. An exception is provided by Church (1988), who supplies a conceptual basis and sample materials for what he calls a 'problem oriented' approach to geomorphological teaching consisting of a series of experimental investigations linked to a lecture course. For example, Church links lectures on global and regional water balances with a practical session that asks students to compile a specific water balance for their own home region, lectures on muskeg are linked to one on the hydrology of permafrost regions and so on.

It is often much easier than might be thought to convert a traditional closed practical into an experimental investigation. For example, the typical controlled investigation that characterizes most practical teaching of statistics in geography can be turned into an experimental investigation by making it more 'open ended' (Wehry, 1970; Finegold, 1972). One strategy is to allow students to choose their data while retaining teacher control over the methods to be adopted. By choosing their own data, students control the research questions asked and can generate their own studies in accordance with their background and interests. This data selection can use normal pencil and paper methods, but, if facilities permit, it is more efficient to store all the data on computer and allow students to create their own subsets for analysis. Unwin (1980), for example, describes teaching principal components analysis in which three data files, each with at least twenty individual variables, are made available which, in turn, creates well in excess of 100,000 possible individual student problems each using six variables. As Goddard (1976) points out, most departments have several data holdings used for research that can be used to establish teaching sets and nowadays it is fairly easy to acquire machine-readable data sets suitable for this purpose.

At a higher level of complexity, practicals can be open ended with respect to technique by providing data and a choice of analytical techniques. Again, these can use pencil and paper, but it is more realistic to use one or other of the 'user-friendly' packages, such as SAS or MINITAB, supplemented by appropriate routines to calculate specifically geographical measures that are not implemented in the basic package.

An experimental approach to teaching statistical methods is not limited to applications of techniques to geographical data. Geography students often lack understanding of fundamental statistical concepts such as independence, randomness and sampling – themselves the foundations on which more complex ideas are built. Various solutions to this problem have been adopted and are reflected in the available textbooks. Some ignore it completely, concentrating on a 'cookbook' type of treatment that emphasizes applications (e.g. Shaw and Wheeler, 1985) or advocate reliance on distribution-free and robust methods (e.g. Cox and Anderson, 1978). Relatively few offer a thorough treatment (see Silk (1979a) for an honourable exception).

If students lack mathematical ability, there is much to be said for a simple experimental approach of the type illustrated by Silk (1979b). This uses a computer program that places point data into a defined area of space in a series of repeated runs by the same student or, if run in the classroom, by different students in the same class. Each simulation represents the outcome of an independent random process so that the histogram of results for, say, the calculated 'nearest-neighbour' statistic is an approximation to its underlying sampling distribution. Along the way, students are introduced to concepts of independence and randomness, the construction of a test statistic and its sampling

```
1     BASIC computer program

10    REM:     A PROGRAM TO ILLUSTRATE THE CENTRAL LIMIT THEOREM
20    REM:     USING RND TO DRAW N SUCCESSIVE SAMPLES EACH OF
30    REM:     SIZE M FROM A UNIFORMLY-DISTRIBUTED HYPOTHETICAL
40    REM:     POPULATION. WRITTEN IN VAX-BASIC, 1988.
50    DIM H(10), P(10)
60    REM:     RANDOMIZE RESETS THE RANDOM NUMBER GENERATOR IN
70    REM:     VAX BASIC. IT MAY BE DIFFERENT ON OTHER MACHINERY
80    RANDOMIZE
90    FOR I = 1 TO 10
100        LET H(I) = 0
110        LET P(I) = 0
120   NEXT I
130   INPUT"HOW MANY SAMPLES ";N
140   INPUT"WHAT SAMPLE SIZE    ";M
150   FOR J = 1 TO N
160        LET A = 0 , 0
170         FOR K = 1 TO M
180   REM:     IN VAX BASIC RND GIVES NUMBERS FROM 0 TO 1
190        LET X = 100 ✱ RND
200        LET I = INT (X/10) + 1
210        LET P(I) = P(I) + 1
220        LET A = A + X
230        NEXT K
240        LET A = A/M
250        PRINT"SAMPLE  " ; J ;  "HAS MEAN OF  " ; A
260        LET I = INT(A/10) + 1
270        LET H(I) + H(I) + 1
280   NEXT J
290   PRINT"HISTOGRAM OF ALL  " ; N ; " MEANS"
300   FOR I = 1 TO 10
310        PRINT H(I) ; " " ;
320   NEXT I
330   PRINT
340   PRINT"HISTOGRAM OF THE HYPOTHETICAL POPULATION"
350   FOR I = 1 TO 10
360        PRINT P(I) ; " " ;
370   NEXT I
380   END

2  Specimen results

HOW MANY SAMPLES  ? 100
WHAT SAMPLE SIZE  ?     25

SAMPLE    1 HAS MEAN OF 48,0984

SAMPLE  100 HAS MEAN OF 47,9043
HISTOGRAM OF ALL   100  MEANS
  0    0    0    3    43   50   4    0    0    0
HISTOGRAM OF THE HYPOTHETICAL POPULATION
237   251   247   268   240   247   228   252   263   267
```

Figure 4.2   An experiment to illustrate the central limit theorem as an example of a teaching simulation

distribution, and gain some feel for what a specific significance test is actually doing.

Figure 4.2 lists a BASIC program of the sort that might be used. It can give as many samples of specified size from an underlying rectangular population distribution as required. Although by no means intended as a statement of the programmer's art, it has been used in this form to teach what happens when samples are drawn from a population. Without any recourse to mathematics, the results given for the calculated means of all 100 samples clearly show what the central limit theorem actually means. Although the population has a rectangular distribution in the range 0-100, the sampling distribution of the individual sample means that is formed in the experiment can be seen to be a normal curve sharply peaked around the population value of 50.

Similar experiments can be devised to illustrate many of the statistics that are now taught in geography in higher education including the perennially difficult concept of spatial autocorrelation. Griffith (1987), for instance, devised a simulation that challenges students to design patterns that either maximize or minimize the value of a spatial autocorrelation coefficient. The simulation is both fun to play and good teaching practice in that it does much to demystify a very simple, yet fundamental, concept (see Unwin, 1981).

Experiments with hardware of one kind or another are the norm in the physical sciences, and various strategies for presenting them have been devised (see Boud et al., 1986; Brown and Atkins, 1988). In geography, use of them is patchy. Human geographers have favoured computer models as opposed to simple hardware models (see chapter 7), even though the latter are possible (Morgan, 1967). Rather more use is reported by physical geographers, who have devised a number of laboratory-scale models. These need not be complex. Newsom (1978) shows how a model of a catchment with a linked series of water stores can be constructed using nothing more sophisticated than plastic tubing and three or four beakers. However, this can be still be used to generate realistic hydrographs to evaluate the effects of changes in soil moisture storage or other physical factors on the peak discharge and recession curve (Kay et al., 1982) (see also Payne and Fetherston (1983) for an example of a cheap stream table).

Rather more sophisticated models are also available. Parkinson and Reid (1987), for example, describe a hardware model that allows experiments on shallow groundwater flow to investigate the relationship between slope and the position of the phraetic divide. An attractive feature of their apparatus is that, in the best traditions of experimental science, it enables precise experimental results to be compared with the predictions of a mathematical model of the same process. Haigh and Kilmartin (1987) describe a sophisticated version of the stream table for use in experimental studies of soil erosion. Their bank erosion channel is a large sand-filled tray that can be tilted to a specified angle across which uniform flows of water can be generated and the effects studied. The teaching method adopted was similar to the 'investigative laboratory' of Thornton (1972) in that, after a general introduction to the device, student groups were asked to produce a prospectus for a proposed experiment, justifying their plan by means of a poster and verbal presentation setting out the experimental design and expected results. After modifications to allow the suggested experiments to proceed, data were collected and the results presented in seminars.

This type of teaching has great potential, but requires considerable investment of resources, which may be difficult to justify unless the specific experiment is well integrated into the curriculum and the benefits evaluated as carefully and critically as possible against alternative uses of the same resources. This is especially so given the possibilities opened up by computer modelling. As chapter 7 shows, computer simulations provide a cheap and sophisticated alternative for a wide range of problems in physical geography, with games offering considerable potential in human geography (see also chapter 5 for discussion of role-playing games).

Taken as a whole, we can identify three key uses of model experiments in teaching.

1 *Teaching about the models themselves*, spending sufficient class time to cover their mathematical formulation adequately. The appropriate models for this purpose are those that meet two criteria: first, that their relatively simple structures make them suitable for teaching at the intended level; second, that they produce outputs which can be treated sceptically. Good examples are provided by the various hydrograph models presented in Kirkby et al. (1987).

2 *Teaching about real world processes*, using models as a vehicle. Understanding the details of how the model is structured and solved is less important than being able to formulate sensible hypotheses about how the real world works. Since the experimental results should be as realistic as possible, this demands use of the most complex models. It is probable, for example, that a few years hence the current generation of complex watershed or general circulation models, that have been developed by large research teams and can run only on the fastest of today's 'supercomputers', will be available on personal computers for introductory teaching.

3 *Introducing students to fundamentals of the scientific method*. Almost all the authors of teaching experiments using simulation models claim that they serve higher-order learning objectives. This is a view strongly articulated by Haines-Young (1983: 126) who argues that 'while we may teach that science progresses by the process of conjecture and refutation, rarely do we construct situations in which students can have direct experience of it'. It follows that what are needed are models that can be tested against the real world; the type of model

used is not an issue. This position can be illustrated by models of almost any complexity, but it is sensible to use fairly simple ones whose structure can be dissected to find out why they do, or do not, fit. However, as no rigorous evaluations have yet been reported by geographers who use model experiments in teaching, at the moment we simply do not know if these higher-order objectives are attained.

Compared with controlled exercises, experimental investigations enjoy the advantage of motivating the students, particularly through the freedom that students gain by picking their own way through the work. However, experimental investigations need to be designed with care, especially with regard to monitoring student progress. Almost all need careful briefings, drawing a fine balance between telling students so little that they do not know what is expected of them and so much that the exercise becomes a chore to be completed rather than an exciting opportunity for discovery.

Supplying supervision as the experiment proceeds is not easy. Students may make simple errors, expending far more time and effort on an experiment than was ever intended. It can be argued that, in an ideal world, supervision and counselling would be available at all times on demand but, leaving obvious resourcing problems aside, this is probably both undesirable and unnecessary. In many cases, there is much to be said for a structure in which an initial exposition of a subject is followed by several days on which students work on that subject in their own time, perhaps using a well-designed resource-based learning package, and then to provide timetabled sessions at which difficulties can be sorted out.

Research projects

A research project is a relatively large piece of student work with two main characteristics. First, the problem tackled is relatively new, so that any information obtained may well have intrinsic worth as a contribution to knowledge. Second, it is carried out by individual or small groups of students acting independently subject only to collaboration with a project supervisor (see chapter 5 for a discussion of personal tutorials).

Research projects are widely regarded by both staff and students as a valuable part of the curriculum (Adderley et al., 1975). Their advantages include the following.

- *Relevance* As the topics are often proposed by students themselves, they should be relevant to individual interests and backgrounds.

- *Responsibility*   Since students must accept responsibility for their own work, they experience the satisfaction and frustration of research over an extended period of time.
- *Integration*   Both general and specific objectives are integrated into the same activity. Students must display an ability to think creatively and critically, but also have to exercise basic investigation and communication skills.
- *Training*   Although there is dispute about the broader value of the skills acquired by undertaking research projects, for example in terms of future employability (e.g. Renouf, 1989), there is agreement that undergraduate research projects do serve as a training for that small proportion of students eventually proceeding to graduate studies.

Having said this, one needs to be aware of the sheer diversity of the research project as used in higher education. First, they vary enormously in content. Projects can be based on fieldwork, laboratory experiments, archive or library studies, or analysis of raw data which either have been supplied or are gathered by the student.

Second, projects can be teacher or student centred. As will be seen below, the overwhelming tendency is for them to be teacher centred, with the teacher acting as the arbiter of appropriate topics and research procedures. However, it is also perfectly possible for them to be student centred in which students themselves are intimately involved in the supervision process, inviting them to provide constructive criticism on each other's work (see chapter 5) and including peer assessment in the assessment process (see chapter 8).

Third, projects can be taken as addenda to traditionally arranged curricula or as the key factor in moulding the curriculum. Although there is little experience of the latter policy within geography, proponents of project-based curricula in other disciplines argue that the subject matter examined can be determined only by the practical or theoretical needs of the problems studied (Morgan, 1983; Woods, 1985). The curriculum is based entirely around projects which are presented to students before any preparation or study has occurred. Students then take responsibility for the entire problem-solving process, identifying and acquiring relevant knowledge and skills as they go along. This approach has been used most in fields like medicine, planning, law and agriculture where, in addition to the usual disciplinary pressure on the curriculum, there are also vocational requirements. At McMaster University (Canada), for example, a course in medicine has eliminated conventional science teaching in favour of organization around significant problems – a strategy that has also been adopted in several Australian medical and agricultural courses (see Boud, 1985; 1988).

Finally, research projects can assume markedly different significance in the curriculum. At one end of the spectrum stands the project undertaken as a part of an undergraduate course (e.g. those described by Silk and Bowlby (1981)). This type of project usually involves a good deal of contact with the teacher, extends over a limited period of time and may well be conducted in groups. At the other end of the spectrum stand those cases where the project represents the entire submission for the degree. This category includes the doctoral thesis, the outcome of three or more years of full-time individual study, and also experiments at undergraduate level to construct complete project-based 'degrees by thesis' (e.g. as reported in disciplines other than geography by Eaborn (1970) and Cohen and McVicar (1976)). In between stand various instances in which a research project represents between 15 and 45 per cent of total assessment, as with undergraduate theses that are equivalent in status to one or more formal written examination papers and the extended essay that is frequently the culmination of a 'taught' master's course.

Each of these circumstances imposes different demands on student and supervisor in terms of scope and expected student commitment, a point which is developed in chapter 5 when discussing the relationships involved in personal tutorials. In the interim, it can be said that the relationships involved in research supervision, with their basis in original work and new scholarship, can be one of the most stimulating aspects of higher education for both teachers and students. At the same time, research projects give rise to several problems, especially when used in undergraduate geography.

First, it can be argued they may be biased towards positivist modes of enquiry since they are most easily cast in this framework (Silk and Bowlby, 1981: 158). Projects that make use of other approaches are possible, but it is likely that they will prove more difficult and, to date at least, very little has been published on how they might be structured (see Seamon (1979) for some tentative phenomenological explorations in this direction).

Second, and more practically, there are the administrative issues that are discussed more fully later in this chapter. In the interim, we note that research projects make considerable demands on staff and student time, often leading to uncomfortably large workloads at peak times in the academic year. Similarly, staff should not assume that projects make for easy teaching. Used properly, they make heavy demands on staff time, with a disproportionate loading often falling on staff teaching in popular areas of the curriculum – a loading that is difficult to tackle in constructing teaching timetables or to allow for in any notional calculation of hours spent teaching.

Finally, the assessment of research projects gives rise to problems. No matter what is done to reduce the overall importance in assessment of the finished project, the final mark is almost always seen by students as their first, sometimes only, priority to the detriment of all other elements of the course. Anxious questions begin to be asked as the completion deadline approaches, especially when students are unfamiliar with the assessment criteria. Failure to give clear guidance as to these criteria can seriously impair the quality of the learning experience. Yet, having said that, the fact remains that research projects *are* difficult to assess. For example, a completed research project can contain work that may be difficult to attribute correctly and displays many different qualities. Some of the difficulties this generates are as follows.

- Is it a group submission? (Did all the students work equally? Were there some members of outstanding merit who did all the work?)
- Is it a well written report of some poor research?
- Is it possible to give credit for all those problems you know that the students had through no fault of their own? (If you do, then what about those undeclared problems that you do not know about?)
- Can you allow for all the 'extra' help that you know that the students had from you, your colleagues or the technicians? (Are you rewarding their forwardness in asking for help?)

There are various solutions to these problems. One is to have the work marked by two or more staff so as to ensure fair assessment. Another is to split the responsibilities of the markers in some sensible way such as into a mark for the technical content of the work and another for the general manner of performance. A third is to ask all examiners to mark to a common itemized checklist of the type suggested by Beaumont and Wyn Williams (1983: 13; see also Brown and Atkins, 1988: 142). A fourth is to involve other students in the assessment process (see chapter 8).

4.4 WRITTEN PRESENTATIONS

Learning how to write up the results of an inquiry is as important a part of the process as carrying out the various preparatory tasks that precede the writing stage. Students often work well in the preparatory stages, only to fail to do themselves justice in their final presentations. In this section, we outline some of the issues involved in helping students to write up and present their results (for oral presentations, see chapter 5).

The act of writing is highly valued in Western society. Writing itself is seen as a creative activity and as an economical means of developing clarity of thought and expression, yet all too often teachers in higher education either assume that students have already been taught how best to write up their work or that the skills of writing are a gift which cannot be taught. Either way, it is concluded that there is nothing much that can be done to help students learn the skills involved and any assistance given is usually confined to, first, remedial work with students experiencing extreme difficulty or, second, making reference to a few standard texts (see, for example, Gray (1970), Stein (1977), Day (1979), Mullins (1980) and, at a slightly more specialized level, Booth (1984)).

Writing, however, is a craft which *can* be learned and improved by dint of hard work on the part of the learner (Jenkins and Gold, 1990). Many North American colleges, for instance, now offer writing courses, perhaps including related skills such as word-processing (see chapter 7). These are mostly courses offered to students on a college-wide basis, but there is much that geography teachers themselves can do to assist before being called on to give a final judgment on a student's writing during assessment (Nightingale, 1986; 1991). Some suggestions include the following.

- Draft essay titles or project specifications more carefully. Ask students to write for an audience beyond the tutor or tutorial group. There is evidence that titles such as 'prepare a review for . . . .' on a particular key text, or 'prepare a local radio talk on . . .', or 'how would you convince a sceptic that a mountain area had been glaciated?' are more effective than the usual neutrally targeted titles.
- Rather than offering feedback at the end of the writing task, use a conferencing system in which you have brief consultations during the production of the written assignment to give the students the opportunity to talk through their work during its gestation.
- Institute a student self-assessment scheme. Under this system, every submitted assignment is accompanied by a standard response sheet designed to make students think critically about their writing by weighing their own work against various objective criteria. Chapter 8 shows how this can be done and provides a representative example of a self-assessment form.
- Encourage students to resubmit a second draft after marking and discussing a first version. Indeed, Kirkpatrick (1987) suggests three stages: a 'draft' stage in which the teacher comments simply on ideas and general organization, a 'revised copy' stage in which the teacher comments on content and a 'final copy' stage at which the correctness and wider value of the piece is commented on. Clearly, this involves a higher level of teacher involvement than traditional writing assignments (unless you involve other students in this process).

If these improvements fail to work, then, as noted above, there is much to be said for setting aside cultural assumptions and directly teaching writing and presentation skills using specially selected examples of how effective academic writers actually go about the task. Numerous methods of direct teaching have been proposed and evaluated (see Brown and Atkins (1988: 177–83); for student advice see Dunleavy (1986: 78–136) and Jenkins and Gold (1990)). The major problem with this approach is that most poor writers know what they ought to produce and are perfectly able to distinguish between good and bad writing, yet still perform badly. Indeed, when confronted with their own work, many turn out to be enthusiastic editors, recognizing over-long sentences and removing clichés and jargon, but will repeat these faults in each new piece of work.

Proposing models of the writing process may work with some students. One of the best-known models is that summarized below by the mnemonic SLOWER:

- Select a topic
  - List all your ideas
    - Order them
      - Write the first draft
        - Examine your draft
          - Revise before handing in final copy

Yet, while the research evidence shows that this is useful advice, it does not go far enough and for some may even be counter-productive. Successful writers only rarely follow such a rigid sequence. Instead they move freely between each

Table 4.2   Faults, difficulties and suggested activities for student writing

Fault	Difficulty	Activities
Lack of references or bibliography	Knowledge of conventions	Guidelines/notes Models of good writing practice Study skill books
Poor presentation	Practice of conventions	Using word-processor Audio recording
Failure to answer the question	Understanding the question	Question analysis Unpacking questions Turning questions to statements Skeleton answers
Lack of organization of materials	Failure to make connections	Structural diagrams Use of filing cards Headings etc.
Lack of clarity in expression	Semantics	Comparison of text Re-reading for meaning Systematic redrafting Editing Presentation in different form Redraft in different styles

step and seem to use the writing process not just to say something in print but also to decide what to say. Writing becomes a way of clarifying thought and is likely to become more so as word processor systems become the norm. Moreover, advice to follow a rigid schedule can be completely daunting for students who have a major 'block' about starting a writing project. Overcoming the block by starting anywhere but the beginning, or by drafting an 'easy' section in its entirety at the outset, may be a much better strategy.

Most authorities agree that by far the best way to teach writing skills is by activities directed at specific parts of the process. Table 4.2 makes some suggestions for the five most common faults in student work; all can readily be incorporated into conventional assignments and tutorials without losing too much of the substantive geography content of those teaching sessions.

4.5 ADMINISTRATIVE AND RESOURCE ISSUES

We have already mentioned in passing certain administrative and resource issues involved in teaching geography through projects and practicals, but their significance for the success or otherwise of teaching is such that it is worth explicitly emphasizing them at this stage.

Staff time and resources

Through making students responsible for their own learning, it might seem that these methods will involve less teaching input and lower provision of resources than other methods. The reverse is the case. Project work and practicals require considerable preparation and supervision. In the long run such courses may be an efficient means of saving staff time, but they are initially expensive in both staff time and resources. Individual teachers may decide to do most, or all, of the preparation for a practical course well before that course starts, but a considerable commitment of their time is still necessary to ensure that classes run smoothly through the year. Research projects, in particular, make heavy demands, often leading to uncomfortably large workloads at peak times in the academic year.

These problems are complicated by questions connected with hours of accounting, in other words, the ways in which an institution or department allocates teaching responsibilities. Many of the hours involved in practical or project teaching are difficult to timetable, as noted above, and so may well be omitted or credited at only a nominal level. The net result can be a large, additional, but hidden, burden of teaching – an issue which may need to be resolved by local negotiation and agreement before undertaking such courses.

Equipment and technical support

Practicals and projects can often require space, equipment, consumables and technical support staff. A common problem lies in the provision of laboratory space and its organization. If the work is always 'clean' and does not require any special environment, then a sensible arrangement is to have separate laboratories allocated to specific groups of students (after the manner of the studios typical of planning schools). These would probably be allocated by year on the programme, serving as the centre for all the work that is undertaken, with individual students able to lay claim to their own bench space and storage for project work. Alternatively, a division into separate functions might be made, for example, on the following lines:

- 'dirty' work such as size of sediment analysis, stream table experiments and the like;
- 'clean' and 'dry' environmental work such as instrument preparation and measurement;
- 'wet' chemical work, including adequate fume cupboard provision;
- computer work using terminals and computers, including typical peripherals such as digitizers, plotters and printers;
- storage and issue of maps and other resource materials;
- general work making use of pencil and paper and reading.

In addition it may also be necessary to have a specialist laboratory available for pollen analysis or other experimental techniques that have particular environmental requirements. Ideally, each laboratory should have enough space, or only be used by appropriate student numbers, to meet standard norms for bench, circulation and storage space (Savage, 1964; Archenold et al., 1978) and be reasonably flexible in use. The traditional laboratory layout, with its fixed benches facing a demonstration bench at the front of the room and with fixed wiring and piped supplies, is rapidly being replaced by arrangements using movable benches with overhead supply lines.

A short walk around the physics or chemistry departments in your institution will be sufficient to convince you that either they have too much equipment for teaching or that geography has too little and, again, standards differ greatly from department to department. In general, the evidence that exists shows that geography departments have relatively good computing facilities (Dawson and Unwin, 1984), but most are deficient both in basic laboratory instruments (recorders, test instruments, microscopes and so on) and in more specialized equipment (e.g. sieve shakers, sample preparation equipment, spectrophotometers). Geography departments could once be relied on to have a good library of maps and aerial photographs, but nowadays most seem unable or unwilling to keep their collections up to date.

Safety

As in the case of fieldwork (chapter 3), the question of safety is worth emphasizing in its own right. Accidents in laboratories lead to wasted time, spoilt materials, broken equipment, possible injury and sometimes even litigation. Such accidents are also more common than we wish to recognize.

A typical laboratory in a geography department has four characteristics that make it dangerous. First, it has often been created by modification of pre-existing space rather than being purpose built. Second, at peak times, it is almost certain to be overcrowded, if only because most departments have far more students than they had when the buildings were designed. Third, many geography students have little or no previous experience of laboratory practice. Finally, and most worrying, many staff seem to lack an appreciation of industrial hazards. Typical faults are a failure to wear protective clothing, inadequate warning notices and supervision, obstacles on walls and floors, and no clear idea of procedures to adopt when an accident occurs. Guides to accident prevention are given by DES (1973) and Everett and Jenkins (1977) and deserve much greater currency in geography departments than they now receive.

4.6 CONCLUSION

Practicals and project work have many advantages over traditional lectures and can result in valuable teaching and effective learning, but their use should not be confined simply to teaching about techniques. With thought they can be used in virtually every substantive course and, as with the subjects of the next three chapters, are a valuable alternative to lectures. However, we know of no sustained work evaluating their effectiveness as a teaching method and the research evidence from the physical and natural sciences is equivocal. Certainly, they are better than lectures, demonstrations and small groups for improving manual skills and observation, but whether they improve memorization or successfully address higher-order objectives is another matter.

In conclusion, we suggest that carefully evaluating your own practice is probably the best way to proceed when looking at how to take matters further. We would suggest the following approach.

- Study the results of existing practicals or projects to identify those that seem unduly difficult.

- Assess practical and project work to ensure that their objectives have been met.
- Look for common strengths and weaknesses. If all your students fail to understand the importance of, say, a null hypothesis in statistics it is your fault, not theirs.
- Use simple observation of how the students undertake the work. Do they spend too long on it? Do they work inefficiently, and, if so, at what points? Are your demonstrators adequately briefed and giving value for money?
- Try introducing a practical project into your lecture course or some lectures into your practical course.
- Help your students to write by introducing self and/or peer assessment forms.

KEY READING

Teaching in Laboratories (Boud et al., 1986) is a most useful source which also has a good grounding in educational theory. The recent text by Brown and Atkins (1988), *Effective Teaching in Higher Education,* has excellent chapters on laboratory teaching and project supervision. The activities which are listed at the end of each chapter are particularly worthwhile. Problems of supervision and possible solutions are detailed in *The Management of a Student Research Project* (Howard and Sharp, 1983), and *Improving Student Writing* (Nightingale, 1986) contains many valuable ideas. Within geography, *Project Work in the Geography Curriculum* (Beaumont and Wyn Williams, 1983), although aimed at school level, has many useful ideas and material. You may like to examine accounts of attempts to create project-based curricula in geographical higher education. In this context, we particularly recommend the essays by Clarke and Gregory (1982) and Church (1988). Nightingale (1991) provides clear guidance on helping geography students write effectively and sets this in the context of the research evidence on student writing.

5

Teaching by Discussion

Watermouth makes students nervous; you never know what to expect . . . . There are classes where the teacher, not wanting to direct the movement of the mind unduly, will remain silent throughout the class awaiting spontaneous explosions of intelligence from the students; there are classes indeed where the silence never gets broken.

Malcolm Bradbury, *The History Man*

5.1 INTRODUCTION

Picture a room in which thirty students sit around a large rectangular table. They have been organized into seven groups of four or five. On the desk in front of one group is a nameplate which says 'Town and Country Planning Association'; in front of another, 'The City of Glasgow'; yet another has the nameplate 'The Church of England'. At the head of the table, and clearly in charge of the exercise, is another group of students who represent a Commission of Inquiry. Charged with the responsibility for gathering information about the state of the inner cities, they call for evidence from the other groups. After hearing the oral presentations and receiving short written statements from each interest group, the Commission retire to deliberate on what they have heard and then present a written and oral presentation of their findings to the class as a whole. During the five sessions of class time that this process takes, the teacher sits unobtrusively in the room, observing and making notes for assessment purposes, but not being allowed, by the rules of the exercise, to speak until after the Commission have delivered their Final Report (Jenkins and Pepper, 1987).

What this describes is a 'simulation': a teaching exercise that duplicates the essential features of the real world, in the form of a game or problem, in which learning takes place through acting out a particular role. As will be seen later, simulations come in various forms, but are only one method used for teaching students through discussion. Among other options available for use in geographical higher education are a bewildering array of alternative types, variously labelled 'seminars', 'tutorials' and 'workshops'.

To avoid confusion and unnecessary fine distinctions of meaning, we define the word 'seminar' in its narrow sense as a traditional group discussion introduced by an essay or other work. It can be regarded as a particular type of 'group tutorial', the general term that we use here to describe situations in which small groups of students and a tutor meet for a period of discussion or other collaborative work. The size of the group may be as few as five or six students, but increasingly, with pressures on staff resources, group tutorials have expanded to ten to twenty students. Group tutorials may be 'subject centred' (tackling themes relating primarily to course content) or 'student centred' (meeting to discuss student needs and problems). These are distinguished from 'personal tutorials' as employed, for example, in the process of preparing a dissertation. 'Workshops', with their connotations of practical work, were treated in chapter 4.

Therefore in this chapter we focus on four types of teaching in which students learn through discussion, respectively entitled seminars, group tutorials, personal tutorials and simulations. The focus throughout is on *non-traditional* group teaching. We emphasize the word 'non-traditional' advisedly. The evidence strongly suggests that traditional group teaching, relying heavily on the seminar, is grossly deficient. Teachers report so-called discussion sessions degenerating into ill-prepared monologues, in which students sit in a stony, but anxious, silence, desperately hoping that they will not be 'picked on' by the tutor and forced to contribute. As the academic year drifts by, teachers find attendances falling and negative student reactions typified by the common quip: 'I don't know what I was supposed to get out of *that*' (Hollis and Terry, 1977: 73; see also Powell, 1974; Rudduck, 1978; Unwin, 1984).

We believe that this state of affairs is not inevitable, but improvements depend on careful reappraisal of the aims and purpose of group teaching methods. Their rationale does not lie in their value in presentation of information, in relation to which they are as effective, but less cost efficient, than the lecture or other traditional teaching methods (Brown and Atkins, 1988: 52), but rather in the quality of learning experience and development of skills. In the short term, non-traditional group teaching methods are used to encourage individuals to develop a range of problem-solving, communication and collaborative skills. In the longer term, the goals of group learning relate to the student's personal growth and development. These partly involve employability, with the evidence supporting the view that the skills fostered by these teaching methods are valued by potential employers (Jenkins and Pepper, 1988: 69–70). A less tangible, but vitally important advantage is that students gain immeasurably from having to take greater responsibility for their own learning, from having to learn how to organize their own collective programme of work and from finding out how they and others respond to the challenges that are set.

5.2 ESTABLISHING THE GROUND RULES

Most geography teachers in higher education will have had little training in how to organize discussions effectively, especially when dealing with groups. Many will also be unsure about how to relate group exercises to other forms of teaching or how to assess group work, especially that involving oral presentations. We offer the following eight general principles (based on Jenkins and Pepper, 1988) that can be applied to whatever method of group teaching is chosen.

1 *The relationship of group teaching to other forms of teaching must be explicitly formulated* There needs to be a reason for teaching in this manner other than the fact that a slot exists on the timetable. If a course is to contain a combination of, say, lecturing and group tutorials, thought must be given to precisely what role the various elements are each expected to play and how those roles interrelate.

2 *Students will need convincing* Students will not normally demand justification for traditional teaching methods but may well blanch at non-traditional group teaching methods, especially if a significant component of their final grade is determined by their performance in group tutorials or simulations. Their concerns and fears about this matter should not be swept aside, but rather the opportunity should be taken to build up the student's confidence in the logic of these teaching methods; stressing the richness of learning experience and the legacy of practical skills that such methods can provide. There is nothing to be gained from secrecy.

3 *Teachers must re-define their roles* The teacher's traditional role, as observed previously, is that of the provider of information and instruction in geography. By contrast, the methods to be outlined here involve teachers becoming organizers or facilitators of student learning. In precisely the same way as suggested in chapter 4, the teacher can change from posing as the authority on the subject to the person who creates the broad structures within which an exercise runs, who ensures that the necessary resources are available at the right times and who advises students about how to approach their tasks. This change in role may feel uncomfortable to some and time may be needed to build up confidence in teaching by these methods. It makes more sense to start in a small way and build up than to start with ambitious projects that flounder with mutual recriminations.

4 *Students require clear guidance as to what is expected of them*   While leaving the thorny question of assessment criteria and procedures until chapter 8, students perform most effectively when they have a clear idea about how to tackle their roles, how much time they are expected to take in preparation and how they should approach the task of working together in groups. Group teaching methods place a premium on good course handbooks and may well necessitate initial sessions to train students in such matters as public oratory and how to organize and structure a group.

An example of how this can be done is found in an advanced level fieldwork-based geography module at Oxford Polytechnic entitled 'Geography and the Contemporary World'. The module itself is based around a *syndicate* approach (Jaques, 1984: 190), in which students are told that each member's activity is expected to contribute to the knowledge and understanding of the group as a whole. During the course, they are required to carry out a lengthy collective research project and to make three oral presentations about their progress (see also chapter 8). To prepare them for these tasks, the course opens with an initial 2 hour session on 'Making Groups Work'. It begins with the teacher's introduction to the importance of effective groupwork in achieving the aims of the course. The students are given time to organize themselves into syndicates and then receive copies of a 'Guide to Groupwork' which contains the sections shown in figure 5.1.

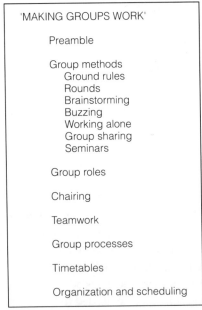

Figure 5.1   The structure of a 2 hour session on 'making groups work'
Reproduced by permission of Educational Methods Unit, Oxford Polytechnic

The students first elect someone to chair the discussion and then work their way through the Guide's various sections. Its preamble explains that working effectively in a group is not something that comes readily, pointing out that:

> You need to learn, *as an individual*, how to be supportive and facilitative of the way that your group works, and your group has to learn, *as a group*, how to work together and make the most of its talents and personalities. Most of your working life will be spent in groups and time spent now learning about making groups work will be invaluable later on.

The students then are led to consider seven areas of concern when contemplating effective group working. The first deals with various methods of working together in a group (many of which are discussed below; see also Habeshaw et al., (1984)). After this, they discuss the functions that need to be covered: who will chair the group and the rules under which they will operate; the desired features of teamwork; the nature of group processes; the importance of operating to a timetable; the importance of organization and scheduling. The Guide comes complete with advice about how to construct flowcharts and the importance of monitoring their own progress. Throughout the process, the tutors take a subsidiary role, merely acting as consultants for student groups whenever they seek assistance.

Evaluation has shown that this exercise is an effective introduction to the art of group working and to the responsibilities that each person is expected to bear as part of a group. Nevertheless, it cannot be expected to have any long-term impact if treated as a 'one-off' session, in which the lip service paid to group skills is quickly forgotten as the students begin the subject-centred or 'geographical' part of the course. Any course developing such skills must necessarily reiterate and reinforce the major points of the exercise. Indeed, in the module discussed above, students are constantly reminded that the initial session on developing group skills is only the start of a process which continues throughout the course and will be reinforced by subsequent monitoring sessions.

5 *All students must be involved* No other form of teaching requires such close attention to group dynamics. Personality, minority status, gender, age and individual social skills can all influence the degree to which a student becomes actively involved in group learning. Mature undergraduates can feel isolated and unsure of how to interact with groups of students considerably younger than themselves. Students from ethnic minorities may well mistrust their fellow students and take chance remarks as indicative of wider prejudice. Female students tend to have lower expectations that they will be taken seriously in discussion, may have difficulty in relating to tutors who, as in geographical higher

education, are predominantly male and may find that certain exercises are designed primarily with male participants in mind (see section 5.5).

A careful watch must be kept for these and any other students who might drift into non-involvement. Their first hesitant steps to contribute to the class should be warmly encouraged and care taken so that they are not shut out by their more vocal colleagues. More generally, teachers must ensure that, although students may take on specialist tasks in a particular exercise, work is evenly distributed among the group and that all participate. Failure to do so can not only lead to students with marginal commitment to the course, but it can also be a major source of friction and resentment within groups, especially from those who have had to shoulder the bulk of the workload.

6 *Room choice and layout are important*   Group teaching often suffers because tutorial classes are allocated to specialist teaching rooms (e.g. cartography or practical laboratories) which have fixed and inflexible fitments around which classes have to operate as best they can. Yet if there is any possibility of choosing appropriate rooms, the available research (e.g. Altman, 1975) suggests that there is much to be gained. The nature of the room, the position of chairs, the arrangement of desks, the location of audiovisual facilities and screens can all exert an influence on even the best-conceived schemes for group tutorials and simulations. While there are limits to the amount of difference that self-conscious juggling of furniture is going to make or, more to the point, that students will be prepared to undertake, the following checklist is useful when organizing group teaching (based on Jaques, 1984: 141).

- What associations does the room have in the minds of the audience (i.e. is it the tutor's own room, a specialist classroom, a 'neutral' room?)
- Is the room a regular venue? Is discussion vulnerable to noise or interruption?
- How possible is it to rearrange the groupings of chairs and tables?
- Is everyone equally spaced? If not, is the spacing chosen appropriate for the exercise in hand?
- Does anyone have a special position, e.g. behind a large desk; at the head of a table? If so, does that particular arrangement suit the task in hand?

7 *Do not assume that students will know how to use visual aids*   Anyone who has been to academic conferences will know that many *teachers* have little idea how to use aids properly. It is quite unrealistic to expect students to be able to do so without assistance. If students are encouraged to use such aids in their presentations, they will need guidance about exactly the same considerations as raised in connection with lectures in chapter 2.

8 *Keeping one's nerve* Finally, it cannot be overemphasized that the teacher adopting non-traditional group teaching methods must have the confidence to persevere with an exercise even if the initial signs are that it is not working as well as desired. Simulations frequently take time to start functioning properly, with participants gradually getting the measure of their particular roles. Equally, student-led discussion sessions sometimes begin with a somewhat stilted discussion that lacks flow and lapses into silence. The temptation for the teacher to intervene under pressure of the anxious silence can be considerable, but should be resisted. Many sessions that start badly can finish well and, given the openness of this style of teaching, a virtue can even be made, when de-briefing, of sessions that do not live up to expectations. Keeping one's nerve is all important.

5.3 SEMINARS

Seminars are as traditional a part of teaching as lectures in geographical higher education. They are used for a variety of purposes, ranging from examination revision to synoptic overview, but most seminars work on the assumption that students arrive to discuss work prepared in advance of the class. This can be some reading or an essay that just one student has prepared. The teacher's task is then to structure and lead a discussion, with the objective being to achieve an intellectual exchange and a deepened understanding.

Traditional seminars occasionally generate lively discussion and can be very useful at graduate level, when new ideas and proposals for research are being discussed. At undergraduate level, however, the odds are against seminars regularly meeting expectations. Seminars that discuss reading that all students have supposedly covered tend either to dissolve into a ritualistic exchanges between the tutor and one or two vociferous students or stumble from one embarrassing silence to the next. A problem here is that of 'diffusion of responsibility', whereby a substantial proportion of the group feel no particular responsibility, *as individuals*, to participate given that their colleagues are not participating either. Faced with silences, the tutor tends to fall back on impromptu lectures on the subject in hand or anecdotes in an attempt to lighten the atmosphere. The result usually falls well short of the goal of intellectual exchange.

Experience with essay-based seminars is equally discouraging. All too often, these begin with an expressionless and halting monologue during the time that the student reads out the essay. This is followed by an uneasy dialogue between the teacher and the student who has produced the essay, perhaps supplemented by the interjections of a handful of more vociferous students, finishing with the teacher's time-filling soliloquy. Unless the topic is unusually appealing or contentious, most students will spend the bulk of the period sitting in silence, anxiously trying to avoid eye contact with the teacher.

A brief analysis of the essay-based seminar's structure reveals that this is always a likely outcome, given that the format effectively excludes most people in the room from the discussion. Only two individuals are likely to have much knowledge about the topic: the teacher and the student who prepared the essay. The other students rely on the oral presentation to inform them, but are unlikely to gain much since the essay is rarely written for that purpose. In the absence of guidance to the contrary, such essays usually accord to the conventions of written rather than oral communication, frequently being too dense in style and insufficiently structured to make effective oral presentations. These deficiencies are accentuated when the essay is to be taken in for assessment at the end of the session. Knowing that the teacher is the arbiter of its quality, the essay will be directed primarily at impressing the teacher rather than informing fellow students.

Lacking an adequate basis for participating as equals, the other students can adopt a variety of strategies. They can ask questions, effectively accepting the inequality of the situation and normally begetting a one-sided and stuttering discussion, with short questions leading to long answers. In such circumstances, substantive points of comment are normally restricted to matters which they regard as 'safe' (Jaques, 1984: 101), about which they are unlikely to be assailed by better-prepared opponents. Alternatively, they can try to sidetrack the discussion on to subjects about which they have background or commonsense knowledge and about which they feel competent to talk, a strategy that is often resisted by the teacher as straying 'from the point'. If neither strategy works, the tendency is to lapse into silence, a course of inaction reinforced by the diffusion of responsibility mentioned above.

The question arises as to whether these types of seminar are structurally flawed or whether they can be rendered worthwhile by reorganization. It certainly *is* possible to get more out of these seminars by constituting them in a different way, so that more people are involved and responsibility for participation is extended. For example, we lay out below a schedule for reorganizing a 1 hour essay-based seminar:

0.00 Introduction to topic. Division of students into groups of three to four with the remit: 'Sketch out a model answer to the question that has been set'.

0.05 Student groups consult and build up the structure of their (collective) model answer.

0.20 Pyramiding: each student group gets together with at least one other group to draw up shared model answer.

0.30 Presentation: each of the enlarged groups elects a spokesperson who verbally presents the group's findings.

0.40 Student-tutor comments on groups' presentations and outlines own findings and approach.

0.50 General discussion. Closing words from the teacher.

1.00 Finish.

The example works on two basic principles: first, that the two people who were previously dominant now play a much reduced role; secondly, that the erstwhile 'silent majority' now contribute collaboratively rather than as isolated individuals. As may be seen, the idea is to get students who have *not* prepared the topic to work together to build up a picture of what an answer to the question could be.

Suppose that the topic set was: 'Examine, with appropriate examples, the role played by working-class flats in the evolving form of British cities since 1870'. The students who have not researched the subject will probably be able to suggest some of the basic ideas about flats (who built them? where? why?), may know a little about the emergence and influence of sanitary and town planning legislation, and will probably have some general knowledge about the location of high-rise estates. However, the extent of their knowledge of specific examples or their ability to knit these fragments into any coherent chronological sequence is usually sketchy. It is precisely these elements that the student who has prepared a written essay can supply. He or she will not read the essay out but will draw on the knowledge so gained to act as tutor. In other words, the student-tutor will listen to and comment upon the conclusions reached by the other students, clarifying points of ignorance or confusion, highlighting ideas of importance and perhaps defending the approach that was taken. The student who has prepared the essay gains from having to act in the role of tutor; the other students obtain practice at the valuable skills involved in formulating good answers to questions. The teacher meanwhile essentially chairs the meeting, taking on the roles of organizer and timekeeper, although he/she will probably wish to add some closing remarks.

While this, and a variety of similar strategies (Coleman, 1978; Broady, 1986), are a considerable improvement on the traditional model, we suggest that structural failings in the existing model of the seminar still remain. The focused pattern of authority and responsibility, the anxiety felt by many participants and the frequent lack of any considered rationale for the prepared essay or class reading are significant flaws. What is required is to return to the first principles suggested in the previous section and explore the various other frameworks available to make group learning more effective. This is the task to which we now turn.

5.4 GROUP TUTORIALS

It is impossible to do full justice here to the many ways in which group tutorials can be organized (Abercrombie and Terry, 1978; Habeshaw et al, 1984; Bligh, 1986; McKeachie, 1986), but a sample of four contrasting types gives some impression of the range and versatility of these teaching methods. The first, *no-tutor* sessions, addresses the problem of tutor domination of discussion. The next method, use of *mini-presentations* and *conferencing*, provides ways of organising and rewarding group oral presentations. The following section shows how *debates* can supply a formal structure for considering key issues and stimulating clearly articulated arguments. The final method to be discussed, *brainstorming*, harnesses lateral thinking to produce group-based creative thought.

No-tutor sessions

The structure of a tutorless tutorial is simple to explain. Students meet to discuss a particular pre-selected topic. Tutors absent themselves from the discussion, but may maintain contact in one of two ways. First, they may leave a tape-recorder running during the discussion. The recording is collected and analysed by the tutor, who gives feedback at the next tutorial or through written comments. Second, they may return for the last quarter of the tutorial. The tutor may ask for a summary of the discussion and then ask questions or give opinions as is felt necessary.

Research in one UK geography department shows that this method is effective in increasing active student involvement in tutorials (Webb, 1980), even if the format tends to reinforce the teacher's position as an authority who supplies evaluative comments about the quality of a discussion after the event. No-tutor sessions add variety to the tutorial mix and are valuable in the early stages of a course, first, as a means of encouraging students to participate and, second, as a possible corrective for courses in which tutors feel themselves to be repeatedly dominating discussion. However, Pepper (1980), applying no-tutor tutorials in his environmentalist course, reported that students may feel uncomfortable about sitting in a room in which the tutor has departed leaving behind a tape-recorder, they may doubt their ability to produce worthwhile discussions when seemingly left to their own devices, and may even feel resentful about the tutor placing them in this position. As stressed often before, the key to effectiveness lies in acquainting students fully with the aims and rationale of the exercise and helping them to learn the necessary skills.

Mini-presentations and Conferencing

The *mini-presentation* (Brown and Atkins, 1988: 64–5) is particularly useful in first year geographical teaching or as part of fieldwork courses that are arranged around student projects. This method asks students, in groups of two to four, to give a joint presentation lasting, say, 10 minutes on the issue that they themselves have researched. The topics chosen will be linked. For example, students might be asked to do library research in order to prepare presentations summarizing the salient features of the following aspects of the geography of the Transvaal in South Africa:

1 coal mining;
2 gold mining;
3 agriculture;
4 rural settlement;
5 the geography of education;
6 the urban geography of Johannesburg;
7 electoral geography.

When these are discussed in subsequent class sessions, the aim will not be to work laboriously through the presentations treating each as a separate subject in its own right, but, through discussion of seven topics, to gain insight into the unique social, economic and political geography of South Africa.

For more advanced students or for students undertaking substantive group research projects, presentations may be given as part of a formal *conference*. Subject only to the constraints of the availability of a suitable setting and a sufficient block of time, conferences can be arranged in precisely the same fashion as those held for professional business or academic audiences, with papers arranged into thematic sessions, discussants and even conference abstracts.

Both these methods provide an excellent opportunity for training students to work in groups and speak in public, but are only effective if certain rules are observed.

● Students must be told that they must not read an essay or a paper, but must present the topic to the audience so that it can be readily understood as an oral presentation in its own right. They should be encouraged to use appropriate audiovisual aids, but instructed as to how to do so effectively. If unfamiliar with this type of presentation, they must be given explicit instructions about what is expected of them and guidance as to what form the discussion will take. Make it clear that they have been given a group topic and will be assessed collectively.

- The presentation must be sharply focused. It is unreasonable to expect the audience to generate worthwhile discussion if the initial paper is rambling and unstructured.
- Presentations should be kept strictly to time. Failure to do so can ruin the timetable of the ensuing discussion and place unnecessary pressure on later contributors.
- The discussion should be chaired, but not led, by the teacher, who will not personally be asking any questions other than perhaps the last. Students should be encouraged to ask penetrating questions, which give the presenting group an opportunity to show their knowledge and ability to handle questions.
- The teacher should make notes about the presentation for assessment purposes, encourage the group to fill in self-assessment sheets and perhaps get other groups to complete peer assessment (see chapter 8). As a tailpiece to the session, or perhaps at a later date, the results of the assessments should be discussed and, if necessary, justified. In this way, assessment can be used not just for rewarding effort but also to supply feedback and encourage critical self-awareness.

Debates

Formal debates provide another format for tutorial discussion. The objectives of a debate are to focus students' attention on important issues, to encourage teamwork and to strengthen their abilities to express their ideas logically. The process begins by specifying an issue for debate, identifying two opposing viewpoints, suggesting strategies by which students might divide up the task and stating the rules of the exercise. An example used for an introductory society-environment course (Pepper, 1985: see also Jenkins and Pepper, 1988) involved the proposition: 'Are there natural limits to what human societies can achieve?'. In tackling this task, students are divided into two groups at a preliminary meeting: 'optimists' who believe that human societies are making steady economic and technological progress to which there are no resource limitations, and 'pessimists' who believe that the limits to progress will soon be reached. The students then proceed on the basis of the briefing instructions shown below.

Your job is now to prepare for the next tutorial meeting, in which you will debate your case with the other side by

(a) advancing facts and arguments from the reading given

(b) presenting them as clearly, logically and convincingly as you can.

In the tutorial, each side will be given 20 minutes to make its case, and everyone in your group will be required to help in planning and presenting the arguments. You must therefore meet other group members during the coming week to plan out who does and says what.

Your debate will be assessed. At the end your tutor will declare winners, losers and scores. Each side can score a maximum of 5 points. Each individual will receive the same mark as that given to the group overall. This is a team effort and you sink or swim with your team. You can get high marks for yourself only by helping your group to score high marks.

The 'reading' referred to in this extract consists of small resource packages of appropriate materials selected by the teacher. These are handed out at the preliminary meeting, at which the tutor discusses how the debate will be structured and the strict time limits that will be operated. A specimen timetable for debating this proposition with a class of ten to fourteen students might appear as shown below. The debate itself lasts 45 minutes, which is followed by the tutor's observations and adjudication, and a further group analysis of the issues raised.

1 Tutor introduces proposition and states rules
2 Outline statement of case for 'optimists'
2 Outline statement of case for 'pessimists'
8 Detailed proposal of case for 'optimists'
6 Calling of 'specialist witnesses' by 'optimists'
4 Cross-questioning of 'optimists' witnesses by 'pessimists'
8 Detailed proposal of case for 'pessimists'
6 Calling of 'specialist witnesses' by 'pessimists'
4 Cross-questioning of 'pessimists' witnesses by 'optimists'
2 Final statement for 'pessimists'
2 Final statement for 'optimists'
———
45 minutes
———

The major constraint on debates is the relationship of class size to time, since the number of students that can be assigned to each team is a delicate matter. The larger the group, the more likely it is that some members will not have the opportunity to present their views and will become marginal participants. Team size must also be adjusted to the length of a class. Five to seven people per team might be optimal for a 45 minute class, while teams of eight to ten can usually express themselves in a 75 minute session (Estaville, 1988: 4).

Brainstorming

'Brainstorming' supplies a formal framework for group-based creative thought. Based on notions of lateral thinking, it is a valuable means by which to expand people's thinking in a particular area and to look for ideas that might not be arrived at by rational methods. Its prime uses are when initially approaching a topic as, for example, when initiating a problem-solving tutorial or as part of the introductory session to a course.

To take an example of the latter, let us consider the type of tutorial that might result when applying brainstorming techniques to an introductory session for a course on the economic geography of contemporary Britain. The students are divided into groups of ten to twelve and each group appoints a note-taker, who uses a blackboard or flipchart to record the group's views. Students are given the following proposition to consider: 'In this course, we are going to be considering the economic geography of contemporary Britain. It would help us at the outset if we could agree on the range of things that we should be looking out for in this course. If you call them out, your note-taker will write them down.'

Certain ground rules are needed to ensure that the exercise achieves its aims of gathering a wide range of ideas that are subsequently sorted and ordered. These rules might well include the following:

- suggestions are called out in any order;
- individuals do not have to justify their suggestions;
- initially no one comments on other people's suggestions.

These rules give group members the freedom to express their ideas, even if they are not sure how to explain or justify them (Habeshaw et al., 1984: 63). After a certain time, or at the stage when suggestions have dried up, the group takes stock of the total list of possibilities. Items can be sifted and ideas organized and arranged in order of priority. When this process is complete, each group's final list can be put on a poster and pinned to the wall (Jackson and Prosser, 1985), with an ensuing verbal explanation by each group of the reasons for their choice. At this stage, when student opinions have been firmly expressed and divergences of opinion identified, the teacher can then hand out the course guides with their provisional list of topics that the course was to cover. The teacher's list can be compared with those produced by the students, and explanations be given for the course's approach and content. It is often possible to take on board student suggestions which would improve the course or would build on any areas that the students would find of particular interest. An amended, and final, list of topics could be issued at the start of the next meeting.

To see the advantages of this procedure, one only has to consider the alternative. The teacher normally hands out course guides at a time when students will have only half-formed ideas and vague expectations of what the course is about. The students will listen passively, perhaps write some notes and tuck the course guide away in their folder. Experience suggests that it may well stay there, largely unread, until the time that assessment approaches. 'Brainstorming', in contrast, allows the teacher to capitalize immediately on the student's initial ideas in a relaxed atmosphere, so that when the course syllabus is given out, students have already had an opportunity to develop and articulate their own thoughts about the matter. Two beneficial results can ensue. First, the students can understand something of the structure and orientation of a course from the very start, rather than expecting them somehow to acquire that understanding during their course of study. Second, it breaks down the idea that the syllabus is immutable. At the expense of making, at most, minor changes to the syllabus, the teacher indicates to students that their ideas are taken seriously and that they are invited to be active participants in their own learning. Experience shows that students appreciate being given that opportunity.

5.5 PERSONAL TUTORIALS

At the start of his influential book *Locational Analysis in Human Geography*, Peter Haggett (1965: vi) noted how he and a group of fellow geographers arrived at St Catherine's College, Cambridge, in the same year as a newly elected Fellow, A. A. L. Caesar. He went on to acknowledge their collective debt to Caesar, noting how, through their later writings, ran 'the marks of prolonged exposure in Cambridge "supervisions" to Caesar's formidable powers of critical dissection and logical re-arrangement'.

Haggett's experience of learning through a close and enduring one-to-one relationship with a gifted tutor mirrors that of many former Oxford and Cambridge graduates. Given the influence that Oxbridge practices have exerted on British higher education, it also partly accounts for the special place that the personal tutorial holds both within that system and in higher education systems influenced by the traditional British model. Yet this ideal is a rarity outside Oxford and Cambridge. Lack of staff resources elsewhere means that the personal tutorial is confined primarily to two specific uses. The first is associated with the teacher's counselling role. Most colleges provide their students with a designated personal tutor to whom they can turn for advice if faced with, say, emotional, financial or health problems or in making choices about their future. Much of this work involves being a good listener and knowledgeable about where a student can obtain specialist advice.

These characteristics are also true of the second type of personal tutorial, namely, those linked with the process of producing dissertations. We mentioned in passing previously (chapter 4) that good supervision is crucial to the success of student research projects. As such, the literature specifically on the success or failure of thesis or dissertation research (e.g. SERC, 1982; Swinnerton-Dyer,

1982; Howard and Sharp, 1983; Phillips and Pugh, 1987; see Brown and Atkins, 1988: 116, for a summary), directs attention to two linked factors: the role of the supervisor and the way the project is managed.

For graduate work, good supervision is widely held to be *close* supervision involving regular and lengthy tutorial meetings. At these sessions, the supervisor and student talk through ideas and problems arising from the project, often basing discussions around interim reports and drafts of chapters of the final thesis. The nature of supervision changes over the course of the project which, in the case of a Ph.D., can be 3 years or more. In the early days, the relationship may resemble that of master to apprentice, with the student knowing much less about the topic than the supervisor and relying on the latter for guidance about how to proceed. Given the requirement for original work, the position is often reversed by the time that the project is completed, with the student knowing more about the topic than the supervisor. By this stage, their relationship may well have changed to an association of equals.

Changes in this traditional tutorial relationship, however, have come about through the pressures being placed on supervisors to ensure that their postgraduate students successfully complete their theses. In the United Kingdom, for example, the various bodies that grant awards for research treat completion as the *sine qua non* of the exercise, with a policy of withdrawing further awards from institutions that do not reach a specified completion rate (Gray and Flowerdew, 1987). Although this has produced some positive side-effects, such as the introduction of training courses, multiple supervisors and research committees on the North American model (Nowell, 1988), supervisors now have almost as much to lose from their students' non-completion as the students themselves. With this in mind, one can envisage the danger that supervisors could try to improve completion rates by favouring predictable topics undertaken by uninspired but hard-working, students with a great deal of direct tutorial assistance.

At undergraduate level, there are few equivalent pressures on the supervisor, but there is also a process of change in the supervisor–student relationship that takes place over the shorter period involved in supervising an undergraduate dissertation. While the teacher–student relationship may deviate less from the pattern of master–apprentice, the supervisor's role does change over the course of the project. Table 5.1 suggests how this might occur.

At one time or another, the supervisor can expect to act as director, facilitator, adviser, teacher, guide, critic, supporter, friend, manager and, eventually, examiner. When the student is struggling to define a topic, there is a need for regular tutorials at which the tutor assists the student to tackle what may well be his or her first piece of substantive research. Students normally have limited knowledge of the literature, lack contact with other workers in the field and

Table 5.1   The changing role of the supervisor of the undergraduate thesis

1 *Selection and justification of a general topic and creation of a short topic analysis*

Tutor's role	Advice on feasibility
Tutor's involvement	High
Resources needed	Low

2 *Formal checking on feasibility of proposed research*

Tutor's role	Validation of proposal
Tutor's involvement	Very high
Resources needed	Low

3 *Preparation of detailed research proposal*

Tutor's role	Interested colleague
Tutor's involvement	Moderate
Resources needed	Library, maps, other documents

4 *Execution of work, data collection and analysis*

Tutor's role	Provision of facilities
Tutor's involvement	Low
Resources needed	Often considerable, e.g. instruments, data, computers, travel expenses, video- or audio-recording equipment.

5 *Drafting of report for assessment*

Tutor's role	Advice on standards and style
Tutor's involvement	Variable
Resources needed	Word-processor, mapping laboratory, photocopying

6 *Assessment*

Tutor's role	Examiner
Tutor's involvement	High
Resources needed	None

will almost certainly incorrectly estimate what can be done in the time available. The temptation not to give advice at this stage, either on the grounds that 'students should learn by their mistakes' or that such advice is simply 'spoon feeding', should be resisted. While remaining a good listener, the tutor can try to steer the student towards sources that will indicate directions to follow, such as previously published studies of similar problems, various local literature sources, topics that have appeared in the media and examples of good quality dissertations completed by previous students.

Once a topic has been agreed, the student's attention should be directed towards demonstrating its feasibility. A useful tutorial device at this stage is for the supervisor to request a formal outline of the project for discussion, perhaps addressing the following checklist:

- description of the proposed problem area and the place of the intended work in it;

- a statement of the aims and objectives;
- a survey of the literature;
- a description of the proposed methodology, whether quantitative or qualitative, in as much detail as possible;
- a short specification of what analytical methods (e.g. literary, field, laboratory, statistical, mathematical, cartographic) are to be employed and why;
- a brief speculation about what the results and conclusion might be.

Experience shows that this can very often be *the* key stage in the tutorial process, since good counselling here can save much time later.

From this point, the tutorial process changes as suggested in table 5.1. While the project is being executed, the supervisor's role often switches to that of facilitator: for example, providing the student with access to appropriate facilities or equipment for the research or supplying introductions to useful contacts. When material has been collected and the student begins the process of preparing the final report, tutorial meetings usually turn to discussion of draft writing, although opinions differ as to the degree of help students should be given when writing up their reports. At one extreme, the master–apprentice model suggests that considerable assistance be given, possibly down to the level of proof-reading drafts prior to their submission for assessment. At the other extreme is the view that the final product should demonstrably be the student's own work, in which case assistance in writing up is frowned on. Whichever is adopted, it is essential that the supervisory relationship is patient, helpful and encouraging. To repeat, this is usually a student's first attempt at a piece of formal academic research. The conventions and practices of written research that may be second nature to the professional geographer may not seem so obvious to the student.

5.6 SIMULATIONS

Use of simulations in geographical higher education developed in the late 1960s, drawing on roots in war-gaming, psychological research on experiential learning, and management and business studies (King, 1981b: Walford, 1981b). They initially developed fastest in secondary education, encountering resistance in higher education as being somehow inappropriate for serious use in teaching, but have subsequently become more popular. Four factors account for their growing popularity.

First, they allow learning activities to be mixed with socializing, a property that makes simulations an ideal element in a course's introductory sessions or perhaps as an 'ice-breaker' in a study weekend. Rowntree (1981a: 137) identified the high levels of motivation and intense social interaction that simulations, particularly games, can generate among students, arguing that 'students become hooked by the relevance of the problem or issue; they are involved as producers rather than consumers of the subject-matter'. Second, simulations provide incisive approaches to issues involving problem-solving, decision-making and forecasting. As noted previously, simulations model the essential concepts and structures of real-world situations. The student learns from having to work within those concepts and structures and, in the process of having to master the factual background, may also learn considerable amounts of factual information. Third, although often involving considerable amounts of preparation, simulations free teachers from formal teaching and allow them to use their time to monitor student learning strategies and become better acquainted with the personalities of the individuals in their group. Finally, simulations are a valuable adjunct in fostering communication and collaborative skills training, although the precise types of skill that are fostered will depend on the type of simulation involved.

This last point is important. Simulation encompasses a family of teaching methods rather than a single strand of methodology. As shown in table 5.2, they vary markedly along the three dimensions of equipment, extent of personal contribution and competitiveness. To elaborate, simulations vary in their equipment needs (high for a board game, low for discussion-based sessions), in the amount of personal contribution required (low for games proceeding according to predetermined rules, high for role-playing exercises free from such rules) and in whether they are competitive or collaborative (whether groups work against one another or together as one overall unit).

Table 5.2 Contrasting dimensions of simulations

Full equipment	———————————	No special equipment
High personal contribution	———————————	Low personal contribution
Full competition	———————————	Full co-operation

Source: Based on Fien et al. 1984: 120

Different types of simulation have different merits and drawbacks for geographical teaching and skills training. Leaving aside the subject of computer simulation, which is considered in detail in chapter 7, we shall consider the value of simulations further by dividing them into two convenient categories: role-playing exercises and games.

Role-playing exercises

Broadly speaking, role-playing exercises are concerned with the simulation of meetings at which such issues as environmental conflicts or locational decisions are discussed. The meeting in question might be a Commission of Inquiry, as in the example at the start of this chapter, or a courtroom scene or a planning inquiry. The teacher is responsible for providing background material and for creating the initial framework and timetable. The student participants are required to take on and play roles to the best of their ability, regardless of whether or not those roles accord with what they really think about the issue. What then takes place depends on the kind of issue involved as well as on the types of rules and structure that have been laid down.

At Carleton University in Canada, for example, a course in Cultural Geography employs documentation to reconstruct historical debates in order to gain insight into images of place (Knight, 1979). One such debate concerned the location of the Canadian capital in the mid-nineteenth century, with the simulation of a debate in the Canadian Parliamentary Assembly being followed in the subsequent week by a simulated meeting in the British Colonial Office. Students took roles that were assigned to them, with background to the historical characters that they were playing supplied by documents issued the previous week.

At St David's University College, Lampeter, an Applied Rural Geography course simulates a planning inquiry to give insight into rural planning problems (Cloke, 1987). Classes of no more than twenty students are divided into two groups: 'applicants' and 'appellants'. Over the course of the next 6–8 weeks, students have to prepare for and submit evidence to the planning inquiry. 'Applicants' have to choose a site for building construction and apply for planning permission; 'appellants' present the case against the development. The procedures followed are shown below (abridged from Cloke, 1987: 37):

1 Divide the class into two groups – applicants and appellants.
2 Organize the election of a chairperson and confidential surgery sessions with a postgraduate or staff member dedicated solely to one or other group.
3 Groups allocate roles to individuals.
4 Applicants select site and publish the plan for their development.
5 Applicants and appellants prepare a full case for and against the development respectively, using evidence from interviews with key actors.
6 These cases are presented and debated at the final 'public inquiry' before a neutral 'inspector'.
7 The decision is given.

Another format used in physical geography teaching employs a simulated application for research funds as a means of integrating communication skills into the curriculum (Keene, 1988). Students are presented with a simulated

ADVERTISEMENT ONE

UNITED NATIONS ENVIRONMENTAL RESEARCH COMMISSION

Applications are invited for a research grant of up to £250,000 for a field project involving a specific environmental indicator that is:

"likely to lead to the advancement of our understanding of environmental change over any chosen time scale within the last three million years".

The UNERC research grant is awarded annually to a group of three researchers of proven ability to undertake a project of up to one year in duration involving field work (lasting up to six months) at any location(s) in the world. The UNERC will provide funding for travel and subsistence during the field work, and for the loan or purchase of laboratory and technical facilities during and after the field work.

Applicants are restricted to ONE environmental indicator selected from the following list. Formal agreement as to which environmental indicator is selected is required before submitting the application form. All teams of researchers will be interviewed on their proposed research programme.

1. Ocean core sediments	2. Ice cores	3. Cavern deposits
4. Lake deposits	5. Fossil pollen	6. Coleoptera
7. Tree rings/growth	8. Diatoms	9. Loess and/or Palaecosols

Use the application form provided (one per team), and read the instructions which indicate the method of application and interview.

Applications must be received by noon on *Tuesday 26 May 1987* (5th week of term). This deadline is fixed so that members of the interviewing panel have adequate time to assess the proposals and prepare appropriate interview questions. Interviews will take place during the 6th week of term.

UNITED NATIONS ENVIRONMENTAL RESEARCH COMMISSION

GRANT APPLICATION FORM FOR RESEARCH ON ENVIRONMENTAL INDICATORS
[*** On this print four pages reduced to half-page. Spaces for answers excluded]

Forms to be completed legibly, typed or in BLACK ink.
Closing date for application is *Noon 26 May 1987*.
PRINT NAMES OF APPLICANTS: 1. ....
2. ....
3. ....
Seminar Group No. .... Time/Date of interview ....
FULL TITLE OF RESEARCH PROJECT:
***
PERIOD OF TIME FOR WHICH THE GRANT IS REQUIRED:
***
FINANCIAL DETAILS OF THE WAY FUNDS WILL BE SPENT:
***
Signatures of applicants agreeing that preparation for interview was shared equitably:
1. .... 2. .... 3. ....
Date: .... For Official Use:
....
[Pages 2 & 3]
STATEMENT OF THE RESEARCH TO BE CARRIED OUT. THIS SHOULD INCLUDE A BRIEF DESCRIPTION OF THE BACKGROUND TO THE PROJECT, AND SHOULD MAKE CLEAR WHAT YOU PROPOSE TO DO, HOW YOU INTEND TO DO IT, AND WHY YOU THINK IT IS WORTH DOING.
***
[Page 4]
BIBLIOGRAPHY
***
INTERVIEWER'S COMMENTS:
***

Figure 5.2 A simulated advertisement for a research grant application
Source: Keene (1988: 87)

advertisement (figure 5.2), which invites them to apply for a research grant from a fictitious 'United Nations Environmental Research Commission'. They proceed over a period of 6 weeks to go through the various stages of preparing a group application for funds, before attending an interview before a panel of student assessors.

These three examples merely skim the surface of a enormous genre (Walford, 1981a), but convey the flavour of this type of simulation. Role-playing exercises require students to take primary responsibility for running the classes themselves, with the tutor becoming a referee, an adviser, a resource and, usually, an observer. They offer students rich and valuable learning experiences, supplying insights and skills training that may not be available from other means of teaching. Yet role-playing exercises should be used with care. Six principles are of value in choosing whether and how to use them (based on Fien et al., 1984: 118).

1 *Do not overuse them* While valuable as occasional techniques for in-depth analysis of important issues, they quickly pall if encountered too often in the student's programme. One of the authors of this book still ruefully recalls the pain of overhearing a student dismissing his cherished role-playing exercise as representing the *Sesame Street* school of teaching!

2 *Role-playing exercises* make considerable demands on tutors and students. They require considerable preparation, make demands on time and resources and fill up large amounts of class-contact time that could have been occupied in other ways. Whenever introducing such exercises, it is important to examine their objectives and ask whether they might not be achieved in some other way.

3 *Do not emphasize winning* Certain students may play roles more effectively than others, but they will 'win' only if a simulation achieves its educational objectives, which may or may not depend on, say, being part of a group that successfully communicates an interest group's viewpoint at a simulated public inquiry.

4 *An equal start* Before commencing a role-playing exercise, make sure, first, that everyone understands the point of the exercise and, second, that they have had a chance to absorb the demands of the role that they are playing before the exercise begins in earnest.

5 *Advising* When advising groups during the exercise, it is valuable for the tutor to question groups about the strategies and decision-making processes that they are using and to indicate the relationship of their activities and decisions to reality. This is particularly the case with exercises lasting for more than one session, when groups may start to lose sight of the overall rationale.

6 *De-briefing* After the game, there is an inevitable feeling that the session

has finished and it is now time to leave. It is important, however, to leave time to give students an opportunity to reflect on their learning experience. This should include a reminder of the game's objectives and an evaluation of the exercise's outcome in the light of those objectives.

Games

Many of the above points also apply to operational games, which are differentiated from role-playing exercises by having more rigid structure and rules, and by giving more definite feedback and pay-offs to certain actions. In some games, students are operators, in others they remain as decision-makers, but the scope of choice is deliberately narrowed in order to focus on a particular sequence of events (Walford, 1981b).

Games vary greatly in their demands on participants' time and in their complexity, but tend to cover similar topic areas, particularly exploration, Third World development problems, locational choice, construction of transport routes, land use and exploitation of resources. Overall, we can recognize three different categories in terms of their origins.

The first type are commercial packages. Care is necessary when thinking of purchasing them for direct or adapted classroom use. While some are produced by major publishing houses, many are produced by a cottage industry with poor standards of quality control. A large proportion are expensive and some are notoriously difficult to obtain. Many are tailored for the school classroom rather than for the higher education market (Walford, 1981a; Fien et al, 1984). When using them, the tutor needs to be aware that the games come replete with the designer's underlying values and assumptions, which may not accord with the values held by the tutor. Monk (1978), for instance, observed that women normally take, or are allotted, minor roles in geographical games and do not regularly have the opportunity to exercise power and influence in locational decision-making or spatial conflicts in capacities other than as citizen lobbyists or as members of local governments. While this situation may reflect reality, the tutor needs to be aware that the allocation clearly veers towards a conservative interpretation of reality. Finally, purchasing expensive games is usually worthwhile only if the game will be used often enough to justify the expenditure. Changing needs mean that this imposes an unnecessary constraint on the teaching programme.

Having said this, there are numerous cases in which purchased games have been directly and successfully incorporated into geographical higher education. Conolly (1981), for example, reported the experience of Sydney Teacher's College in Australia in which several such games were fully integrated into the curriculum. These included the 'Fishing Game', in which participants adopt strategies to achieve a trade-off between income and security in uncertain environmental circumstances, 'Lynwood', a town planning game, and 'Starpower', a game designed to simulate the meeting of two contrasting cultures (for information about availability, see Key Reading). Corbridge (1985) described his experience of using 'The Green Revolution Game' as an entrée for students into the social and environmental structures under-pinning peasant crop decision-making processes in the Third World. He stressed the vital importance with such a game of having sufficient time to play it through to its conclusion. 'The Green Revolution Game' takes the best part of a day to complete properly (see also Peacock, 1981: 141). Cut-down versions simply do not provide the full experience and may disappoint students and tutor alike.

The second type of game is an inevitable development of the last category, namely, games in which the salient features of commercial games are comprehensively rewritten to suit the circumstances of different courses. Mackinnon (1984) took ideas from existing freight distribution games to devise a game to demonstrate the use of spatial optimizing techniques. Gold et al. (1990) extend notions from commercial cultural conflict games into outdoor fieldwork activities in order to examine different perceptions of place. Thus instead of showing how a group builds up its own culture and had difficulty understanding a group with a totally different culture, their simulation showed how two groups of 'journalists', with opposing briefs, could devise diametrically opposed reporting from precisely the same visual evidence. In both cases, the end product moved on substantially from the original versions.

The third type are *ad hoc* games produced by individuals with a specific teaching interest in order to fill a specific niche in their own courses. Some of these may go on to become commercial games and enter the public domain, but that criterion in itself is not a prerequisite of quality. In reality, devising games is not a difficult activity. The essential elements of gaming can be quickly learned, either from studying existing games or from practical manuals (e.g. Jones, 1987), and the games thus produced have the great advantage of being tailor-made to fit course needs rather than having to adjust the course, even if only subtly, to accommodate a purchased game.

Whatever type of game is employed, the conditions surrounding their use remain precisely as made for role-playing exercises. Proper briefing is always vital, perhaps playing several rounds of the game as a demonstration before beginning in earnest. Equally, full 'de-briefing' is always necessary to ensure that participants have fully grasped the wider, as well as the specific, objectives of the game. Above all, operational games only work properly if they meet the true requirements of a specific course.

5.7 CONCLUSION

In this chapter, we have dealt with teaching methods that seek to help students learn through discussion. With the exception of the personal tutorial, used both for moral guidance and for project supervision, we have concentrated on methods that involve groups. After showing the deficiencies of traditional seminar teaching, we have sought to offer practical guidance as to how group tutorials and simulations can be used as a valuable alternative. In conclusion, we offer four final observations.

1 Group tutorials and simulations that increase student participation are not a 'soft option' for the tutor. While tutors may spend their class contact time advising and observing, an enormous amount of effort is normally expended in making sure that the exercise works as it should. Adopting these teaching methods may simply redistribute work, cutting down on lecture preparation but greatly increasing administration time.

2 These methods are also expensive in student time. Many of the examples cited above require that students spend considerable amounts of time outside the classroom in consultations, preparation and even lobbying. This needs to be recognized when estimating student workloads on a course.

3 Beware of the temptation to use group teaching methods for novelty or time-filling purposes. That strategy frequently backfires if there is no proper rationale for, say, expending long periods of time in obscure role-playing exercises or proceeding through endless, often repetitive, stages of operational games.

4 Do what feels comfortable. As we have stressed on many occasions above, these methods involve a change in the teacher's traditional role. Make sure that the role you adopt is one with which you feel happy.

KEY READING

There are many useful overviews of group teaching methods, of which we recommend the former University of London Teaching Methods Unit's invaluable compilation *Improving Teaching in Higher Education* (UTMU, 1976), the late Jane Abercrombie's oft reprinted *Aims and Techniques of Small Group Teaching* (1979), Jaques's monograph *Learning in Groups* (1984), Bligh's invaluable collection *Teach Thinking by Discussion* (1986) and Sinclair Goodlad and Beverley Hirst's *Peer Tutoring* (1989). On simulations, the new edition of Morry van Ments' *The Effective Use of Role-play* (1989) is valuable. Two journals of interest for simulations are *Simulation/Games for Learning*, produced by the Society for the Advancement of Games and Simulations in Education and Training based at Loughborough in England, and *Simulations and Games*, published by Sage Publications.

6

Resource-based Learning

The greatest revolution in education has come not from teaching machines or computers, but from the greater availability of a wide variety of printed materials.

W. J. McKeachie, *Teaching Trips*

6.1 INTRODUCTION

In chapter 4, we discussed various examples of practical and project classes which made extensive use of handbooks, workbooks and other printed materials in the teaching process. Here, we develop the underlying notion of *resource-based learning*, primarily from printed materials, as a means of either replacing or complementing other forms of instruction. To gain some indication of the potential and variety of resource-based courses, we first consider some examples of geographical courses (several of which were previously introduced in chapter 4) as a prelude to defining resource-based learning. After that, we examine the reasons for the growth of resource-based learning, the ethical and practical problems that it raises and the circumstances in which it is best used. We end with a series of pragmatic, yet vital, administrative issues.

6.2 WHAT IS RESOURCE-BASED LEARNING?

Many geography courses already exist which use few or no lectures, where the course material is delivered largely through print and other resources. One example comprises part of the geography programme at Carleton University in Canada. The first year geography course contains no lectures but instead:

a printed study guide leads students *individually* [our emphasis] through the course texts, the primary source being Peter Haggett's *Geography: A Modern Synthesis* (1975). For each unit of study (roughly one week's work on one chapter of the text) the guide specifies detailed learning objectives, lists the reading, poses questions and gives answers about the reading and provides tests for self assessment. Students can ask questions of instructors or graduate assistants during designated tutorial or testing sessions. When students judge themselves to be sufficiently prepared they take a short test on the whole unit, with an opportunity for a review and retesting if they fail. (Fox et al., 1987: 3–4)

The second example comes from Canberra College of Advanced Education in Australia. In a course on spatial data analysis, students individually work their way through a practical workbook and take a test or review exercise at the end of each unit. Should the student's performance in that test be unsatisfactory the 'tutor has the option of requiring the student to revise areas of weakness or undertake a second attempt at the review exercise before proceeding to the next unit' (Cho, 1982: 136). As such, the course operates on the basis of a Keller Plan (see chapter 4). In a similarly designed course on 'Environmental Systems' at the University of Colorado at Colorado Springs in the USA, grading of tests and certain remedial instruction is done by student 'proctors' who receive academic credit for their role in the course (Beyer, 1988).

In the United Kingdom, students of the Open University can take courses such as 'Changing Britain: Changing World' (Open University, 1985), in which students mainly learn at home using specially written print-based course units. These materials are complemented by audio-cassettes, television broadcasts, optional tutorials and a week-long compulsory residential course. At Southampton University, a second year course on physical geography techniques contains no lectures, but is instead based around workbooks and tape–slide programmes designed by geography staff (Clarke and Gregory, 1982: see also chapter 4). At Plymouth Polytechnic, a third year course on 'Issues in Geography' is based around study packs, largely containing 'key offprints or extracts with some explanatory and linking text' (Jones, 1986: 162). Students borrow these materials on a short loan basis from a resource centre.

A somewhat different example of a resource-based course is a first year course on 'Geography, Environment and Society' at Oxford Polytechnic. Here again, there are no lectures, although the occasional plenary sessions allow all students to view films or take part in a simulation. Most of the instruction is through teaching packages written by the staff, but often students use previously published material from textbooks, Open University units and journal or newspaper articles. A Course Guide leads students and staff through each week's assignment and activities, while students individually read a package and attempt an assignment on the material. There is a weekly group tutorial linked to each package consisting of about twelve students led by a member of staff.

The above examples, which are by no means exhaustive, hint at the sheer diversity of such courses. They differ in their degree of emphasis on print materials; they also differ in educational philosophy, in where the students study, methods of instruction, how students are assessed and in the terminology used (e.g. open learning, distance education, Keller Plan). In this chapter, however, we are essentially focusing on those courses, or parts of courses, which are largely or partly based on specially designed print-based 'learning packages' (some consideration of interactive video and computer-based instruction is contained in chapter 7). In saying this, we do not imply that the printed materials must be custom written for the course – indeed, an established textbook is often used. Rather, 'resource based learning' (RBL) here refers to courses, or parts of courses, with a particular style of instruction in which students primarily learn from

> specially prepared teaching materials. That is, the teaching will have been largely pre-planned, pre-recorded, and pre-packaged. It will be presented in instructional texts, audiotapes, videotapes, assignment exercises. (Rowntree, 1986: 11)

Some of these courses, albeit a minority adopt the psychological principles of behavioural reinforcement, in which good performance is rewarded and poor performance penalized. The best known of these courses are the Keller Plan schemes (Keller and Sherman, 1974; see also chapter 4). Those responsible for such courses follow the strategy of defining the course objectives and dividing the course material up into units. The students then study the material individually at their own pace. When they feel that they have mastered the information, they take a test. Should they reach a specified level of competence or 'mastery' they are allowed to pass on to the next unit. If they fail, they are usually required to take the test again. By their nature, Keller-style courses are teacher centred, despite being otherwise known as the Personalized System of Instruction. Indeed the only degree of control that the student actually exerts is over the pace at which they master the material and, in many Keller courses, that is also defined by the teacher. (The reading suggested at the end of this chapter gives further guidance on this very particular form of instruction and on other contrasting courses.)

6.3 THE GROWTH OF RESOURCE-BASED LEARNING

Various factors help to explain the growing popularity of RBL. These include the following.

● *Increasing access* Many authorities, both within and outside the higher education system, have argued for the desirability of extending learning opportunities to students unable to attend on a full-time basis because of family, occupational or other circumstances. The growth of 'distance education', in which students work primarily at home at their own pace and in their own time, makes RBL an attractive option. If higher education institutions cater for more mature and part-time students and play an increased role in re-training or refresher courses, then it may well be decided to deliver more of their courses in this way.

● *Providing basic course material* Some teachers have developed print-based materials to replace, at least partially, the conventional role of the lecture in imparting information. These materials can comprise anything from an extended lecture handout right up to a complete specially designed course. They also ensure that students have a full set of notes from which to revise.

● *Helping overcome differences in background knowledge* Students often enter higher education with widely varying levels of existing knowledge about the subjects that they are to study, which can be a major problem. Equally, there may be optional courses for which a certain level of background knowledge may be valuable as, for example, in the case of a course in soil analysis which may require students to have a basic grounding in chemistry. In both cases, an appropriate RBL package can be a way of supplying the necessary background knowledge.

● *The positive example of Open University materials* The experience of the Open University in Great Britain and comparable bodies elsewhere has shown what can be done with RBL. The quality of their materials and the commendable integration of learning objectives and self-study shown by their courses have convinced many observers about the value of this approach to teaching. We know of numerous teachers who have integrated these materials, including the specially designed television programmes, into their courses.

● *Efficiency* Budget cuts have forced many geography departments to re-examine the efficiency of their teaching, in which staff time is a very costly variable. As many departments seek to teach more students with fewer staff, one answer might be to introduce RBL as partial replacement for face-to-face contact time.

● *Technological changes* These have lowered the production costs and ease of distribution of RBL courses. Good offset-litho printing and cheap simple desk-top publishing packages are now well within most departmental budgets. As more staff become proficient at basic word-processing, lecture notes can easily be converted to student handouts, and, in turn, readily transformed into RBL packages. In the USA, for example, 'quick copy' services will take responsibility for arranging copyright permission, and reproduction and sale of packaged reading.

● *Shifting the load*   By this stage, we do not need to emphasize that increasing workloads are causing academics to look carefully at how they allocate their time between the different components of their job. In this context, RBL courses seem a sound option, since they allow teachers to shift a proportion of their responsibilities for facilitating learning on to their students and thereby save time spent in, and preparing for, the classroom. More positively perhaps, they allow teachers to concentrate much of their preparation for teaching into certain periods of the year, effectively freeing up blocks of time for research.

● *Coping with large numbers*   Following on from the last point is the particular situation faced in handling large introductory courses, where the pressure on staff time is at its greatest. Here perhaps an available textbook can be used or modified and the course probably needs little modification from year to year. For such courses, the cost of releasing staff to prepare special materials can be justified by economies of scale.

● *Staff enthusiasm*   Innovation is an important stimulus in any occupation and there are many teaching staff who have enjoyed the challenge of trying this new form of teaching. In addition, since many RBL courses are produced by groups of teachers acting collaboratively rather than individually, many have found the experience of writing a course together to be an enjoyable and valuable staff development exercise.

These, then, are the major reasons for the present and likely future growth of RBL, but there are also some serious drawbacks in establishing such courses. First, they can be deceptively expensive and hence an inefficient use of resources. Institutional circumstances can play an important role in this respect, since the presence of a well-equipped print room, an educational consultant ready to offer advice and the availability of special grants to support such initiatives can provide hidden subsidies that may make the difference between RBL being viable or non-viable. In addition, students may be inexperienced in using RBL materials and training may be necessary in order to help them obtain the best results from this style of teaching.

Second, care is necessary so as not to reduce the quality of the learning experience, particularly for students new to higher education. While it may be attractive from a tactical point of view to handle large first year classes by RBL methods, it is important to ensure that the impersonality of a large introductory course should not be compounded by delivery in an impersonal manner. As we shall argue later, there are ways of making RBL 'personal', but it is salutary to know that even many Keller-style courses use lectures, not so much to teach information but rather to motivate and inspire students and to provide a social occasion.

Finally, it would be politically naive not to recognize that the introduction of RBL has wider implications. Too often this method has been seized on by academic staff who wish to downgrade teaching. Administrators, likewise, have seen it as a way of achieving budget cuts through reduced staffing. Such attitudes have often led to resistance from academic staff to the use of RBL, with trades unions being concerned about the threat to jobs – issues which we consider further later in this chapter.

These are real drawbacks, which require care to be taken when introducing RBL. Overall, we would argue that, in many institutions, it is most effective when used to complement other forms of instruction. In conventional courses, it works particularly well when staff (and students) wish to maximize the value of classroom time. They do not want that time to be wasted on imparting information or getting a basic understanding of course content, a task which can be accomplished better by students working on RBL materials before they come to class. Table 6.1 summarises what we see as the potential benefits and disadvantages of using this style of teaching.

6.4 DEVELOPING RESOURCE-BASED COURSES

Having made a decision in principle to base all or part of a course on RBL materials, the following practical questions have to be faced.

1 *Allocating work* Is the material most effectively developed by one person or should more be involved? How much technician and secretarial time will be required? If several people are to be involved, how is co-ordination to be achieved? Staff development, enhanced group morale and even tangible research products can emerge from such an exercise, but poor leadership and planning could result in much tension and poorly designed materials.

2 *Production costs* Some sources suggest that around 50 hours preparation time are required to create materials for 1 hour of RBL. Clearly, the commitment will depend partly on what is being produced; our experience is that producing these courses can be very time consuming and that it is necessary to plan well ahead to ensure that the materials are there well before the course starts. (Perhaps this is a point to recall that lectures do have certain advantages, including being able to prepare them the night before!)

3 *Existing materials* Can one use or adapt material that is already produced? Does one have to re-invent the wheel or can a course be based substantially around an available textbook? British academics have too long allowed themselves the luxury of saying that no textbook really suits their course, whereas North American geographers are willing to make compromises in attempting to ensure that students have an adequate written basis for their studies. Perhaps one could

Table 6.1   Advantages and disadvantages associated with the development of resource-based learning

---

Potential advantages

Increases student activity
Can enhance student motivation and performance
Students can work in their preferred way and at their own pace
Can develop student responsibility towards study
Weaker students can focus on essential objectives whilst stronger students can be 'stretched'
Remedial work can be aided, catching weaker students earlier.
Useful for reinforcement and revision
Once provided, independent learning materials, together with student responses, are likely to be more comprehensible than traditional notes
Student absence or distance is more easily accommodated
Teacher can see a student's progress and problems more easily
Class discipline may present fewer problems
Teacher may be able to operate within a more flexible timetable

Potential disadvantages

Students may be required to work harder, thus breeding resentment
Some students become lonely and find the process very difficult
May diminish student motivation, particularly if overused or inappropriately used
Differences between students may be exacerbated
Self-study areas in college (such as library resource centre) may have inadequate capacity
May make heavy demands on college resources such as typing, paper and reprographic systems
Storage of, and access to materials may be difficult
High initial effort is needed to write independent learning materials, particularly those that involve construction of materials rather than compilation of study-packs
Updating of materials can be a considerable task
Can stultify creativity and intellectual growth
Can lead to too much assessment

Source: Yorke, 1981: 52; reproduced by permission

adapt the course to the best available textbook? Will students really lose out? Would staff time not be better spent by adopting a textbook and then concentrating on devising materials and activities that would complement or criticise it?

4 *Production standards*   As noted above, the success of Open University materials has been a powerful stimulus to the wider adoption of RBL, but their high quality and, consequently, high production costs could actually deter some people from attempting to produce their own. It must be stressed that high

quality production can be useful in increasing the impact of materials, but is not essential for educational effectiveness. As Rowntree (1986: 4) notes: 'you don't need high-tech. printing technology to produce self-instructional materials . . . perfectly adequate results can be obtained using a typewriter and the kinds of low cost methods of reproduction available to most educational . . . establishments.'

5 *Choosing the media.* In this chapter we have assumed that most course materials will be printed. This is generally the easiest and most effective medium – but many courses would benefit from the use of several complementary media. Film, tape-slide presentations, interactive video and photographic collections can all play a part if used effectively.

Having considered these and other questions, you may well decide to continue with a conventional course or limit the extent to which RBL materials are introduced into a course. However, if you have decided to go ahead, the following principles should be considered.

1 *Design materials for students* Since what is produced will be a public document, there is a great danger that one writes or includes things to impress colleagues. That it will be seen by one's peers can be a stimulus to producing good materials, but beware the danger of impressing colleagues. Always use direct simple language wherever possible.

2 *Choose reading carefully* RBL is often based upon previously published material such as journal articles. Considerable care is needed to ensure that students working on their own can understand the material. Your latest research article may be a very good communication to your peers, but it is unlikely to be what students need. The reading has to interest and engage the students so that they will want to read on and complete the reading.

3 *Gauging the tone* Try in your writing to create the tone of a personal tutorial since, unless devising a group task, you are writing for the individual student working by themselves. Rowntree (1986: 11) comments that: 'you should write as if you were talking to a learner with whom you are not too well acquainted and you will probably succeed in being conversational without sounding over familiar.' It is the skill in writing the 'written equivalent of a one-to-one tutorial' (Rowntree, 1986: 119) that can result in a 'mass produced' course directly involving the individual learner.

4 *Giving adequate guidance* It is important to write down everything that the student needs to know, or might reasonably ask, about how to tackle a piece of work. The alternative is a large number of individuals banging on your door, mostly asking the same questions.

5 *Cut the content* Deciding what to include and exclude is a key decision in any form of teaching, but it becomes even more important when using RBL.

While it is advisable to be all-inclusive when supplying students with instructions, the same is not necessarily true of substantive content. In particular, there are great temptations, first, to think that everything has to be included and, second, to underestimate how long it takes students to study RBL material. A basic rule of thumb is to think what you want to write, and then halve it.

6 *Establish clear learning goals*   Make very clear to students what they should have learned as a result of reading the material or watching a film. For instance: 'at the end of reading this package you should be able to explain the role of the North East of England in the world economy (a) in *c*.1960 and (b) in the 1980s.' Occasionally it can be useful to specify what they are not expected to do.

7 *Encourage students in active learning*   Our contention, by now familiar, is that students learn by being active. Reading is an activity, but it needs to be complemented by a whole range of activities otherwise, as in a lecture, students' attention can quickly decline. Encourage students to make notes, complete diagrams, calculate or write in their own examples. After students have worked at an activity, give them feedback on how they have fared, for example, by providing answers at the end of their resource pack. Even in an RBL course mainly directed at the individual student, it can be valuable to include some packages which require students to work through the material in small groups.

8 *Recognize different patterns of usage*   Unless attempting to write a tightly programmed learning package, recognize that individual students will differ in the way that they use your material. Not all will start on page 1 and work steadily through the package. Students differ as learners, and one of the advantages of RBL materials is that their flexibility allows a variety of ways to approach the material. For this reason, it may be very important to include some additional optional material that many students may ignore or just quickly glance through. For example, take the case in which students are required to read an article on city classifications which uses analysis of variance to demonstrate variations within a set of cities. Those students with knowledge of this technique will be able to read the material without difficulty, but it may well be valuable to provide information on that technique, perhaps as an aside to the main text, for those who lack this knowledge.

9 *Include study skills*   To be effective, RBL requires adequate skills at such activities as reading, watching a film and using a computer package. Indeed, systematic development of these skills can be an important objective in its own right for developing RBL courses. Certain basic strategies concerning skills should be built into one's packages. Make it clear that different texts and tasks benefit from very different reading strategies, for example, certain background information can be quickly skimmed. Students should be directed to build up a map or structure of what they are reading linking together the varied materials in a package. They need to be directed to analyse particular readings in depth

to understand the fundamental ideas, but it is also important to specify how long an entire package and its separate components should take. If given no direction, it is possible for interpretation of a supposedly simple table to take a hour of a student's time.

10 *Specify when work has to be completed*   One of the arguments for resource-based courses is that they allow students to pace their own learning. Some students, however, may well need help to structure their time properly and to take responsibility for their learning. Furthermore, the competing demands of other more conventional courses may lead students to leave work on the resource-based course until the assignments or examinations are due (e.g. see Jones, 1986). One answer to this problem is to require regular attendance at seminars and the regular completion of work, but this can remove much of the students' responsibility for organizing their time and pacing their learning. There is a difficult, but necessary, balance to strike here.

11 *Provide appropriate work space*   These courses often assume that students will work individually at home or in the library, but you may require them to consult specific bulky materials only available in certain defined places or to use particular fixed equipment. It may therefore be essential to establish specialist resource rooms to accompany such courses, as occurs in many institutions that run Keller Plan courses.

12 *Link RBL with other learning activities*   RBL courses need to be integrated into the general curriculum in terms of development of knowledge and skills. In the same way, RBL itself can be put together with other forms of activity – perhaps using lectures to set an agenda for the course and group tutorials to draw out wider issues through discussion (see chapter 5).

13 *Involve library staff*   In developing resource-based courses, librarians can be both your allies and your enemies. The librarian can assist in finding key sources, clarifying any uncertainties over copyright law and perhaps arranging for certain materials to be set aside for consultation. However, librarians may well ask justifiably awkward questions in key committees about such a proposed course. They may worry that, instead of sitting in classrooms, students will be crowding into the library to read their packages. This has implications for the way in which students use the library and the competing needs of other students who want to use the books – which, after all, is what the library is for. Moreover, librarians emphasize that a fundamental purpose of higher education is to develop students' ability to find their own information. They may well cite, as we do, the importance of students becoming 'autonomous learners' and ask how packaging all the information in a course text will aid them to achieve that aim. There may well be an element of role protection in these arguments, but be prepared to argue your case. Recognize the validity of these concerns and accept that, while certain distance-based courses have to be based upon

a tightly integrated package, this is not necessarily the way that all packages have to be designed.

6.5 ADMINISTRATIVE ISSUES

We have already mentioned certain administrative issues that are likely to be faced when implementing RBL. Some of these echo points made in chapter 4, but RBL also brings certain problems of its own.

Staff time and resources

In the long run such courses may be an efficient means of saving staff time but, as we have noted, they are initially expensive in both staff time and necessary resources. Individual teachers may decide to do most, or all, the preparation themselves well before a course starts, but if the intention is to introduce a 'package centred' course, and certainly if it requires the preparation of specialist computer packages, high quality maps or tape–slide presentations, then these resources may go beyond an individual teacher's capabilities or available time.

There are several answers to this problem, with the solution depending on particular circumstances. If decisions on teaching responsibilities are taken at the department level, then the department could decide to release a group or an individual from immediate teaching responsibilities to enable them to prepare such a course. Similarly, a department could allocate a proportion of its revenue and secretarial time to developing a course. Alternatively, resources may be competitively available at an institutional level or from outside sources. For example, the physical geography techniques course at Southampton University, mentioned earlier, was partly funded by a grant from the Nuffield Foundation. Some institutions set aside funds to support specific teaching innovations.

Hours of accounting

The ways in which an institution or department allocates teaching responsibilities can present a further problem. Many systems employ some notional idea of the amount of contact hours that teachers at different grades are expected to perform per week as part of their contractual obligations. In the non-university sector of British public education, these are actually formalized in the shape of national guidelines (albeit subject to local variation). Arrangements whereby teaching staff are contracted to teach in the classroom for a given number of hours per week often take no account of the preparation time that is required to produce that teaching. Under such conditions, expenditure of many hours of time to prepare a course that requires few classroom contact hours is not a sensible strategy. All that may happen is that the department or institution could seek to recoup the hours saved by RBL activities by allocating the teacher additional tasks to fulfil the contractual arrangement. The solution to this problem needs to resolved by local negotiation and agreement before undertaking such courses.

Copyright

Many package courses are based upon previously published materials. Undoubtedly, as we have noted, this is a sensible way to proceed but one has to check carefully the copyright of any sources one wishes to use. National laws on copyright vary enormously in this respect, with US law, for example, being far more liberal than British law. Subject librarians or audiovisual staff are often the best immediate source on the specific legal position. Requests can be made to publishers requesting permission to use particular sources. Many geography journals, if asked, will grant the right to make extensive copies for student use. Certain journals clearly state that subscribers can make copies for students, good examples being the *Journal of Geography in Higher Education*, *Geography*, *Area* and *Transactions of the Institute of British Geographers*. Many newspapers will also grant individuals and institutions the right to make copies of articles as long as they are solely for educational use by students at the institution. Commercial publishers, however, will often request a fee. Finally, do not forget to protect your own copyright on what you have produced.

6.6 CONCLUSION

The experience of geographers and others suggests that RBL can play an important, and probably increasing, role in geographical education. There is much that can be learned and adapted from the work of distance learning institutions and from courses based on Keller principles. We reiterate that RBL is not necessarily an effective means of cutting costs or time; indeed, it can often be more expensive than conventional teaching, certainly in the short term. Having said this, RBL can be very effective in the right circumstances in both educational and cost terms, particularly as part of courses designed to prepare students for classroom activities.

In moving to adopt any aspect of RBL, our suggestions are as follows.

- Consider perhaps replacing a small part of a lecture course that you might be giving this year by a presentation using packaged material.

- Consider preparing a full course guide for a course that you will be teaching next year. The guide should give details on all class sessions and full instructions on assignments. Experiment by designing part of the course around a specially designed package or a published textbook. Involve students in redesigning the experimental section of the course for the following year's students.
- Find someone in your institution who teaches an RBL-based course (it can be in any subject area). Ask to sit in on some of the formal sessions, discuss the course with some of the students or even take the course yourself. Decide whether this method is potentially of use to you or your department. If so, decide how you can implement it.
- Ensure that the geography course as a whole does not overuse packages, but employs them as part of the wider mix involved in delivering the curriculum.

KEY READING

There is a developing literature on 'distance education', which makes considerable use of RBL. Particularly recommended are *Course Development: A Manual for Editors of Distance Learning Materials* (J. Jenkins, 1985), *Making Self-instructional Material* (Harrison, 1985) and *Teaching through Self-instruction* (Rowntree, 1986). Further useful supporting readings can be found in CNAA (1983), Levine (1985), and Calfee and Drum (1986). There are now detailed discussions by geographers on a variety of approaches to RBL. Of these, we would recommend Backler (1979), Cho (1982), Clarke and Gregory (1982), Limbird (1982), Whitelegg (1982), Jones (1986) and Fox et al. (1987).

7

Computer Assisted Teaching and Learning

Thinking about the computer's role in education does not mean thinking about computers, it means thinking about education.

A. B. Ellis, *The Use and Misuse of Computers in Education*

7.1 INTRODUCTION

The resources that academic geography departments have invested in computing facilities during the 1980s have had a major impact on undergraduate geographical teaching in two main ways. First, perhaps the greatest effect has been the creation of courses that make computer technology an object of study. Many courses are now offered in subjects such as 'automated cartography', 'remote sensing' and 'geographical information systems' in which the focus is teaching *about* computers. Second, the computer has also been used as a tool for teaching and studying *geography* - an approach variously known as computer assisted learning, computer assisted instruction or computer-based learning. It is with this second category that this chapter is concerned.

At the outset, we stress that our view of the computer's current or even potential impact remains sanguine, particularly since its major impact on geographical education to date has been more on course content than on teaching methods. While we believe that computers have a valuable role to play right across the geography curriculum, we are not seeking to encourage wholesale automation of geography teaching, nor to develop a comprehensive theory of educational technology, nor even to list the computer programs available for geography teaching. The first of these goals would be foolish, the second premature and the third impossible.

Rather, our aim in this chapter is to explore ways in which computers can, and do, support geography teaching at first degree level. In the sections that follow, we examine specific examples of what computers can do in delivering the geography curriculum. First, we describe the range of computer resources currently available and look at the educational uses that can be made of a selection of these. In these sections we seek to demonstrate that most computer resources can be used in a variety of ways in an educational context; very few are entirely prescriptive as to how they should be used. Second, we examine some of the teaching and learning activities commonly encountered in geography and consider the computer resources that are best able to support them. Our intention here is to show that most educational activities can be supported by a number of different computer resources. Thus, if you do not have access to one particular resource, this need not jeopardize the application you may have in mind; other materials can probably be pressed into service to provide the necessary support.

By exploring the field from these two contrasting perspectives, we hope that whatever your starting point, you will be able to see what can be done with computers in the geography classroom. We also hope to illustrate the message contained in our opening quotation – that in matters of educational technology, it is the educational goals that matter most.

7.2 COMPUTER RESOURCES AND THEIR EDUCATIONAL USES

Over the past 20 years, a wide range of computer resources (see table 7.1) have been developed specifically for educational use, and many resources that were designed for other purposes have been pressed into service for teaching and learning. Such resources vary in their degree of generality. Some, for example, have geographical subject matter or skills built in, others have not; some are designed specifically for educational use and may therefore adopt a particular instructional style, others do not; some are meant to be used in a narrowly defined way (by individuals, by small groups or for giving demonstrations), others are designed for more flexible use.

Table 7.2 indicates how a selection of these different types of computer resource perform on the basis of these criteria. As may be seen, there is a spectrum from the most specific resources (e.g. computer assisted instruction and 'drill and practice' tutorials), through focused-but-flexible resources (such as simulations), to wholly general purpose resources (e.g. generic information processing software).

Since the mid-1970s, geographers have tended to design and use highly specific computer resources in their teaching, but the benefits of using so-called 'generic software' have now become better recognized (Forer, 1987a,b; Rees, 1987). Generic software includes databases, spreadsheets, word processors and expert system shells, contains no geography at all and usually no teaching or learning mechanisms. However, by adding geographical data from independent sources

Table 7.1 Types of computer resources

Drill and practice
Mechanistic computer exercises, designed to provide practice and reinforcement in particular knowledge and skills.

Computer assisted instruction (CAI)
A genre of instruction that ranges from repetitious 'programmed learning' through to 'intelligent tutoring systems', based on principles developed in artificial intelligence.

Computer managed learning/instruction (CML or CMI)
Software that manages conventional and/or computer-based teaching material, particularly that involving mastery learning or self-paced instruction. CML software keeps records of student progress and performance on the basis of regular tests, recommends future learning activities and presents summary information to teachers.

Presentation software
Software (usually graphic) designed for use as a demonstration or presentation tool.

Computer-based games
Programs which present a simulated situation in which students act out a role, interacting with the computer.

Simulations
Programs which model some feature, event or process in the real world, which can be explored in an *ad hoc* manner or subjected to systematic experimentation.

Model-building tools
Software (e.g. programming languages, spreadsheets, expert system shells, graphic modelling tools, etc.) used to create models of the real world.

Generic information processing software
Widely available commercial software that process particular types of information (e.g. word-processors, spreadsheets, databases, etc.).

Geographical information handling software
Programs that can be used to explore geographical data using standard methods of spatial analysis and display (e.g. thematic mapping packages, image processing software and geographical information systems).

continued

Table 7.1   *continued*

Hypertext and hypermedia
Hypertext software enables units of textual information to be
    arranged in complex networks so that users can follow multiple
    and arbitrary pathways through it, and create entirely new
    connections between these items. Hypermedia systems enable
    information of many sorts (text, images, maps, sounds, speech,
    etc.) to be built into such networks.

Data logging
Hardware that can monitor and measure events and processes
    in the real world. Information may be passed to a general
    purpose computer for subsequent processing, and may also
    be used to control equipment.

Videodisc
A mass storage device that can store huge amounts of information
    in video form (some 55,000 frames per side of a 12 inch disc).
    The information can be any combination of photographs,
    diagrams, maps and moving footage, with commentary, sound
    and music recorded on its soundtracks. Can be used to teach
    knowledge or skills when combined with tutorial software.

Optical disc
A mass storage device that can store huge amounts of information
    in digital form (some 550 megabytes per standard 4.75 inch
    disc). The information may include text, numerical data, maps
    and images. With appropriate software, optical discs enable
    users to browse through, retrieve, analyse and display
    information from very large data sets.

Interactive video
Video discs which are linked to computer software to create
    interactive learning systems.

Multimedia systems
Essentially the same as interactive video, but using either or both
    video and optical disc storage devices.

Computer communications
Communications facilities may be used to connect personal
    computers together into local area networks (LANs), to connect
    a single personal computer together with larger shared
    minicomputers or mainframes, or to connect various computers
    nationally or globally in wide-area networks (WANs).

and by devising appropriate exercises and student training, such software can provide a wide range of highly effective learning activities. For example, generic software can be used to explore data from field surveys, laboratory experiments or secondary sources, to set up and run simulation models (e.g. of population growth or migration) or to prepare course essay papers or dissertations. These programs are equally applicable to subjects other than geography, and therefore student skills can be applied across several courses with only a single training experience. General purpose packages are also widely used in the outside world, and their use therefore serves to enhance students' personal and vocational skills as much as their aptitude for studying geography.

*Applic. to
how*

Table 7.2   The contrasting characteristics of computing resources

Facility	Software type			
	CAI D&P tutorial	Simulations	Geographic tools	Generic tools
Geographical content	✓	✓	✓	–
Educational origin	✓	✓	(✓)	–
User control	Low	Medium	Medium	High

Each type of computer resource can be used in a variety of ways in geography teaching, a theme that will be illustrated here by reference to three examples: simulation software, computer-based games and the video disc.

Computer simulations

Computer simulations, which share the same intellectual roots as simulations generally (see chapter 5), are one of the more commonly used types of educational computer software in geography (Shepherd, 1985). Long gone are the days when spatial diffusion and drainage network evolution exercises were laboriously hand-run by students. Today, fully interactive computer simulation programs, often involving high resolution colour graphic displays, animation and sound effects, have removed the unnecessary burden of manual operationalization of models and make it possible for students to model many elements of the real world. Computer simulation programs therefore fulfil both an 'emancipatory' and a 'revelatory' role in geography teaching.

Most simulations have been developed for physical rather than human geography, given that they are easier to construct where a system can be clearly defined and its behaviour expressed mathematically or algorithmically. While several deterministic and stochastic models have been developed as teaching tools in human geography (Marble and Anderson, 1972; Stephens and Wittick, 1975; Dethlefsen and Moody, 1982; Midgeley, 1985), their normative bases mean that they are perhaps better used to demonstrate the poverty of current theories of human spatial behaviour or to show the complexity of social processes than to simulate real-world behaviour.

By contrast, computer simulation has provided considerable benefit for students of physical geography, especially with regard to meteorology, biogeography, geomorphology and hydrology (see Kirkby et al., 1987). As an example, consider the RAIN program, developed to illustrate the hydrological cycle (Riley, 1990). Figure 7.1 indicates the systems view of the world built into this program, with its interconnected 'stores' and 'transfers'. Students are able to define inputs of water into the system and experiment with different parameters in order to observe the passage of this water through the system (see also Burt and Butcher, 1986).

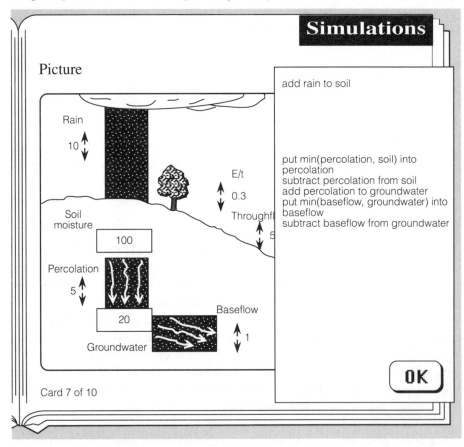

Figure 7.1   The RAIN simulation
Source: after Riley (1990)

Computer simulations have various advantages as tools for the study of social and environmental systems (Kirkby and Naden, 1988). These include the following.

- *Providing demonstrations*, as when simulation programs are used as an 'electronic blackboard' during lectures to illustrate graphically patterns and processes in the real world (see below).
- *Carrying out experiments*, in which students can adjust the values of selected parameters in a model, either to re-create a predictable response or to appreciate the effect of variable changes on model outcomes. Thus, in a population growth model, students might manipulate birth or death rates to see the effect on the size of future populations. They can also experiment systematically with a model's parameters in order to understand the complex interrelationships that exist in natural or human systems. In a water pollution simulation, for example, students could explore the interactions between water temperature, water velocity, and the type and quantity of pollution.
- *Replicating a known feature or event*, as with programs that simulate spit growth or river meander formation. For example, the SPITSYM simulation program (McCullagh and King, 1970; King and McCullagh, 1971) – developed in relation to the Hurst Castle spit on the English south coast – can be used to challenge students to discover the parameters that re-create the form of this particular coastal feature.
- *Relating model behaviour and outcomes to the real world*, as when comparing the numerical or graphical output of a simulation with published data, or with data gathered by carrying out appropriate fieldwork. Kirkby and Naden (1988), for instance, describe how hydrological models can be calibrated to specific run-off records, so that appropriate local fieldwork can be undertaken. Haines-Young (1983) uses biogeographical examples to illustrate how testing a simulated world against reality encourages students to learn by an active process of conjecture and refutation (see below).
- *Exploring alternative realities* In a climatology course, for instance, a climatic model can be used to explore the possible effects on the atmosphere of changing the solar constant, the amount of dust in the atmosphere or the relative proportions of land and sea areas on the earth's surface (Cerveney and Balling, 1984). Alternatively, a course on society and environment might use a global atmospheric model to explore the concept of 'nuclear winter' or a Limits to Growth type of model to examine possible future effects of resource depletion, pollution or uncontrolled population growth (Deutsch et al., 1977).

- *Providing an environment for problem solving*, in which students apply their knowledge of a system to solve problems arising in its function or to improve elements of its operation. (Examples of the role of computers in problem solving are discussed later.)
- *Acting as a focus for evaluating geographical theory*, since criticizing computer models allows students to understand the difficulty of creating testable theories in geography. Criticism can be done in two ways: by using appropriate simulation programs or by reading and discussing critiques published in the literature. For example, the well-known Club of Rome 'Limits to Growth' model exists in simpler educational form as a BASIC program from the American Huntingdon II Project, and has also generated a considerable literature (e.g. Clark and Cole, 1975). This literature, and the computer models it analyses, provides students with a rich resource for the study of the limitations of simulation modelling as a tool for social and environmental engineering.

Taken as a whole, computer simulations present students with a simplified, but instructive, view of the real world, in which time and space can be compressed or dilated. They allow social and environmental systems to be subjected to controlled and repeated experiment, yet the experiments are undertaken without any adverse effects on the real world. In particular, potentially dangerous situations can be explored in complete safety. Indeed, on occasions, simulations can be more productive than either the direct examination of objects or events in the real world or the intensive study of empirical data. They are also effective in overcoming the fears of less numerate students towards the in-depth study of physical processes, particularly if the programs are used to provide a visual introduction to a new topic. In certain circumstances, they can also take pressure off departmental resources by providing a substitute for fieldwork.

Nevertheless, despite their attractions as teaching and learning tools, computer simulations must be handled carefully in order to provide the fullest educational benefits. The following suggestions are offered on how to make the most of them in geography teaching.

- It is essential to train students in the art of devising hypotheses if they are to use simulation programs to ask effective 'what if . . .?' questions about the world and to participate in the process of discovery learning. Erecting hypotheses is a skill that does not come naturally to all students, even to those who have an aptitude for grasping concepts.
- Ensure that students are given sufficient access to a computer to enable them to undertake adequate exploration of the simulation model. If a

specific program is to be used individually by students, and only a limited number of computers or terminals are available, then schedule the use of the software over a period of days (or even weeks) following the introductory classes on the topic.

- Avoid using complex and highly realistic models. These can obscure the major components and behaviour of the system being studied and can deprive students of the motivation for looking closer at the model, of the satisfaction of discovering unrealistic model behaviour or the challenge of identifying the cause of this misbehaviour.

- Avoid using simulation programs that demand too little student thinking or which require too little student interaction with the model. Some simulation programs ask users to enter a single number and then expect them to wait until results are produced. Far better to use a program that offers students alternative ways of interacting with the model.

- However good the program, its effective classroom use demands considerable amounts of the teacher's time. To derive the full benefit, students will need a careful introduction to the simulation, organized access to computer facilities during the work and thorough debriefing afterwards, perhaps by written assignments or subsequent field work or laboratory experiments. Without these activities, all of which require a major input of preparation, marking and classroom time by the teacher, the use of computer-based simulation programs can easily degenerate into mere recreation or mindless key-pecking.

Computer-based games

Computer-based games share similar characteristics to the games described in chapter 5. Unlike computer simulations, they have been developed particularly well in relation to human geographical contexts, dealing with situations such as agricultural decision-making, industrial location and travel (e.g. Watson, 1984; Midgeley, 1985; Kent, 1987). Available for both group exercises and individual student use, they focus around students pitting their wits against the computer in a competitive situation. The user is usually able to select a level of difficulty at which to play the game, and the program often provides a number of geographical arenas in which the game is played out. Some games involve little more than arcade-type skills of hand–eye coordination, but others involve geographical skill and knowledge.

Taken together, they have a number of uses in geography teaching.

1 *Assisting student learning*   At a relatively crude level, games programs can be used to reinforce and test factual geographical knowledge (e.g. Lewis 1979),

the idea being that the entertainment component provides students with an incentive to learn. Malone (1981), however, suggests that teachers should be extremely careful when assuming that the computer motivates students to learn. His evaluation of many games programs led him to suggest that the *task* set for students by a game should provide the motivation, and not the packaging or surface form of the game, for example, slick graphics, animation or sound effects.

2 *Encouraging acquisition of skills*   Games formats can also be used to teach students geographical techniques or statistics through interactive experiments. A simple example is the Hunt the Hurkle game, which is designed to help students to reinforce their grasp of the principles of grid referencing by having to trace the location of a mythical animal hiding in a grid. Griffith (1987) provides a more sophisticated example of a game designed to help understand the concept of spatial autocorrelation, with other experiments of this kind being reported by Silk (1979b).

3 *Influencing student attitudes*   Students' attitudes to society and the environment can also be fostered by using appropriate computer games. Examples of games programs that can do this include those that deal with pollution control, environmental management or disease eradication. Games can also be used to shape students' attitudes to learning, especially where the computer plays a relatively small part and the game is itself shaped around group collaboration (see the previous discussion in chapter 5).

Overall, the message when using computer games in geographical teaching is much the same as that already noted for computer simulations. Game-playing exercises can, and usually do, place considerable demands on teachers. If you intend to use computer software during game sessions, then student use will need to be carefully scheduled and organized. In particular, different strategies will be needed if only a single computer is available, as opposed to when there is a roomful of networked microcomputers.

Video discs

Although video disc technology has been available in educational circles for over a decade, its full potential is only now being realized (Braun, 1978; Wood and Stephens, 1978). This potential derives from the video disc's massive storage capacity (some 55,000 frames of video information per disc side), its ability to store information of various types (single images, film and video sequences, sounds and commentary), its ability to display this information one frame at a time or in moving sequences and the possibility of retrieving a single frame from anywhere on the disc in a matter of seconds.

Video discs can be used in several ways for teaching: as a classroom teaching aid, as a medium for group learning, as an individualized tutor and as a visual archive (Bayard-White, 1985; Laurillard, 1988). We shall now explore its potential in geography.

1 *Video playback*   At its simplest, video material on a disc can be presented as short sequences of moving images with accompanying sound or commentary, requiring little or no interaction by the user. Both the Domesday (e.g. Maguire, 1989) and Ecodisc (McCormick and Bratt, 1988) video discs devote an entire side to such images: the former provides 120 short broadcast clips to illustrate the nature of life in Britain during the 1980s; the latter contains a television program that describes the nature reserve which is the subject of the interactive material on the other side of the disc. Replay of this type, however, is far cheaper by conventional film and video, making it difficult to justify using videodiscs solely for this purpose.

2 *Multimedia teaching and training*   A more powerful teaching resource is created by connecting a video disc player to a computer to create an interactive video (IV) system, which 'combines the rich and varietal sensory experiences offered by television with the detailed control characteristics of computer-based learning' (Duke, 1983: 24). IV systems have many uses. For example, appropriate tutorial software can be used to present short video extracts, still frames and spoken information on a particular topic and to ask the student appropriate comprehension or test questions at key points. Evidence from industrial applications of this technology suggests that learning time for certain topics can be shortened by up to 60 per cent, and retention and recall can improve by anything between 25 and 80 per cent.

3 *Multimedia databases*   IV systems can also be used in less structured ways. Laurillard (1984) suggests that their vast information capacity and instant access capability offers considerable potential for greater student control of learning. In contrast with the 'programmed learning' approach typical of many commercial training systems, she sees a combination of video disc databases and flexible interrogative software as a powerful resource for autonomous student learning. The BBC's Domesday Project represents one example of this approach, providing discs with a cornucopia of visual, cartographic, textual and numerical data, together with powerful facilities for browsing, analysis and display. The more recent Countryside disc provides similar resources for the study of rural environments in the United Kingdom. Both these examples make use of hybrid (interactive video read-only memory (IV-ROM)) video disc players, which can read digital data (typically text and numerical information) stored on one of the video disc soundtracks.

4 *Experimental environments*   Some video discs are organized in such a way as to provide students with a simulated world or electronic environment with which they can experiment. An early example of such a system is provided by the Tacoma Narrows Bridge video disc (Zollman and Fuller, 1982), which uses archival news footage of a collapsing bridge, together with interrogative and simulation software, to teach students the principles of structural engineering. Another example is provided by the Ecodisc (noted above). This holds large quantities of information about a British nature reserve, and the accompanying software enables students to use this information for a number of educational experiences. They can wander around the reserve on a 'surrogate walk', they can watch the ecology developing for 50 years into the future, they can sample the local flora and fauna, and they can devise a plan of action to achieve certain management goals for the reserve.

In summary, use of the video disc, and especially the IV system, has distinct advantages for geography teaching. It supplies a 'sensory rich' learning experience in that it combines both visual and aural information, it allows students to learn at their own pace, it *can* be an acceptable substitute for expensive or time-consuming activities such as laboratory or field work and it is flexible in usage, with the same video materials on a disc being used for different purposes, or by different levels of learner, simply by providing several computer programs with the system. Naturally, as with all self-directed learning activities, both teachers and students need to adjust their attitudes to make it work effectively.

Looking ahead, however, technological advances in other storage technologies may limit the further development of the video disc. Just as the video disc appears to be making an impact, optical disc technology in the form of the compact disc read-only memory (CD–ROM) now seems set to provide all the facilities we have outlined above (except, for the moment, motion video), but by means of a completely digital – rather than video – technology (Ambron and Hooper, 1988; Megarry, 1988). Some material previously issued on videodiscs is already being made available on CD–ROMs (the BBC Ecodisc is a prime example). If the CD–ROM does indeed usurp the position of the videodisc in education, then little will need to be modified in our educational discussion above: just substitute 'CD–ROM' for 'video disc', and expect to read increasingly about 'interactive multimedia' rather than 'interactive video'. *Plus ça change . . .*

7.3 EDUCATIONAL ACTIVITIES AND COMPUTER SUPPORT

Shifting the focus of the discussion, we now examine the various teaching and learning activities that can take place in geography courses and the ways in which these activities can be supported by appropriate computer resources. We begin with teacher-centred uses of the computer and then consider a wide range of student-centred activities.

Course preparation and management: computers as personal assistants

Computers can be used in various ways to support conventional teaching.

- Assembling material for reading lists and lectures by searching through on-line bibliographic records (e.g. GEOBASE, which provides on-line access to GeoAbstracts) or CD–ROM databases.
- Producing class handouts and reading lists with a combination of word-processor, drawing program and desk-top publishing software.
- Producing overhead projector foils on a pen plotter attached to a personal computer, and 35 mm slides using 'presentation software'.
- Culling data for practical exercises from digital databases, or generating random data by a simple program written in a common programming language (see chapter 4).
- Indexing and selecting teaching resources (such as 35 mm slides) using information retrieval or database software.
- Managing the progress of students through a course. Computer-managed learning (CML) software can be used to test students at regular points during a course, and to recommend subsequent learning activities.
- Handling student assessment grades. This can be done by using computer-based objective tests (see chapter 8), with some institutions making use of computerized test databases from which individual teachers can draw an appropriate test set for a particular assessment (Byrne, 1976). Alternatively, the computer can be used to collate and present student grades. Webb (1987) describes how general purpose spreadsheets, with their easy-to-use facilities for entering, updating and weighting student grades, can be used to do this.

Expository teaching: the computer as presenter

Computers are a poor substitute for the conventional lecture, but can do much to add sparkle or variety to a lecture presentation. In particular, the computer can be employed as an 'electronic blackboard', using one or other of the following resources.

- Programs that create video 'slides', and allow these to be displayed on a television screen in any sequence. These include standard graphics programs (computer-aided design (CAD), painting, business graphics programs), as well as purpose-built 'slide projection' emulators. However, unless they are used imaginatively, such slides often do little more than equivalent diagrams drawn on a blackboard or displayed on an overhead projector.

- Standard data analysis or thematic mapping packages. These can be used in a lecture to provide live illustrations or to test theories. At the University of Washington, for example, a purpose-built data analysis and mapping program called Sociology Showcase was developed specifically for use in lecturing to classes of between 400 and 800 sociology students (Stark, 1986).
- Computer simulation programs that produce animated graphics output. The introduction of short computer simulation sequences can breathe life into a static model or forbidding formulae (Sumner, 1984a), and are ideal for visualizing the dynamics of geographical processes such as convective uplift, population migrations or sediment transport and deposition.

Care is necessary if a computer is to be used effectively as an 'electronic blackboard'. Some practical tips here are as follows.

- Avoid using text-only displays, unless they are in bold checklist form and meant to serve as an advance organizer. Play to the computer's strengths: generate graphical displays, display animated sequences, run simulations, respond interactively to student suggestions.
- Choose programs that produce uncluttered screen displays, and which can be used with minimal keyboard interaction.
- Make sure that all students can see and read the computer display, which may require having a large screen or multiple monitors. It is also possible to send computer output directly to an overhead projector, although a perfectly legible display on a computer monitor can sometimes be badly degraded if converted into video form for projection.
- Provide students with paper versions of screen material, particularly if the screen's contents are unclear, or if you require the students to have detailed transcripts of computer-generated information. Students cannot concentrate completely on the subject if they are too busy copying down what they see on the screen.
- Use demonstration programs in short bursts, interspersed with discussion or summarizing note-taking by students (as suggested in chapter 2).

Group discussions: the computer as catalyst

Although group discussions were discussed fully in chapter 5, it is worth noting the possibility of using the computer in such contexts as a powerful learning stimulus. The idea is for a teacher to sit down with a small group of students and to work through an appropriate computer program in response to their questions and stimulate further discussion. To derive the maximum benefit from this style of teaching, the following guidelines should be adopted.

- Ensure that the discussion group is no larger than six to eight people (including yourself), and that seats are arranged in an arc around the computer screen.
- Use a computer whose keyboard you can cradle in your lap.
- Use programs that can be rapidly navigated and preferably have been designed with small group discussions in mind. For example, ITMA, the British educational software development group, specialises in developing programs that can be used with minimal typing, with each program coming with its own specially designed 'drive chart' (Burkhardt et al., 1980; Fraser, 1981; Birkhill, 1983). Other software useful in this respect are standard spreadsheet programs (such as Lotus 1-2-3) and information retrieval programs (such as dBASE). Some geographical simulation programs may also be useful, particularly if they are easy to operate in the context of fast-moving discussions.
- Master the software before using it in class, so that you can use it quickly and effectively.
- Encourage students to provide appropriate questions or 'what if . . . ?' suggestions.

Working with a computer in small group discussions has a variety of advantages, in terms of examining ideas in a thought-provoking and structured way with few of the time constraints associated with traditional forms of computer-based learning. Against this, care must be taken to avoid the teacher posing as the guardian of the computer, perhaps by rotating the keyboard from student to student, although this implies suitable student preparation.

Tutoring: the computer as teacher

Although few institutions now have the resources to provide the Oxbridge style of personal tutorial (see chapter 5), pursuit of the underlying ideal led to much interest in the 1960s and 1970s in computer tutoring. Much of the early software to emerge was based on the then current technology of programmed learning, in which the computer presents material on a chosen topic, poses questions, provides appropriate feedback for the student's response and then branches to the next relevant topic according to the validity of the student's answer. More recent developments have seen a considerable elaboration of branching methods of programmed learning materials, with a relatively sophisticated methodology of 'instructional science' emerging (Riegeluth et al., 1978). These developments are usually described as computer-based instruction (CBI) or computer assisted instruction (CAI). Among the claims made for this application of computers are that it individualizes teaching, allows students to learn at their own pace and provides the feedback necessary for students to correct their learning mistakes and reinforce their positive learning gains.

In the commercial training field, this kind of instructional material is successfully used to deliver relatively standardized training to repeated cohorts of trainees. By contrast, geographers teaching at degree level seem to have ignored this training potential, even for teaching students basic technical skills – an area of tuition in which this technology excels. Geographical skills that could benefit from the CAI treatment include use of laboratory equipment, use of computer hardware and software, and fieldwork, survey and statistical methods. Moreover, there are already some commercial computer programs available that might be evaluated for geographical teaching purposes, for example, in teaching students how to use general scientific equipment such as measuring gauges, increasing student familiarity with basic mathematical and statistical procedures, and for training students on how to use software. However, it must be stressed that the programmed learning style adopted by most tutorial software is primitive when compared with the approaches adopted by human instructors. Programs written in this mould are largely unable to locate and treat the sources of students' learning difficulties, are typically unable to adjust to different levels of student expertise or familiarity and lack in-depth knowledge of the subject being taught. For this reason, geographers may prefer to use tutorial style software in a limited way, perhaps introducing new concepts or techniques in a formal classroom setting themselves, and then recommending use of appropriate software for remedial, reinforcement or practice work.

Another approach to using the computer as a tutor lies in IV (see above). This technology has the advantage of being able to store and deliver information of many kinds, thereby making multimedia training sessions possible in a desk-top computer environment. Yet, while there are considerable opportunities for using IV to teach place knowledge (particularly by using the technology as an 'intelligent database' to encourage active learning), the applications for doing so again have not appeared.

Looking to the future, it is possible that 'intelligent tutoring systems' may be provided with the ability to reason about objects, events and processes operating in space, and coaching software may help students to overcome individual learning difficulties (Sleeman and Brown, 1982; O'Shea and Self, 1983; Woolf and McDonald, 1984). Nevertheless, considerable research progress still has to be made before such systems become widely available for routine geography teaching, and care should be taken when considering the adoption of this style of computer support (Ridgway, 1988).

Seeking help: the computer as adviser

Increasing pressure on staff time, a theme that we have already touched on many times in this text, imposes the need to find ways of coping with the everyday inquiries made by students when encountering specific learning problems. Computer assistance is an idea that seems particularly attractive in this context and can be used in the following ways to solve at least some student learning problems.

- A fairly simple form of remedial help can be provided by 'drill-and-practice' programs, which can be used independently by students to identify and fill gaps in their knowledge.
- Bibliographic databases (such as GEOBASE) can help students when they are trying to locate information for an essay or course paper. Less obvious, perhaps, is the potential for using an expert system 'shell' to codify rules for selecting appropriate information sources. Indeed, expert systems could be used to advise students on a wide range of practical work, such as helping them to select appropriate data collection methods, satellite image classification procedures, laboratory experimental procedures or techniques for exploratory data analysis.
- A more exciting use of the computer lies in diagnosing the nature of a student's learning difficulties. In mathematics, for example, programs have been devised that can identify student mistakes and misconceptions when handling calculations (Brown and Burton, 1978). It might be possible for similar principles to be transferred across to geography, where they could help to diagnose student difficulties in learning, say, statistical methods.

Clearly, there is considerable scope for computers to act as advisers on geography courses, but there is virtually no software as yet to help them play this role. Even if this shortfall is made good, a more significant issue needs to be resolved: whether it is acceptable for interaction between student and teacher to be replaced by interaction between student and machine. Lack of space, however, does not allow this complex ethical question to be discussed here.

Data exploration: the computer as analyst

As we have seen in chapter 4, there is much to be gained by giving students the opportunity to analyse geographical data for themselves. Computers can support this type of work in several ways.

1 *Exploratory data analysis* Computer-based exploratory data analysis (or EDA) is well established in geographical research, occupying a central role in the hypothesis testing approach to the subject (e.g. Rivizzigno, 1980). A number of computer programs (such as MINITAB) are available for the interactive statistical analysis of numerical data (Anon, 1984) and database programs (e.g. dBASE) can be suitably adapted, especially with regard to data searching (Daines, 1984).

2 *Geographical data visualization* Mapping is of central importance to EDA and knowledge of how particular computer maps are created is valuable if students are to understand the biases, assumptions and shortcomings of the maps when exploring their data (Hughes, 1976, 1979). Davidson and Jones (1985) describe how inexpensive mapping programs can remove the drudgery from map construction and provide ideal tools with which students can learn the principles of both analytic mapping and map communication (see also Hershey and Whitehead, 1989). A number of computer programs are also available that create statistical graphics, and these can be used to convert numerical data into appropriate summary displays. Moreover, standard commercial data analysis programs (e.g. SAS, SPSS-PC, dBASE, Lotus 1-2-3) increasingly provide built-in or add-on facilities for creating such graphics and also for producing maps. Figure 7.2 illustrates the type of screen display typical of desk-top mapping software.

3 *Interpretation of remotely sensed data* The interactive manipulation of satellite scenes is an area of degree-level work which would be unthinkable without computer support. Fortunately, several relatively inexpensive image processing programs are available for use in higher education (Mather, 1989), and teaching data sets are becoming available on floppy disc for computer analysis.

4 *Geographical information handling* The geographical analysis of spatial data requires geographical information systems (GIS) as well as computer mapping software. This type of software is now available on desk-top computers and can be used for spatial analysis by undergraduate geographers (Fisher, 1989). Some GIS software (e.g. PC-MAP) provide grid-cell operations; other types (e.g. PC/ARC-INFO) operate on geographical data represented in vector form. Because of its wide applicability and power, GIS software stands to revolutionize the way in which geography is taught at undergraduate level.

Computer-based EDA implies ready access to appropriate computer-readable data, which, until recently, has been a major deficiency in the resources available for computer-based teaching. Fortunately, within the past few years, large packaged data sets have become available from a variety of sources. For example, national population census data for several countries are available commercially on CD-ROM, coastline and political boundary data for the entire world have

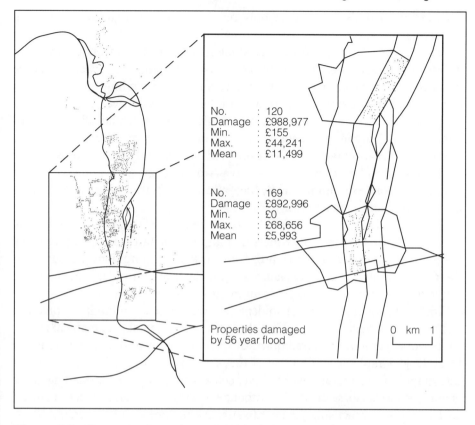

No. : 120
Damage : £988,977
Min. : £155
Max. : £44,241
Mean : £11,499

No. : 169
Damage : £892,996
Min. : £0
Max. : £68,656
Mean : £5,993

Properties damaged
by 56 year flood

0 km 1

Figure 7.2 Computer-based geographical data analysis

also been distributed on optical disc, and NASA has issued hundreds of *Voyager* images of the outer planets on CD-ROM which could be profitably used for the comparative study of planetary geomorphology and meteorology.

Yet even though the problems of finding suitable data are easing, there is another challenge in the adoption of computer-based data exploration. It is often claimed that computer-based data analysis is the prime example of the 'emancipatory' role of the computer in geography teaching, removing as it does the time-consuming tedium from much practical work, yet caution is needed. 'Emancipation' can be a two-edged sword, for four possible dangers lie in unthinking introduction of computer-based data exploration.

First, computer-based data analysis can exchange one form of slavery (e.g. performing calculations or drawing maps and diagrams by hand) for another (manipulating a keyboard, learning to use a computer operating system, becoming familiar with the command languages of a succession of computer packages). When this happens, data-centred work can end up exercising relatively low level technical skills and achieve only relatively limited higher level learning objectives.

Second, not all the activities that students are freed from undertaking are necessarily unwelcome. Pencil-and-paper 'data dredging', for example, can be productive in developing new hypotheses and understanding the procedures of empirical investigation. There are similar dangers in over computerizing fieldwork, for if computers are used to collect data automatically (e.g. with environmental probes and data loggers), then students may be shielded from valuable personal contact with the reality and consequently lose the opportunity to develop hypotheses about how the real world behaves. Hypotheses do not only come from examining 'data'; they also come from pondering the world during first-hand contact with it.

Third, in using the computer as a tool for routine EDA work, students may develop a 'black-box' mentality towards computer facilities, assuming that they have no need to understand how programs work or the conditions that surround their use. Teachers need to explain the algorithms and formulae hidden within software, and particularly their assumptions and limitations.

Finally, it is not unknown for student involvement in the minutiae of practical work to deflect them from thinking about the fundamental geographical issues. At its worst, computer-centred practical work can remove students even further from the geographical subject matter they are supposedly studying: examining cartographic data structures without ever constructing maps; understanding query languages and database principles without engaging in exploratory data analysis; spending hours practising keyboard skills at the expense of discussing ideas, concepts or theories. In some teaching situations, too much attention may be focused on technology and too little on information and skills.

Reading: the computer as study aid

The idea of using computing facilities to augment or replace standard print media sources has long been suggested, with the latest speculation focusing around 'dynamic books' that can provide readers with guided tours around their contents, precis a selected passage or summarize the line of argument running through the entire text (Kay and Goldberg, 1977; Goldberg, 1979). Such systems still lie in the future, but it is worth briefly reviewing the possibilities now available to whether the computer may be able to do better than the printed page.

Book substitutes   There have been many attempts to use computers as a substitute for books. In the 1960s and 1970s, some so-called instructional programs appeared which did little more than display pages of text on a printer terminal or VDU screen. A similar 'page-turning' role is played by broadcast teletext, which displays 'frames' of text or numerical information selected by the user. The problem with both these is that they do little more – and sometimes considerably less – than printed books. Displaying static text on screen is no substitute for high quality printed books illustrated in full colour. It is perhaps fortunate that few such facilities are available in geography.

A step up from this is the computerized textbook on floppy disk (such as the British Viewbook and Hyperbook systems), which is accompanied by software that provides text-searching facilities, colour coding of key words and phrases, cross-referencing of concepts and the ability to extract passages of text for direct inclusion in a word-processed essay. More recently, 'electronic textbooks' have been made possible by advances in desk-top publishing, optical disc technology, free text retrieval software and bit-mapped graphic displays (Yankelovitch et al., 1985). CD–ROM, in particular, is being hailed in some quarters as the 'new papyrus' (Lambert and Ropiequet, 1983). Linked with appropriate software, CD–ROM makes it possible for students to browse through the content of textual materials in any order, to find specific keywords and phrases instantly, to point to a word or phrase and find related words or illustrations, to insert 'bookmarks', to annotate specific passages of text and to leave an audit trail of those passages used during a particular consultation (Weyer and Borning, 1985). It is now no longer the lawyer, journalist or business person who has the privilege of referring to material in newly developed electronic archives; geography students can also consult electronic versions of journals and reference books, in addition to the more traditional paper and microform versions.

Computer-illustrated books The computer-illustrated (or computer-enhanced) textbook is made up of a textbook accompanied by ready-to-use interactive software (Harding, 1988). In some ways, the computer-illustrated book is a modern version of the educational slide pack with supporting notes. The difference is that the textbook and accompanying software are designed to be used together by the student, with the strengths of each medium (print and software) being put to best use to create a multimedia study package. Although there have been previous attempts to write geography texts with program listings included (e.g. Cole, 1975), the first computer-illustrated text in geography has yet to appear.

Demonstrators Computer-based demonstrator programs have made a significant impact recently, due largely to the rapid growth of GIS software. One of the first, and perhaps the most widely known, demonstrators is GIST, developed at Birkbeck College, London, to illustrate the principles of geographical information systems by means of text, graphics and animations (Raper and Green, 1989). At its worst, the demonstrator concept can easily degenerate into an

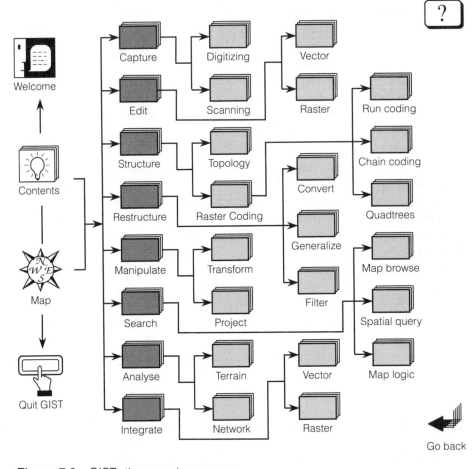

Figure 7.3   GIST: the opening screen
Source: Raper and Green (1989)

uninspired 'slide show' or electronic 'page-turner'. Yet at its best, the demonstrator can provide a truly complementary approach to the textbook, which can be used by students to preview a conventionally taught course or as a refresher to review course contents. Its key strength lies in the integration of several types of information, textual and graphic, and the opportunity for interaction with the student. Figure 7.3 illustrates GIST's content 'map'.

Conjectures and refutations: the computer as model builder

Simulations and games permit students to learn through 'guided discovery'. However, the specific geographical content of simulation and games software, and the educational aims built into them, frequently constrain students and make it difficult for them to explore concepts and theories freely. What is needed is software that takes students beyond revelatory experiences and enables them to exercise conjectural forms of thinking. One way to do so is for students to build computer models of real world systems, since the process of constructing a suitable computer program can often provide a deeper understanding of real-world systems than reading about them in a text or exploring ready-made simulation models. They can also gain first-hand experience of the difficulty of building models and of the limitations of current geographical theory (Moffatt, 1986).

Several resources are available to support this type of activity.

General purpose programming languages The use of 'high level' programming languages for building models has a long tradition in geography (Harbaugh and Bonham-Carter, 1970; Dawson and Unwin, 1985; Kirkby et al., 1987). Against this, learning to design even relatively simple models in languages such as BASIC, FORTRAN, PASCAL or C takes a considerable amount of time, and the provision of student training in computer programming can eat into time set aside for other study activities.

Logic programming languages Many claims have been made for the educational use of logic programming languages, such as PROLOG, on the grounds that logic is the common denominator of all academic disciplines (Ennals, 1981, 1982). These languages are widely available on personal computers and can be used to compile knowledge databases on geographical phenomena and to explore lines of reasoning based on that knowledge. Although few examples have been published, this type of software tool can also be used by geography students to build and test their own models of the world. However, the syntax of languages such as PROLOG is often difficult for students to grasp if they have already developed a procedural style of programming with the languages described above and especially if they are unused to couching their ideas in a rather formal logical form.

Special purpose simulation languages A number of programming languages (e.g. DYNAMO, GPSS and SIMSCRIPT) have been designed specifically for modelling discrete and continuous systems. They provide facilities for most of the awkward tasks involved in numerical modelling: generating standard distributions, performing integration, handling time steps and queues, performing statistical analysis and generating reports (Roberts, 1983). At a more advanced level, the visual interactive simulation (VIS) system enables the step-by-step output from a discrete model to be displayed graphically in real time and for users to interact dynamically with the model as it is running (Bell and O'Keefe, 1987). The object-oriented programming language SMALLTALK can also be used for geographical model building. This allows 'objects' to have visual representations attached to them, so that their movement in space can be displayed graphically on screen (Goldberg and Robson, 1983). By using tools such as these, students can keep their sights focused on the higher levels of model structure and behaviour and avoid wasting time on developing software that handles the underlying mechanisms.

General purpose spreadsheet software   The three previous resources involve students in writing computer programs. For those who are unhappy with this approach to model building, it might make greater sense to turn to other tools that can be used with less training. Spreadsheet programs such as Lotus 1-2-3, Supercalc, Multiplan, Excel or Wingz meet this requirement, for they can quickly be used to set up a population forecast, an ecological model (Silvert, 1984), or an impact model for a new shopping centre. Spreadsheet programs have a number of advantages for student use in that they are robust, easy to use, have powerful calculational facilities, can be programmed for special tasks and are widely available on most personal computers. In addition, many can generate various types of graphs and charts, so that the results of a student's model can be displayed graphically. Most can export information to other programs, so that output from a student's spreadsheet model can be passed to, say, a mapping program for graphic display of the model's outcomes. Most can also import data, so that population data from a census file or streamflow data from hydrological fieldwork, for example, could be brought in to calibrate and test a model.

Interactive simulation environments   This kind of program permits students to define, manipulate and modify models by using a graphical 'direct manipulation' interface. They do not require any conventional programming skills at all (Wedekind, 1982). An example of this innovative type of program is STELLA (Richmond, 1985), which allows users to create a wide range of social and environmental simulation models within the general framework of Systems Dynamics. With STELLA, students can use a mouse to select graphical symbols on screen that represent system components and assemble them into a working model simply by creating a logically coherent structure diagram. Using such programs, students can quickly build models of dynamic systems, examine model behaviour and easily modify not only the parameters of the model but also the structure of the model itself. Riley (1989) explores some of the educational implications of using this type of model-building tool in geography.

Expert system 'shells'   Expert systems, and the closely related logic programming languages, have enjoyed considerable exposure during the 1980s (O'Shea, 1982;

Ennals, 1986). They offer great potential for engaging students in conjectural modes of thinking. Expert systems enable 'knowledge databases' to be constructed on the basis of carefully phrased rules that specify the relationships between items of information. Expert systems can use this information to answer questions, make diagnoses and give advice, and they can explain their line of reasoning when drawing inferences. They can also acquire new knowledge, either by learning from their own performance or through 'knowledge-building' dialogues with experts. This type of system offers enormous potential in areas such as medicine, mineral prospecting, business or agriculture, where decisions have to be made in a risky or uncertain environment, and where inferences must be drawn on the basis of complex and often incomplete information.

At present, geographical expert systems are not readily available and, in any case, the educational challenge we are proposing here is for students to create their own expert systems, i.e. models of the world they are studying. To do this, they can use an expert system 'shell'. Expert system shells are programs that contain all the knowledge-building and inference mechanisms of a working expert system, but without the resident knowledge base; this is provided by the user. Shells can be used to encourage conjectural thinking by acting as a 'sounding board' for half-formed student ideas, or as a recipient of newly acquired knowledge. For example, students might be asked to describe some part of the world to a shell program, so that it could build up a knowledge base on the topic. In order to provide this knowledge, the students would carry out a thorough investigation and present this knowledge in a series of precise 'rules'. In other words, students would play the role of the 'knowledge engineer'. When the knowledge base is built, the students could then interrogate it, ask it to draw (and explain) inferences and generally test its robustness. This could help them to identify weaknesses in their own understanding of the geographical system being studied, and so lead to further refinement of the knowledge base.

Having said this, we must again counsel caution. Most of the expert system shells currently available for personal computers work best with only relatively small problems, can rarely produce geographical displays and usually can only handle problems that are amenable to a rule-based solution.

Problem solving and design: the computer as tool

Growing educational and vocational interest in problem-solving approaches creates an agenda in which computers could play a major role. For example, students could be presented with a computer simulation of an ecosystem that shows signs of malfunction or of being in a state of disequilibrium. Their task is to investigate the system in order to identify the cause of the problem, suggest (to the program) appropriate solutions to the problem and explain (again to the program) why a particular diagnosis and prescription were made. In this example, the student is required not simply to understand the model, and therefore how part of the world behaves. The challenge is to use this understanding to solve a particular problem. If students understand the system, then they will be more likely to come up with effective solutions to its problems.

Unfortunately, the intelligent models necessary to permit this kind of exercise have yet to appear in geography, although some have been developed on an experimental basis in other disciplines. In medicine, for example, the well-known MACPUFF model replicates the human respiratory system, which can be thrown into malfunction for students to correct. Similarly, in electrical and electronic engineering, the SOPHIE model of faulty circuits is used to teach students trouble-shooting abilities (Brown et al., 1975). Interactive video systems offer considerable scope for this kind of work, and the Ecodisc system described earlier can be used to manage a small habitat in order to achieve specific goals. An alternative approach is for students to use spatial optimization software to minimize patient travel times to hospital, or to locate shopping centres in the most appropriate locations.

Design activities have a similar role to problem solving exercises, and have the added advantage of encouraging students to think creatively (see Ehrmann, 1987). By undertaking design exercises, students are encouraged to synthesize existing knowledge, to exercise their imagination, to put theory into practice and to operate in the real world of practical decision making and problem-solving. Design-related activities encourage students both to use existing knowledge and to create new knowledge for themselves, and also to apply and devise strategies for solving design-related problems.

Many existing study activities in geography can be turned into design work relatively easily: asking students to design a nature trail on a field course rather than simply following one; challenging them to plan a by-pass for a local town rather than read the literature on existing plans; asking them to produce a detailed site plan of a new shopping centre in a greenfield location at the edge of a large town. Taking this last example, it might appear initially that students will be engaged more in a task about drafting skills or civil engineering than learning geography. However, as a learning device, this design exercise can provide a powerful introduction to several interrelated aspects of the real world: the scale and layout of typical out-of-town shopping centres (especially their large car parking space); the need to link retail developments to existing infrastructure; the three-dimensional problems of terrain modelling; the geotechnics of site preparation; the broader issue of site selection. This type of design exercise can be supported by such computer tools as a geographical information system to select an appropriate site within a study area, a civil engineering package to model the shopping centre in relation to terrain and transport infrastructure, and a CAD program to create a scaled plan of the centre in its chosen location.

Writing: the computer as editorial assistant

There are various ways in which computers can be used to assist the many writing activities that students routinely undertake as part of their courses of study.

Reading and information gathering Many college libraries have installed computerized catalogue search facilities for rapidly locating reading material on a particular topic (Shepherd, 1984). Occasionally, they also offer programs that provide on-demand guidance on how to consult certain types of printed material, which can be particularly useful both to students who are new to the college library and to final year students gaining access to dial-up bibliographic search services.

Such catalogue systems, however, are relatively limited. Most concentrate exclusively on book holdings and do not readily accept individual lecturer's own reading lists or bibliographies. Therefore it might be worthwhile supplementing the main library search facilities with desk-top computer software that can be placed in a geography department map library or study area. This can then be used to search for journal articles or other specialized reading material held within the department. In order to track down relevant references beyond the scope of the college's library, students might also be encouraged to use remote bibliographic databases, such as GEOBASE. Nevertheless, the cost of using dial-up search services might mean that this must be done sparingly, perhaps using the expert services of a subject librarian to construct the necessary computer search requests.

Organizing ideas During the early stages of tackling an assignment, some type of organizer is invaluable when trying to impose some order or structure on a mass of notes and half-formed ideas. Walton and Balestri (1987) suggest that creative writing and computer programming have much in common, and that the adoption of a 'top-down' design approach, commonly advocated for program design, is also to be recommended for the creation of written work. This approach seems to be particularly well supported by the 'outline' type of software (typified by Brainstorm, DAYFLO and Agenda), which enables writers to create a hierarchically structured set of ideas, starting with broad ideas or topic headings and then fleshing out each idea with a module of written text, or a further set of lower level headings. One advantage of students using this type of software is that they end up using the same tool throughout the writing process.

Writing up the assignment   This issue was discussed in chapter 4, but it is worth noting the value of using a text editor or word-processor when a written assignment is being prepared. One of the major benefits of the word-processor appears when the first draft is complete – it enables students to do something they are traditionally loathe to do when preparing written material, i.e. revise their initial drafts. Finally, when the presentation stage is reached, students can use spelling checkers to correct the prose, graphics packages to create appropriate graphs and diagrams, and even a desk-top publishing (DTP) package (such as Ventura or Page-Maker) to produce a polished final document. In the near future, students may also be able to turn to a 'writer's assistant' for support in clarifying their prose (Williams and Holt, 1989).

The use of new technology to support an established educational activity inevitably leads to a rethinking of that activity. Word-processing illustrates this dictum perfectly. The benefits of using word-processing are now well known, particularly in raising the standard of students' written presentation. Moreover, it is often students with no previous typing skills, and only basic writing skills, who appear to gain most. For this reason, it is often useful to introduce 'computer illiterate' students to a reasonably simple word-rocessing program as a starting point in their use of the technology.

Adoption of this technology poses a challenge for existing educational practice in relation to student writing. Part of that challenge is the practical problem of servicing the needs of students using the word processing equipment, with the necessity for teachers or their surrogates to be on hand to solve the many technical problems that occur, from lost files to printers that fail to print. More significant are the implications for the involvement of teachers in students' efforts at written composition (see chapter 4).

Making presentations: the computer as communicator

The importance of preparing and giving presentations has been stressed at many stages in this text. Computers offer various possibilities in this respect, for example, asking students to prepare and deliver a short presentation, perhaps no more than 10–15 minutes in length, which is to be illustrated using appropriate computer software. The topics can be allocated by the teacher or chosen by the students. The presentation is made to a group of a dozen or so students, and leads into a general discussion. Such presentations can be used to good effect in seminars, particularly in the second or third year of a course when students have acquired the necessary computer skills.

Given that this form of presentation is to be made to a small group, the requisite equipment need only be a standard personal computer aided by software to explore data or to produce graphic displays or slides, animated sequences and simulations. More imaginative approaches are possible using IV or hypermedia systems. For example, Walker (1988) describes an innovative video disc system which is designed specifically for this type of use in geography. The system contains a wealth of visual material (such as maps, photographs, video clips), and the accompanying software allows students to select material, add captions, set up text pages and define appropriate presentation sequences.

A variation on this exercise allows students to create a presentation that is to be delivered by the computer, rather than orally by themselves. There are two ways in which this can be done. The first is for the student to create the electronic equivalent of a poster, but using the characteristics of the computer (such as animation, sound and interaction) which distinguish it from the normal paper medium of the poster. Electronic poster displays can take several forms: a 'rolling demo', to be viewed in an entrance hall or common room, or to be available on open days; and a 'hands-on demo', perhaps to accompany some other activity or display in a geography department. (The latter has much in common with computer exhibits in museums.)

The second way sets students the task of creating demonstrators, as described earlier. An excellent tool for doing this is hypertext software, as represented by the innovative HyperCard program for the Apple Macintosh computer. This software enables units of information to be defined as 'cards', each of which can contain any type of information – text, graphics, animated sequences or sound. Sets of cards can be linked in any arrangement that suits a particular use. Each set of cards is called a 'stack', and represents a highly flexible multimedia database through which others can browse. Dyer (1988) provides an example of how such software has been used by art and design students to create visual presentations as an alternative to the traditional written essay or folio. It takes very little imagination to see how such a tool could be used by students in the equally visually rich subject of geography.

7.4 ISSUES IN COMPUTER ASSISTED LEARNING

During the above discussions, we perforce omitted a number of concepts and theories of current concern in the design of computer assisted learning materials, including conversation theory (Boyd and Pask, 1989; Pask and Boyd, 1989) and constructivism (McAleese, 1990). We were also unable to do full justice to many significant issues that arise in implementing and using the computer in teaching and learning, for instance, the potential application of computers to distance or open learning (see Whiting, 1988). Nor have we attempted to list the 'best' type of computer assistance for particular aspects of geography, be it climatology, urban geography or historical geography. Similarly, we have not explored the potential of computer-assisted learning in different types of course structure, nor have we said much about the particular needs of 'problem' groups of students, such as the disabled, the home-bound or the socially or economically disadvantaged.

Thus, before drawing this chapter to a close, we have selected four topics for further discussion that we believe have considerable significance for the future teaching and learning applications of computers.

Claims and reality

Many high-sounding claims have been made about the computer's role in teaching and learning (e.g. Chambers and Sprecher, 1980; Stonier and Conlin, 1985). Among the most common are that it motivates students to learn, individualizes the process of teaching and learning, encourages students to participate actively in learning; makes it possible to introduce students to previously obscure or difficult subject matter and to realistic examples, and enriches a course by providing added variety and encouraging active student involvement in learning. Of course, similar claims have also been made for educational television, programmed learning and other audiovisual media. So, is the computer really a different kind of technology?

Some see the combination of graphics and animation as uniquely appealing for teaching geography (Batty et al., 1985), others see the interactiveness of the computer as its paramount virtue (Stark, 1986), while yet others see the computer's versatility as its chief asset – Weizenbaum (1976), for example, calls the computer a 'universal machine' because it can be instructed to behave in an infinite number of ways. Stonier and Conlin (1985: 29) provide a typical statement of this view:

> Computers are the most important pedagogic invention since grandmothers. No technology to aid learning, from prayer wheels and medieval stained glass windows to overhead projectors and videotapes, approaches the potential effectiveness of computers – not even books.

Is this merely hyperbole, or do the educational benefits actually live up to these claims?

Although there is encouraging evidence from other educational application areas the information gathered so far in geography fails to point unambiguously to areas of the curriculum for which computer-assisted teaching outperforms other methods (Shepherd, 1983; Forer, 1984). There are many problems in using computers for teaching geography, such as the high resource cost, the need to train teachers and students in their use, lack of easy access to computer facilities, the preparation of supporting teaching materials and the time needed to locate, acquire, test and implement software. Moreover, despite more than a decade's sporadic exploration and experiment, there are few established guidelines as to what makes a good item of educational software and few principles to suggest which computer approaches are best suited to putting across particular geographical skills and concepts (although see Ellinger and Frankland (1976) and Laurillard (1978, 1988) for relevant discussion).

Evidence about the cost effectiveness of using computers in teaching is somewhat clearer. Information gathered during the National Development Programme for Computer-Assisted Learning in the United Kingdom during the 1970s led to the conclusion that computer based teaching is nearly always *more* expensive, in unit cost terms, than conventional teaching (Fielden and Pearson, 1978). The realization of this same truth on the other side of the Atlantic led one American expert to comment: 'Don't try to justify CAI [computer assisted instruction] as a labour-saving technology – at least not yet. It must first be justifiable as an improvement in the quality of education' (Nievergelt, 1980: 12). Little that has happened during the 1980s has changed the fact that using computers in teaching is almost always likely to represent additional cost. However, we hope that in this chapter we have convinced you that the added cost can be justified by the improvements that the computer can bring to the quality of teaching and learning.

Ménage à trois *in the classroom*

Relationships between teachers and students are of paramount importance in education and are almost always disturbed by the introduction of new educational technologies. The computer is no exception to this general rule. Its use can reinforce established relationships, modify others and help to forge entirely new ones. Some would see this as a valid reason for rejecting the new technology out of hand. The sophists of ancient Greece, it should be recalled, objected to the use of written records for instruction on the grounds that this would eliminate the intimate interaction between tutor and student.

We would encourage you to consider an alternative, and more positive, view. By using your knowledge of the ways in which computer use can affect the relationships between teacher and students, it may be possible to broaden and enrich existing relationships, and also to foster the development of a wider range of relationships in your courses. The computer need not be treated as an intruder; it can become a valuable partner in the process of teaching and learning.

Figure 7.4 summarizes the relationships that can occur in the computer-supported classroom. The specific relationship that requires most comment here is that between an individual student and a personal computer, since it is the

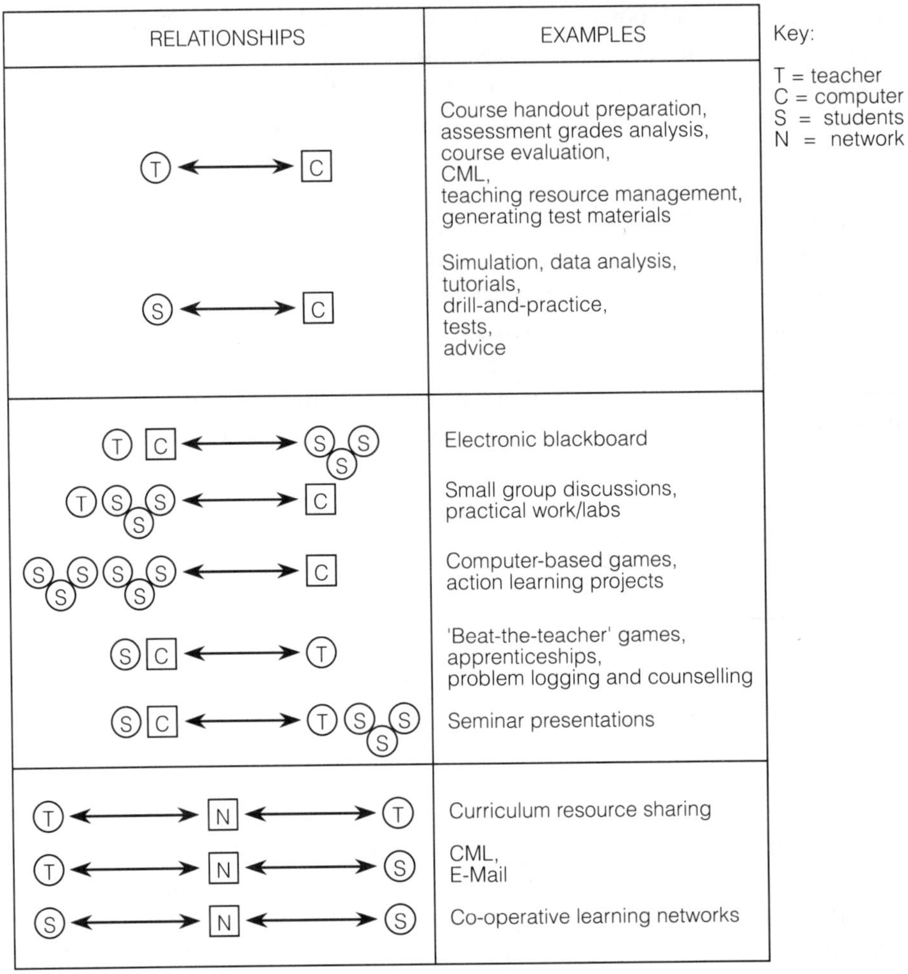

Figure 7.4   The computer and classroom relationships

C, computer; N, network; S, students; T, teacher.

one that typically comes to mind when one considers the educational use of computers. It also stands at the heart of the notion of 'individualized learning', which has been much vaunted since the introduction of programmed learning and teaching machines in the 1950s and 1960s, and which is now closer to reality given the rapid spread in ownership of personal computers.

The growing proportion of student work in contemporary geography now being carried out on a computer, on lines already suggested in this chapter, leads to important issues. For example, student immersion in private computer work can lead to a significantly reduced interaction with staff and other students and, in its extreme form, leads to students who become computer addicts (see also Shotton, 1989). In response, it is probably a mistake to let the goal of 'individualized learning' totally dominate student use of computers. Experience shows that many students will learn more effectively when they work in small groups than when they are assigned solitary computer work. Several types of small group work can be organized around computer exercises, as already noted above. These can involve co-operative work (e.g. teams of students attempting to solve an ecological problem with a simulation model) or competitive activities (e.g. teams competing to produce the best optimal location pattern in a given period of time). A new form of software called 'groupware' that assists collaborative work by providing a shared computer environment is also beginning to appear (Grieff, 1988); this may become important in the near future as a means of encouraging and supporting student co-operation in learning tasks. These could supplement the co-operative learning environments reported by Levin (1987).

Who controls the computer?

A major issue in the relationship between teachers, students and computers concerns the locus of control in learning activities – i.e. who controls how students learn. We have already considered this issue in previous chapters, strongly advocating various forms of student-centred learning. It is generally assumed that by providing students with computer-related work, one is automatically handing over to them the control of their own learning, but this is not necessarily the case. Many forms of computer assisted learning carry the potential, and often unrecognized, danger of replacing teacher control of the learning process by computer control. Tutorial style software, for example, can hold a tight rein on student learning, and many simulation and data analysis programs are designed in such a way that students are unable to exercise more than a minor degree of initiative and freedom in exploring geographical knowledge.

An awareness of the straitjacketing effect of certain kinds of computer work led Papert (1980) to ask: 'Should the computer program the student?'. Put another way, should teachers and programmers dictate, through computer software, the style of learning to be adopted by their students, or should they be looking to implement computer resources that encourage students to devise their own learning strategies?

Many of the computer resources that we have described in this chapter tackle this problem, because they provide environments in which students can work out their own routes to geographical understanding. The existence of flexible, student-centred computer resources, however, is not in itself enough to transfer control of the learning process into student hands. Even when computer resources are designed for flexible use, their deployment is still determined largely by teachers. For example, data analysis, mapping, interactive video, expert systems, simulation and modelling software can all be used in a teacher-centred way as presentation aids in expository teaching. Unless care is exercised, this type of computer use can be an even more significant barrier to student learning than poor software (Shepherd et al., 1980). As we have tried to show in this chapter, there is much to be gained from handing over computer resources for students to use in their own ways as tools for independent learning (Laurillard, 1987).

At the same time, it is equally possible to undermine meaningful learning by giving students infinitely flexible and unconstrained tools. A clear example of this danger is provided by the use of hypertext software to create 'knowledge browsers', in which students are free to roam around an electronic archive with no restrictions on where and how they proceed. Hammond (1989) and Hammond and Allinson (1989) have convincingly shown that this can be counter-productive, and that students require 'navigational aids' (such as indexes, 'maps', tours and quizzes) to help them make sense of the vast quantities of information now available to them. Elsom-Cook (1989) suggests that what is needed is a tutoring system that can move back and forth along a scale from totally constrained guidance at one end to total freedom at the other, as the occasion and student requirements dictate.

Preparing for computer use

The final issue we want to consider concerns how you should set about preparing yourself – and your students – to make effective use of computers on your geography courses.

The first act of preparation is to take a realistic look at the time and effort that effective use of the computer will demand from you. These include identifying, evaluating, acquiring and implementing new hardware and software, producing data sets and documentation, familiarizing yourself with new items of equipment and software, setting up and clearing away computer equipment, and evaluating and revising your teaching in the light of experiments with computer-assisted teaching. This will all have implications for your teaching and administrative load which needs to be thought through carefully. Possible responses lie in reorganizing the timetable, reducing course content and changing teaching and classroom organization.

If you are contemplating teaching with computers for the first time, our advice would be to use the machine to support just one – or at most two – classes or topics in the first year of adoption, and set aside time to prepare yourself for these ice-breaking sessions. A particularly effective way of introducing the computer into a course for the first time is to use a simulation or game program in an informal small group tutorial. This way, if things go wrong, discussion can take over, and the small size of the group will limit any psychological 'damage' that might result. The computer pool is a deep one and so we would advise you to jump in at the shallow end. You do not have to take the computer on board in a big way for it to make an impact on your teaching; the 5 minute computer demonstration within a 1-hour lecture can be just as effective as 2-hour, computer-centred practicals or laboratory classes.

If you are a more seasoned user of computers in geography teaching, then other concerns will be uppermost in your mind. A perennial issue is whether you need to develop your own software in order to support your courses. We would advise that you think long and hard before going down this road, even if funding for software development is readily available (Groop et al., 1985). The creation of good quality educational software is extremely time consuming: it can take many days – even weeks – to devise a single working program for students to use. Your time might therefore be better spent in modifying an existing program, or in adapting a general purpose program (such as a spreadsheet or database) for geographical use, perhaps by acquiring appropriate data or by writing a 'macro' to make it simpler for your students to use.

Yet, if you enjoy the excitement that comes from developing software of your own, using a conventional programming language, concentrate on developing programs that you, rather than your students, will use in the classroom. Since the user interface takes the most time and effort to get right, writing programs for your own use in class can avoid the expense of producing foolproof software for others to use. The time saved in this way will probably triple your productivity. Alternatively, use a modern programming environment, such as Hypercard, to create materials that can be used by students for active learning (Riley, 1990). Whichever set of tools you decide to use, consider joining a courseware development team, either in your own department or with others in your institution, or even from other institutions. The benefits of sharing software production work can be considerable. Finally, make good use of the wealth of experience provided in books written on educational software design (e.g. Burkhardt et al., 1980; Beech, 1983; Heaford, 1983; Steinberg, 1984; Alessi and Trollip, 1985; Alexander and Blanchard, 1985; Watson, 1987).

Turning now to the preparations necessary for your students, it is important to recognize that they too will need time to be trained and to practise appropriate skills if they are to make the most of computer-based geographical work. Many geography degree courses package computer skills teaching into separate 'practical' course units (on the lines discussed in chapter 4). In a vocational degree course, or a joint honours degree which links geography and computing, this separation can work well. Yet we would again suggest that the general separation of substantive geography from technique can often be counter-productive. In some geography degree courses, training in computer skills is consigned to a final year 'advanced option' course unit, either because the degree programme as a whole is too inflexible to admit this element in earlier years or because there is a feeling that computer skills are for the select few. Our view is that computer skills are best introduced from the first week of the first year of a geography degree course, within the framework of a substantive course unit, and that this training is reinforced and extended in other courses and in subsequent years. Useful discussions of how such training sequences can be designed are provided by Reeve (1985) and Rees (1987).

In introducing these skills, however, care must be taken over possible gender problems. We know from research in other disciplines (e.g. Rosser, 1989) that women students may not perform as well as male students in computer-based courses. For example, an Australian study of women in computer science courses concludes that:

> stereotyped gender roles circumscribe the aspirations of students and potential students . . . . Computing is commonly seen and presented as heavily technology-centred and reliant upon mathematics. These subjects and orientations have been traditionally and formally less accessible to women. (Kay et al., 1989: 525)

While there is no comparable research that can indicate whether or not female geography students are seriously disadvantaged compared with their male colleagues, it remains an issue which requires attention if all students are to fulfil their potential.

One final question involves the desirability or otherwise of teaching computer programming skills. Opinion differs as whether or not these are essential for students to make effective use of computers for geographical study. Reeve (1985) and others argue that the existence of so much 'packaged' or 'canned' software makes the lengthy acquisition of programming skills an unnecessary – and time-consuming – diversion. The opposite view is taken by Dawson and Unwin (1985), who suggest that only through the development of their own computer programs will students gain a proper appreciation of the algorithms and data structures used in geographical software.

A middle road is advocated by those who have used general purpose software such as spreadsheets (Lee and Soper, 1987) and statistical programs (Griffith, 1987) with students to explore the operation of geostatistical concepts. Most such programs permit students to enter formulae or high level control instructions, but hide them from the other trappings of programming languages. Students therefore gain access to 'programmable' software without the need to learn a complete programming language. As we saw earlier, the 'visual programming' languages available for computer modelling similarly help students focus on geographical matters, and enable them to avoid the rather messy and frustrating aspects of writing programs in conventional, text-oriented programming languages.

7.5 CONCLUSION

In this chapter, we have argued that computers can be used to support all aspects of geographical study. They can also make a major contribution to students' acquisition of general study skills (reading, writing, information gathering and analysis, numeracy, graphicacy, oral skills and teamwork skills), and can help to foster certain attitudes and values, both in relation to geographical issues and to learning itself.

Computers themselves can be fitted into teaching in various ways: there is no universal rule as to how they should be used in geography teaching. At one extreme, they can be used in an entirely teacher-centred manner, perhaps providing 'electronic blackboard' facilities in class. At the other extreme, they can be used by students working independently or in groups. Neither of these is necessarily the 'best' possible approach in all circumstances. Each use will demand different types of preparation, different computer facilities and contrasting styles of classroom management. What is important is to recognize the educational strengths and weaknesses of computing.

These are many and varied. Computers can add variety to existing teaching methods, help teachers tackle difficult areas of the curriculum and open up new learning horizons for students. They can be used to help students understand geographical theory as well as to give them practical experience of solving real-world problems. They can be used individually by students to develop autonomy in learning or by groups of students to foster co-operative approaches to learning. Finally, they can be employed at several different stages in teaching a particular topic: as a previewer or advance organizer, or as a means to extend new ideas.

While making these points, however, it is important to guard against the unfounded claims and inflated expectations which are rife in the world of information technology. It is highly unlikely that information technology represents a golden age of educational excellence to which we have just been handed the key. A degree of realism is needed when using the computer. Wheeling a computer into classroom will not necessarily improve student performance dramatically, nor will it significantly reduce learning time. Moreover, adopting computer assistance takes time and money, and is not guaranteed to work perfectly at the first attempt. Nevertheless, unexpected benefits do occur, such as added motivation for previously dull or boring topics, increased autonomy in your students' learning, and general enthusiasm for the process of learning by your students.

The invigorating effect of computers can also rub off on the teachers, who can be provoked by the novelty of the new teaching medium to reassess areas of their teaching. If the teacher's enthusiasm for teaching is stimulated by introducing computers, this may well have a beneficial impact on students' education, although in an indirect way. At the same time, enthusiasm for computers should not lead to abandonment of existing teaching methods. Computer use should be integrated with other teaching methods; some of the most effective uses of the technology occur when the computer acts in a supporting or complementary role to other teaching approaches. Most important of all is to learn from experience when *not* to use the computer.

Our suggestions for further action follow in this cautious vein.

1 Examine a course that you currently teach, and identify *one* element or topic that you think could benefit from using the computer. Determine the type of support you require (e.g. data exploration software, simulation program, computer-based game) and acquire the appropriate software for implementation.

2 Track down software for potential use in your teaching. This is a difficult task – there is a great deal of software around and no comprehensive catalogue is currently available. One list of (largely British) educational software appropriate for geography teaching has been drawn up by the Geographical Association's Educational Computing Working Group (Fox, 1984); other lists have been produced by software distribution groups such as MECC in the USA and CHEST in the United Kingdom, and a number of computer manufacturers and publishers produce their own less comprehensive lists. Several geographical journals publish reviews of selected software (notably *Teaching Geography*, the *Journal of Geography*, and the *Professional Geographer*), but they rarely carry lists of all currently available material. Hobbyist magazines (such as *BYTE*) can also provide useful pointers to what is currently available for a particular application. It is also worth identifying whether a national database of educational software has been set up in your country (e.g. Unwin and Maguire, 1989).

3 Identify resources for the purchase of equipment and other resources necessary for computer-based learning in the next academic year. There are a number of not so obvious sources of funds: it may sometimes be possible to purchase hardware or software on the back of a research project; the cost of purchasing hardware for teaching may be shared with those spending money on 'administrative' machines; it may be possible to enter into a joint purchasing agreement with another department and share the time made available on the equipment to both sets of students; lobby your institution's computer centre

to allocate some of its central computer funds for the purchase of departmental workstations.

4 Try and acquire the support of a computer-skilled technician for the computer activities in your department. If you have no such staff, try to enlist the services of a faculty or college computer technician, perhaps on a rota basis with other departments. Alternatively, ask the more computer literate of your students to lend a hand in setting up computers for class use, or in tracking down hardware and software faults when they occur.

5 The next time you travel to another institution for a geographical meeting or conference, take the opportunity to see how they use computers in their courses. Ask yourself how these ideas could be adapted for use on your own courses.

6 Ready access to computer facilities is one of the major factors influencing the level of use of computers in education. If such access is poor in your department or college, press for improvements.

7 If you find, as do many teachers in higher education, that the time and effort needed to develop computer-based work is at the expense of other academic activities, then consider converting your experiments into an action research project and publish the results. By doing this, you will add to your personal list of rewardable work, you will benefit your students and teachers elsewhere will benefit from your experience.

KEY READING

An early guide to the subject of this chapter is *Computer Assisted Learning in Geography* (Shepherd et al., 1980), which reviews many of the educational issues involved in using computers in teaching and contains a comprehensive bibliography up to 1980. The microcomputer context is more clearly provided in *Exploring Geography with Microcomputers* (Watson, 1984), and also in *Microcomputers in Geography Teaching* (Midgeley, 1985). At a more practical level, Kent (1987) provides a number of useful class exercises built around selected items of software.

An effective way of keeping up with developments in computer-based learning, both in geography and elsewhere, is to browse through journals which report recent developments. From the enormous selection now available, we would recommend two journals from North America, the *Journal of Geography* and the *Professional Geographer*, which carry occasional articles on teaching with computers in geography at school and college level respectively. In Britain, the equivalent outlets are *Teaching Geography* and the *Journal of Geography in Higher Education,* and antipodean practice is regularly reported in the *New Zealand Journal of Geography.* Educational applications are equally well reported in other subject journals: *Physics Teacher, Biology Teacher, International Journal of Mathematical Education in Science and Technology* and *Science Education.*

8

Assessing Students

'We haven't gone into the question of assessment yet,' said Bob Busby. 'We wanted to get the basic structure of courses agreed first.'

'But assessment is vital,' said Robyn. 'It determines the students' whole approach to their studies. Isn't this an opportunity to get rid of final examinations altogether, and go over to some form of continuous assessment?'

'Faculty Board would never accept that,' said Bob Busby.

'Quite right too,' said Rupert Sutcliffe. 'Continuous assessment should be confined to infant schools.'

David Lodge, *Nice Work*

8.1 INTRODUCTION

So far we have left aside any detailed consideration of assessment – defined here as the process which measures educational attainment on the basis of student performance and which provides feedback to the student about the strengths and weaknesses of that performance. Yet assessment has been an important underlying theme in many of the previous chapters, in terms of both *formal* testing procedures used to learn about the student's knowledge, skills or attitudes and *informal* assessment (for example, the encouraging nod or appreciative comment that the teacher might make to students after a tutorial presentation).

It is now time to examine assessment in its own right. In doing so, we shall frame our discussion around six broad questions which will be considered sequentially in this chapter.

1 What is the current state of assessment practices in geographical higher education and how might they be improved?
2 What functions does assessment serve?
3 What should be assessed?

4 When should assessment be made?
5 What are the relative merits of different types of assessment?
6 How should one approach marking and grading?

8.2 EXISTING PRACTICE

There is considerable choice available when selecting assessment options, yet experience shows that only a fraction of these are normally employed in geographical higher education. In Britain, for example, the key method of undergraduate assessment remains 'Finals' – end of course examinations requiring essay type written answers. As table 8.1 indicates, the overwhelming majority of the 89 courses listed by British geography departments slavishly relied on such examinations as the principal form of student assessment, with a written dissertation or extended essay providing the only other significant element. In the USA, geography courses again follow the predominant national patterns of assessment (Milton, 1978: 106). Although comparable data on a departmental basis are more difficult to compile, the norm is that of periodic testing using both essay type and multiple choice questions.

Table 8.1 The percentage of total student assessment accounted for by traditional written 'final' examinations

Percentage	No. of courses
0–25	1
26–50	7
51–70	37
71–100	36
Not specified	5
	86
Specifying different system	3
Total	89

The courses listed here contain a minimum of a half-degree study of geography. It should also be noted that the word 'department' is used as a general term, although in practice terminology and organizational structures vary considerably.
Source: Compiled from *A Matter of Degree, 1986-7* (Geo Books, 1986).

In neither case is there much sign of change. In our experience, individual teachers tend to view assessment, normally referred to simply as 'marking', as one of the least interesting aspects of their jobs. It may be a necessary chore but it is scarcely a subject for research and innovation. Their attitudes are reinforced by institutional factors. The need for comparability between different departments of the same college and between the college and other academic institutions tends to make divergence from the traditional pattern difficult to achieve. This is reinforced by use of external examiners in those countries that follow the British model (Lawton, 1986). Under this system, the student's performance is assessed by a committee composed of internal examiners, who teach the course, and external examiners, who have no direct contact with its teaching. The latter are appointed by the college or validating body and often possess considerable personal authority, but normally use their powers purely to moderate marks, to ensure that courses are carried out in accordance with regulations and to maintain standards. They have no specific remit to act as a catalyst for change in assessment patterns, even if they were personally inclined to do so.

Continuance of the status quo also stems from the social dynamics of the classroom. The duty to assess confers the power to influence a student's future. A student leaving college is 'marked for life'; those who have failed their degrees approach employment 'in much the same way as a stigmatised convict leaving prison' (King, 1979: 104). That power can be used, consciously or otherwise, to boost the teacher's authority. Students can be teased with obscure clues about forthcoming examination questions or obliquely reminded of the dire consequences that can follow failure to do as they are told. When doing so, teachers subtly remind their students where power resides.

There is little sign that this use of assessment to boost authority will be lightly abandoned; indeed, it is actively enhanced by a set of practices that can only be described as 'mystification'. Students seldom have much idea of how things are assessed and are rarely encouraged to express their views on the matter. Teachers, for their part, are rarely keen to tell them; indeed, the very act of inquiring as to why specific marks were given or particular conclusions were reached is apt to be treated as tantamount to an attack on the competence or impartiality of the teacher concerned. This cloak of mystery is normally justified by arguing that confidentiality is necessary when allotting marks and grades, and countered with assurances that the system has endless safeguards to guarantee complete fairness. Yet besides making it difficult for students to challenge the outcome of assessment, this defensiveness also serves to prevent students from playing any active or constructive part in the assessment process.

In answer to these points, we would argue that there are few inherent advantages and many potential obstacles to quality teaching in existing assessment practices. It is important to recognize that traditional forms of assessment reward certain types of knowledge and skills, but undervalue others. Moreover, traditional assessment creates a particular framework within which learning takes place; change that framework and you can completely change the way in which students learn.

We would argue that assessment should not be taken for granted, but that we examine all the various options that can be adopted. We would begin our analysis by stating six principles that we believe are essential for improved assessment practice.

1 A variety of assessment methods are possible and, in many instances, will be desirable.

2 Assessment can, and arguably should, be made be an integral part of course planning. While more comments are made about the relationship between assessment and curriculum design in chapter 10, it is important to stress that decisions made about the timing, content and administration of assessment can have important implications for curriculum design and vice versa. It is very helpful to think through assessment procedures at the outset, identifying educational objectives clearly, rather than wait until a course is running before concocting a scheme of assessment.

3 Good assessment should be valid, reliable and effective, by which we mean that it should measure what it is supposed to measure, that it does so consistently year by year and that it makes the best use of both the students' and the teacher's time.

4 If something is valued, then it should be assessed and good performance rewarded. 'Sound curriculum planning demands that the system of assessment should match the course's stated objectives' (Jenkins and Pepper, 1988: 72). If those objectives include encouragement of communication, presentation or collaborative skills, then ways need to be found to assess and reward good performance in these areas.

5 Frankness about the objectives of assessment and active involvement of the learner in the assessment process work to the benefit of teacher and student alike. Mystification, as described above, only serves to waste valuable opportunities to improve the quality of the relationship between teacher and learner.

6 Associated with point 5, a balance needs to be sought between assessment as a pressure that motivates students to work and assessment as a threat which spoils the learning experience.

8.3 THE FUNCTIONS OF ASSESSMENT

Geographers undertake assessment for a variety of reasons. These include the following:

- indicating the comparative merits and failings of individual geography students on a consistent basis to the outside world;

- communicating information to students about standards and about what parts of the syllabus are important relative to those that are not;
- motivating students by setting them targets for quality of work and deadlines for completion of that work (although, again, there is often a thin line between encouragement and coercion);
- providing feedback to students about their strengths and weaknesses;
- providing feedback to teachers about the success or otherwise of their teaching.

Collectively, these point to the role that assessment procedures play as an important medium of communication between teacher and learner. As with other forms of communication, however, it must be realized that the process sometimes contains hidden dimensions, which may be as important as those which are openly recognized.

A good example comes from the fact that classroom contacts often communicate clues that allow students to go beyond the information officially given by the syllabus and discern whether or not there is a 'hidden curriculum' (Snyder, 1971) – an agenda of implicit demands made of students which may run counter to the explicit aims of the official curriculum. The hidden curriculum is not that which is expressly taught, either as syllabus or attainment targets, but consists of the 'hidden' clues or messages that students pick up during a course. When analysed, these allow the student to make informed guesses about the teacher's intentions and about which parts of the syllabus can be selectively ignored.

Assessment is very important in this process since it effectively shapes the hidden curriculum that students identify. Thus, one study of college examinations analyses it as a 'game' with stated and implicit rules, which one student identified in the following way: 'I tend to spend a lot of time on things I am really interested in, so I won't get a good degree. If I swotted away diligently, I would get a better degree but I wouldn't be so intellectually broadened' (Miller and Parlett, 1974: 56). If this is how a significant number of students identify the assessment 'rules', then there is a hidden curriculum with a clear set of aims – which are presumably very different from the stated or implicit aims of the staff.

Naturally, students vary in their ability to interpret clues (Miller and Parlett, 1974) and in the degree to which they are motivated towards directing their studies purely to elements likely to be assessed (extrinsic motivation) as opposed to being intrinsically motivated by interest in what is being learned (Elton, 1988). Nevertheless, unless care is exercised, the discovery of a 'hidden curriculum' is likely to create uncertainty and push students towards spending far longer contemplating assessment than the teacher ever intended. This can impose a price on the teacher–student relationship, at worst resulting in assessment deadlines dominating the way in which students approach learning.

8.4 WHAT SHOULD BE ASSESSED?

Geography courses vary in the balance of skills, attitudes and knowledge that they seek to develop in students. A course in map design might emphasize acquisition of skills in graphic interpretation and presentation; an advanced option in the philosophy of geography may highlight abilities to conceptualize; a basic geographical course in computing might emphasize technical skills in programming; a project-based fieldwork course might stress the importance of developing collaborative skills when working in groups. The cardinal rule, as mentioned earlier, is that, if something is valued, then it should be assessed and good performance rewarded, but this leaves the problem of finding a coherent framework for accommodating assessment of qualitatively different skills – whether physical, social or cognitive.

An answer proposed by some geographers (e.g. Helburn, 1968; Monk, 1971; King, 1976; Humphrys, 1978; Halloway, 1984) has been to formalize sets of educational objectives. The main stimulus of this approach has come from Bloom's threefold classification of so-called 'instructional objectives' into 'cognitive', 'affective' and 'psychomotor' (e.g. Bloom, 1956). 'Cognitive' objectives are those connected with thinking and intellectual processes, 'affective' with attitudes and feelings, and 'psychomotor' with skills. Each of these three 'domains' are themselves arranged hierarchically. Thus the 'cognitive domain', for example, begins with the intake of factual information and continues through memorization, comprehension, application, analysis and synthesis, to the 'higher' levels of evaluation and judgment.

Working on this basis, we show in table 8.2 the appropriate assessment strategy for the various objectives, along with the relevant role of the teacher and the student (based on King, 1976). As can be seen, the 'cognitive continuum' begins with memorizing and recall of factual information for which the appropriate form of assessment is an objective test, in which the learner takes a largely passive role relative to the authoritative teacher. A series of progressively higher levels are then identified up to that where the learner is required to show independent and creative thought, such as in work connected with research projects.

Three other objectives are also identified. The testing of attitudes and orientations is considered a difficult area for assessment, since the teacher must decide whether a 'successful outcome' would be achievement of certain specified values and attitudes by the students or the development of *any* soundly based and academically defensible values, whether or not these were the same as those held by the teacher. If the former, testing is relatively straightforward since it essentially measures congruence, whereas the latter involves much greater complexity, with the teacher having to devise clearly defined standards to ensure

Table 8.2 Objectives and assessment strategies

Objective	Appropriate assessment
Memorizing factual knowledge	Objective tests
Understanding key concepts and principles	Short essays
Ability to think critically	Medium or long essays
Independence, creativity and problem-solving	Project or dissertation
Orientations and attitudes	Individual and group projects, dissertations, long essays
Practical skills	Continuously assessed practical work
Oral skills	Vivas, assessed classroom presentations, assessed games and simulations

Source: After King, 1976: 228

fairness in assessment. King (1976: 231) concluded that assessment in this area should be used chiefly for 'formative evaluation of individuals' progress (i.e. for diagnostic feedback to the student) rather than as a summative final grade'. Relatively different forms of testing are required for the other two objectives. Practical (motor) skills, a collective title for a group of skills that are highly regarded by geographers (e.g. map drawing, surveying and computer literacy), demand tests of technical proficiency best achieved by continuously assessed practical work. In contrast, oral skills, that traditionally undervalued aspect of higher education, can be examined formally through a viva, but are better assessed through observation of classroom presentations, assessed games and simulations and other forms of group learning.

In responding to these ideas, it is important not to treat application of Bloom's taxonomy to problems of assessment in geography uncritically. Certainly, it has its attractions, providing a catholic view of the possible content of assessment and identifying the complexities involved. However, the problem of the underlying philosophy, which sounds suspiciously like conditioning, needs to be considered. Tightly specifying objectives after the manner of Bloom and measurement of congruence involve a particular philosophy of education that emphasizes 'correct' answers and conformity. It is possible to espouse a quite different philosophy – one that emphasizes the acquisition of the known much less than elaboration and modification of that which is known in order to reach new conclusions. Eisner (1975) suggested that courses of this type would have 'expressive objectives' – objectives where the outcome is not specified but emerges through the 'educational encounters' (situations in which students progressively work on tasks or problems) of the teaching process. Assessing expressive objectives is difficult, yet is necessary to give proper credit to those capable of heterodox, yet creative, thought – a characteristic that is traditionally prized in higher education. To do justice to students, we would argue that assessment in geographical higher education requires a balance between instructional and expressive objectives – a mixture which tests and rewards, on the one hand, positive acquisition of knowledge and skills, and, on the other hand, innovatory thought and intellectual development (Humphrys, 1978).

8.5 THE TIMING OF ASSESSMENT

The question of timing is more than just a technical issue, since it affects the uses to which assessment is put. Traditionally the student's acquisition of knowledge and skills is examined at the end of a course. The alternative is to test the student's abilities at intervals, regular or otherwise, during the course, with the marks being carried forward to the final grade. Each option has its advantages and drawbacks.

The prime advantages claimed for end of course assessment are that it tests the final outcome – the skills and knowledge that the student takes from a course – and hints at long-term retention. This timing can have a beneficial effect on the atmosphere in the classroom, since it frees both students and teachers from having to worry about assessment for much of the year. This in turn reduces the tensions that students experience during their everyday work and lessens the conflict between the teacher's teaching and examining roles (Rowntree, 1981a).

On the debit side, end of course assessment, by its very nature, gives no credit for work done earlier by students and reduces the possibilities of feedback to students about their performance. The assumption that it tests overall knowledge and skills may be countered by the fact that in practice only a very small proportion of a student's total abilities are tested. Students may do very little work for much of the course and concentrate their efforts into a short period just prior to the final tests. Related to this, not all students are able to build up to a peak of performance at just the right time, and some succumb to stress and stress-related illness.

A similar balance sheet of benefits and disadvantages can also be drawn up for the alternative system, normally referred to as *continuous* assessment, but also known as 'periodic' or 'intermittent' assessment. This gives reward for work done during the course as well as at the end. If used properly, it allows feedback to learners about their performance, both through the marks given and through the teacher's comments and suggestions, and does so at a time when the student can actually capitalize on the advice being given. Continuous assessment, as noted earlier, can be used to motivate attendance or study. Perhaps its greatest advantage is that it gives full rein to self-assessment. This practice, in which the students are invited to assess the worth of their own work according to specified criteria (see next section), allows students to acquire self-critical awareness of their strengths and weaknesses. If carried out on a regular basis, with full provision for dialogue, self-assessment provides students with the opportunity to participate in and gain from the assessment process.

Continuous assessment, however, also has its drawbacks. Overuse of continuous assessment can have a deadening effect on the student's enthusiasm for study. Constant pressures to meet assignment deadlines can lead to a pattern of learning dominated by specific projects, depriving students of the opportunity to stand back and glimpse the wider canvass through independent reading. Widespread use of continuous assessment on different courses can cause student workloads to be bunched at particular times, unless steps are taken to distribute deadlines throughout the academic term. At its worst, this can lead to a complete weariness with a course, no matter how interesting the subject material. Finally, as Goodall (1977) noted with regard to the geography programme at Reading University, introduction of continuous assessment has to be handled sensitively so as to allay the doubts of staff and students about its intrinsic worth.

These, then, are the relative merits and demerits of the two systems, but we stress that they are not mutually exclusive. It is possible to arrange a course so that a given percentage of the final mark is built up cumulatively from assignments completed during the course, with the remainder resting on a final examination. It is also possible to devise a system whereby a selection of material completed for deadlines during the course – such as completed statistical or map practicals – is resubmitted at the end of the course. In this way, students can present work for final assessment with some confidence about the likely outcome, perhaps with the opportunity to act on the teacher's comments and improve on substandard items (see later comments on essays).

Whichever option is adopted, it is essential that the timing of assessment accords with the flow of learning in the course. Before exploring that notion further, however, we must now examine the wide range of assessment techniques actually available.

8.6 METHODS OF ASSESSMENT

Methods of assessment are tackled here under the five headings of objective tests, examinations, coursework essays, projects and oral presentations. Most can be used as the sole method for assessing a particular course, but it is often beneficial to combine several methods to ensure variety and to balance out the advantages and drawbacks to the individual student of different types of assessment.

Objective tests

Objective tests provide a useful point at which to start this survey, since they are one of the most widely used form of assessment procedures – widespread in North America and often employed elsewhere in self-instructional courses and in distance learning materials (e.g. as used by the Open University in Britain). Used equally appropriately in either continuous or end of course assessment, they are called 'objective' because they yield answers or responses that may be marked objectively as being correct or incorrect, leaving no room for idiosyncratic, personal or subjective judgment (Gibbs et al., 1986: 27).

Figure 8.1 shows examples of six different types of objective test that have at least some value for higher education. The first three (short answer, completion, true–false) can be very useful for classroom feedback – indicating to the teacher and the students themselves how well they understood material – but have limited value for formal assessment. The remaining three types, however, can be used for formal purposes, particularly since the mark that can be obtained by guesswork would normally be fairly low (around 20–25 per cent). The fourth option, called 'matching' provides an accurate test of factual knowledge, especially if the number of options in List Y is greater than the number in List A (to avoid the student deriving the fifth answer purely by a process of elimination). The remaining two types are variants of multiple choice questions, in which students are presented with a proposition and asked to select the most appropriate answer from a list of options. Sometimes, the response to be selected will be the *correct* answer. The example shown (from Stratton, undated: 16), has the problem that, as with all multiple choice questions, there is the possibility that students can guess the correct answer C, but to be sure of getting the correct answer they would need to know the correct formula for deriving the standard or z score:

$$z = \frac{\text{raw score} - \text{mean score}}{\text{SD}}$$

The response sought may also be the *best* rather than the 'correct' answer. Indeed, the sign of a good question is one where the options offered are closely related to the designated answer, thereby requiring the student to make subtle distinctions. In the example shown (based on Open University, 1977: 58), the most appropriate definition is 1, since 'teleological' is defined as the doctrine of final causes – the view that developments are due to the purpose or design

Short Answer

Q. Name three of the 'first generation' New Towns that were designated in Great Britain between 1946 and 1950:

1 ....
2 ....
3 ....

Completion

Q. Central place theory was originally formulated by .... in Germany in the 1930s.

True–false

Q. Are the following statements true or false?

1 'Modern crofting was founded by the 1886 Crofters' Holdings Act.'	TRUE/FALSE
2 'The run-rig system was introduced by Jethro Tull.'	TRUE/FALSE
3 'Kelping was widely practised in the interior parts of Highland Scotland.'	TRUE/FALSE

Matching

Q. Match each of the writers in List Y with one of the books in List X by filling in the boxes below the lists. Do not use any of the boxes in List Y more than once.

List X

1 *Towards a New Architecture*
2 *Yesterday: A Peaceful Path to Real Reform*
3 *When Democracy Builds*
4 *The Culture of Cities*
5 *The English House*

List Y

A Hermann Muthesius
B Lewis Mumford
C Patrick Geddes
D Frank Lloyd Wright
E Ebenezer Howard
F Walter Gropius
G Le Corbusier

List X	1	2	3	4	5
List Y					

Multiple Choice: Correct Answer

In a test with a mean of 100 and a standard deviation of 12, a raw score of 124 is equal to a standard score of
A +24
B –2
C +2
D 84 per cent

Multiple Choice: Best Answer

What does the term 'teleological' mean when applied to the early attempts of geographers to study the relationship between people and environment?

1 the view that the earth has been designed for human purposes by a 'supreme being';
2 the argument that human beings are an integral part of their environment;
3 that poeple are at the mercy of their physical environment;
4 that people should always seek to change their environment to suit their own ends;
5 that the environment never changes.

Figure 8.1   Examples of some common forms of objective tests

that is served by them. Definitions 4 and 5 are inappropriate responses to this question; the two remaining answers are both relevant, but only part of the answer. Response 2 is a condition of 1; response 3, by a strict deterministic interpretation, is a consequence.

Provided that they are properly constructed (e.g. see Clift and Imrie, 1981: 84–6; Brown and Atkins, 1985), objective tests are a useful way of assessing students' abilities to 'apply techniques or operations, define terms and categorise instances, describe the consequences of theories . . . and explain events in theoretical terms' (Stratton, undated: 7–8). Such tests are quick to administer and, given the necessary computing facilities, their multiple choice basis allows automated marking and summation of results, potentially saving valuable staff time. They can be incorporated into the framework of a lecture session, for example, as part of a session of the type suggested in chapter 2 (see figure 2.1). When used in continuous assessment, they can supply an indication of the students' individual and collective progress and provide immediate indications of areas in which remedial action is necessary. Finally, they can reward students who have a good grasp of material, but cannot express themselves fluently in written essays.

They also have drawbacks. Objective tests may be amenable to 'objective' marking, but are difficult to construct so that the results are valid and reliable. Moreover, since multiple choice questions are usually expensive to devise, they are far less suited to smaller teaching groups than to large groups for which economies of scale can be produced. Their greatest drawback, however, arises from the fact that, while suitable for testing knowledge of facts and routine procedures, they are poorly suited to testing the higher cognitive skills. They cannot assess a candidate's abilities in marshalling evidence, making judgments and presenting an argument – which may well frustrate the student and make the test seem trivial. Any course that lays stress upon such abilities will clearly need to look to other methods for all, or part, of student assessment.

Essay-based examinations

The term 'examination' is often treated as synonymous with an essay-based test held at the end of a course, but in reality examinations can be administered in many ways, each with its own appropriateness for different circumstances. Examinations can be used as the sole form of assessment or in combination with other methods. They can just as easily be held during a course – a timing that can greatly enhance assessment feedback to students. They can be essay, laboratory or computer based, or have a combination of essay and multiple choice questions. Furthermore, when using essays, the essays themselves can be short or long answer. Short answer essays are commonly used in conjunction with multiple choice questions. They may be simply an addition to the question, as in the rubric: 'outline, in no more than 50 words, the reasons for your choice'. They may be questions in their own right, as in the case of supplying brief definitions:

> Define the meaning of the following terms (in each case, using no more than 100 words):
>
> (a) economic rent
> (b) zone in transition
> (c) isotropic surface
> (d) counter-urbanization
> (e) agglomeration economies

By contrast, long answer essays may require much greater marshalling of evidence and evaluative discussion. They have various formats according to the different ways in which examinations are administered. Table 8.3 shows the broad spectrum available, ranging from 'unseen' or 'closed book' examinations, in which students are presented with questions that they have not previously encountered and asked to supply answers within a 2 or 3 hour period, through various gradations ('open book', 'take home') to 'seen' or 'pre-published' examinations, in which the papers have been given to the student some time beforehand.

Unseen examinations   Looked at in more detail, the typical format of an 'unseen' examination is for students to answer three or four questions in 2–3 hours in

Table 8.3 Major types of essay style examinations

Type	Characteristics
1 'Unseen' examinations	Formal tests normally requiring immediate medium to long essay answers to questions that cannot be predicted with certainty
2 'Open book'	As above, but with candidates allowed to take relevant books and/or notes into the examination hall
3 'Take home'	Akin to unseen examinations in that the student is presented with a paper in which the questions can be unexpected, but also akin to 'seen' examinations as the answers are compiled in the candidate's own time and submitted after a given period, perhaps 2–3 days
4 'Seen' examinations	Formal tests requiring medium to long essay answers, but with the questions being given to the candidate some time beforehand.

essay style. The question paper normally permits the student a choice from six to nine possible questions, sometimes constrained by being divided internally into different sections from which it is possible to answer only one or two questions. The unseen examination is intended to test the students' ability to produce their own work, to recall information, to quote and marshall relevant material from memory and to organize themselves to complete the task in a limited time period. Such tests are intended to test what was earlier described as the 'higher' intellectual abilities of conceptualization, analysis, synthesis and evaluation – an emphasis revealed by the frequency with which words such as 'analyse', 'assess', 'explain' and 'evaluate' occur in the questions that are set.

The argument that such examinations do assess these qualities reliably is not without merit, but over-reliance on such tests faces certain uncomfortable truths. First, for many students, written final examinations primarily assess rote learning abilities rather than creativity and original thought. Second, the questions are often predictable, since examiners tend to focus consistently on a core of significant issues (Unwin, 1990). When this occurs, students can improve their performance dramatically by using past papers to make informed guesses about likely questions. Third, the unseen written examination is selective in the skills that it rewards, valuing fluent literary expression under pressure, but giving no reward for other skills which could legitimately be assessed. Lastly, there is the problem of criterion- and norm-referencing. It is logical for students to pass a course and achieve good marks if they fulfil certain predetermined criteria. This system of 'criterion-referenced' measurement is reliable if the criteria are well defined so that the standard of the assessment remains the same from year to year. However, this is hard to achieve with a written unseen examination because it is difficult to find a new selection of essay questions that will be the same standard as the year before. This can be solved by using 'norm-referencing', which assumes that students are the same standard from year to year and that therefore any variation is due to the paper or its marking (Ward, 1980: 105). Under norm-referencing, the same percentage of students is passed every year; this system may be suitable for large national examinations, but is potentially unjust for the small number of examinees handled each year by the average geography department.

'Seen' examinations   'Seen' examinations address some of these problems, although they themselves have drawbacks. Seen examinations are intended to take the element of guesswork and luck out of the examination process and can reduce the associated stresses. Great care must be taken, however, in selecting questions. If questions are angled too much to specific topics of the course, the student can feel that much of the course is irrelevant for assessment purposes and cease to pay it much attention. Equally, if the questions are too

straightforward, preparing answers to them can simply become a test of memory.

The style of questions that are employed depends on exactly *when* the questions are to be presented to students. If it is only a matter of 2–3 days before the examination, the questions set will probably differ little from those used in unseen examinations. If, however, they are published well in advance of the time for the examination, there is an opportunity for a quite different style of examination to be used. Students taking the advanced geography option on 'The Future City' at Oxford Polytechnic, for example, sit a seen examination which counts for 50 per cent of total assessment (the other 50 per cent is derived from coursework assignments). They receive the question paper at the start of the course, fully 10 weeks in advance of the examination, with a typical examination paper appearing as follows:

> 1 Discuss what is meant by the statement that British urban planning in the post-1945 period was marked by a 'clean-sweep approach'. To what extent can this approach be linked to the future city notions of the Garden City and the Modern Movements?
> 2 Assess, from a geographical standpoint, the view that developments in information, transport and energy technologies will bring about fundamental changes in both the form of the metropolitan city and the organisation of urban society during the next 50 years.

The fact that only two compulsory questions are set derives directly from the principle emphasized above, namely, that assessment creates a framework for learning. The aim of this examination is to focus students' attention on the development and unfolding over the weeks of the two basic themes of the course – the historic growth of consensus about urban imagery and the relationship between society, technology and the city – with a synoptic question being asked about each of them. The opening session of the course contains explicit discussion about the nature of the questions and the wider purpose of the assessment is to test their ability to weave answers together from the various elements of the course and the associated reading. Students are told that neither question can be answered by just attending occasional sessions and regurgitating material, and are also informed that early distribution of the examination paper is taken into account when marking their papers.

Such a procedure has its advantages. The examination effectively rewards work carried out during the course and eliminates the element of luck in the outcome of assessment. Experience also shows that students are able to cope adequately with questions that are markedly more complex than normally set in undergraduate examinations. Against these points, it must be said that students can become bored with prolonged preparation for particular topics. There is little conclusive evidence that students actually plan their preparation much differently from the last minute 'cramming' associated with unseen examinations; indeed, the authors' own experience is that the pressure on key sources in the library in the days immediately before the examination is little different from that before an unseen examination. There is also a tendency for the teacher using seen examinations to overestimate the literary standards that students are likely to achieve. In many cases, the actual quality of writing is not significantly different from that associated with other forms of examination.

Open book examinations   Open book examinations are taken in much the same way as unseen examinations except that the student is allowed to take appropriate published works of reference or notes with them into the examination room (how many books or what type of notes is usually subject to the teacher's specific instructions). This type of examination reduces the emphasis on memory, tests skills of information retrieval and reinforces the significance of reading course materials. At the same time, it can give a false sense of security, since students still need adequate preparation before being able to use reference works effectively. In addition, unless care is taken, the answers can suffer by the students' spending too much time consulting reading and not enough in writing the answer.

Take home examinations   The take home or 'open time' examination consists of an unseen paper which is given to students, with the completed paper to be returned after a set period of time (usually 3–7 days). The student may use books and notes and even consult with other people about the paper. This type of examination also reduces the need for rote learning, reduces examination stress and tests a student's skills at information retrieval. It has claims to being a logical extension of essay writing, with the opportunities for cheating (e.g. through plagiarism or impersonation) being no greater than for assessed course essays. Against this, it is important to recognize, first, that submitted answers can vary considerably in quality, making it difficult to achieve a reliable standard in marking, and, second, that severe problems can again occur in college libraries when students converge on specific books or periodicals at the same time.

Making a choice   These, then, are the major variants of essay style examination available. All can be held either at the end of or during a course and all can be used in combination with other forms of assessment. None of them represents a 'best buy' (Ward, 1980: 76) – a testing procedure that would provide valid, reliable and efficient assessment of a wide range of abilities and would do so in a manner that gave feedback to students and avoided placing them under undue stress. When measured by those criteria, all have advantages in some respects, while compromising on others. We would conclude simply by offering the following principles for making a choice:

- Unseen end of course examinations should not be adopted simply because that is the traditional pattern of assessment.
- If satisfied that an examination is the best way to proceed for all or part of total assessment, ensure that the skills and knowledge that you wish to test will be revealed by the type of examination that you select and by the type of questions that you ask.
- Recognize that such examinations favour those with skills at written communication; others may well require counselling about how to tackle examinations regardless of how many examinations they have taken in the past. If in doubt, give clear instructions in advance about the kind of questions students can expect and provide students with models of good practice and with marking schemes if possible (see also section 8.7). In particular, thought should be given to explaining and showing students what is meant by the *directive terms* (Halloway, 1984: 288) used in essays, such as the following:

  > *discuss* with reference to . . .
  > *describe* and *account for* . . .
  > critically *examine* . . .
  > *compare* and *contrast* . . .
  > *evaluate* the contribution of . . .

- Be careful when writing examination papers to produce questions that are clearly worded and can be answered comfortably within the allotted time.
- Preparation for examinations should not be a test of endurance. Even with unseen examinations, general guidance as how to approach revision should be given.

Coursework Essays

Much of what has already been said in the previous section about examination essays can also be applied to coursework essays; indeed, there are few generic differences between a coursework essay and an essay completed as part of a 'take home' examination. Coursework essays share the same rationale of being regarded as the major way to assess students' understanding of a subject and their ability to organize their thoughts into logical, critical and reflective argument. They are commonly employed as a means, sometimes the only means, of encouraging study during a course and of giving feedback to the student. For the teacher, however, writing good essay questions remains a matter requiring much care and thought if they are to supply valid, reliable and efficient assessment of the student's ability. Four rules for good practice are of assistance.

1 There are many possible ways of carrying out individual student assignments. Durbridge (1981), for example, took a standard type of essay question on the subject of urban land use: 'Land values are both the product and the determinant of the pattern of urban development. Discuss.' She then showed how it could be rendered into seventeen different types of assignment *besides* the standard essay. With this in mind, it is worth considering carefully whether the essay is the appropriate form of assignment.

2 If you decide that a standard written essay meets your objectives, we reiterate that such a task favours those with skills of written communication. All students should be offered counselling as to how to set about the task of producing written answers and given explicit instruction about what constitutes good practice. This can include advice about directive terms (see above) and the characteristics of good essays, as well as assistance with structuring an argument, referencing and ways to increase legibility.

3 Try to place yourself in the student's position when setting an essay. How does the workload fit into the general programme for the course? Will it enhance learning in the course or will it interfere with other desirable developments (e.g. general reading)? Is the language used clear and unambiguous?

4 Essays are a valuable channel for feedback to the learner. One way to achieve this, as well as to make the students more aware of the quality of their work and understand the criteria on which it has been judged, is to include a scheme for self-assessment. An example of an appropriate rubric by which students can carry out this task is shown below:

Consult the standards and criteria outlined in the Course Guide. Against those criteria, re-examine your essay and write below what you consider to be:

(a) its strengths;
(b) its weaknesses;
(c) specific changes that you would make if you had to complete the same essay again.

Finally, allocate a grade to your essay.
Please note that the essay will *not* be accepted for marking without your considered answers to this form.

This can be used at the head of an A4 sheet of paper, leaving ample space for students to fill in their self-assessment underneath. The teacher then adds a written reply and awards a mark or grade. Ideally, the next stage is an individual tutorial at which the essay is handed back with further informal comment about its quality. Any serious gap between the teacher's grade and the self-assessment grade should be explained. Finally, if the essay was poor but could be redeemed by rewriting, it may be possible for the student to re-submit a second draft, albeit for a scaled-down proportion of the original mark. This procedure allows the student to gain far more from the assessment process than merely receiving back an essay with a brief written comment. It also permits students to take greater responsibility for their own learning (see the discussion of writing in chapter 4; see also Boud, 1986).

Projects

The subject of projects was discussed in detail in chapter 4, with the distinction made between controlled exercises, experimental investigations and research projects. Each of these provides different learning opportunities and sets its own problems for assessment, although ideas for good practice in project assessment mirror much of what has already been said about essays.

Controlled exercises, whether in the laboratory or field, normally comprise part of a series, with each part requiring submission of a work sheet or field diary for assessment. The exercises are completed as instructed, and responses are then marked and handed back, usually with brief comments. This process of formal and informal assessment can be fairly haphazard, but attempts have been made to produce a more formal approach. Returning to consider the assessment structure for two examples cited at the beginning of chapter 6 (see also chapter 4), we find that the self-paced second year course in physical geography techniques at Southampton University requires students to hand in weekly exercises, which are assessed and annotated by staff within a week of completion (Clarke and Gregory, 1982). The student receives personal and class feedback to pinpoint errors and weaknesses. At the end of the course, the student re-submits three of the exercises, taking account of staff comments whenever necessary, for a numerical assessment which counts for 15 per cent of the final mark. In the spatial data analysis course at Canberra College of Advanced Education (Cho, 1982), the Keller Plan involves students working their way through twenty-five units, each with their own learning objectives. Mastery of one unit has to be shown before moving on to the next, and so work sheets have to be marked promptly to permit students to progress. The heavy workload that this can produce has led to thought about employing multiple choice testing and computer marking.

Experimental investigations allow students some degree of choice and initiative. Frameworks may be supplied to the students, but the student has the opportunity to move beyond mechanical performance of set tasks, although one may grow out of the other. The physical geography course at Southampton University seeks to go beyond the more constricted framework of the controlled experiment by use of a 2000 word essay, on a topic selected from a short list, which counts for 20 per cent of the total mark. This exercise is designed to test the skills learned in the course's various components (modules). In completing it, the student needs to think beyond the level and coverage of the course material, but is limited to closely related topics (Clarke and Gregory, 1982: 127). Similar demands are made of the learner in the case of the seminar and simulation presentations discussed in chapter 5, with the added problem of projects being carried out by groups rather than individuals. While it is argued that weaker students may be carried by the more able, it is difficult, although not impossible (e.g. see Gibbs et al., 1986: 103-8), to disentangle the individual contribution from the collective effort. Hence, although the issue remains controversial, we would simply repeat the point made in chapter 5: namely, that it is perfectly valid to require individuals to act as a group or syndicate who pool their expertise and act together in producing the end result. Provided that all students are made fully aware from the start that this will be the case, they can legitimately be assessed as a group.

Research projects allow for the greatest amount of student initiative and may call for display of the higher cognitive abilities of synthesis and evaluation. Research projects may be carried out on a group basis, as with Reading University's course on 'Social and Behavioural Geography' (Silk and Bowlby, 1981), or done on an individual basis. Either way, the criteria for assessment are likely to be influenced by those formulated over the years for dissertation studies (see chapters 4 and 5).

Dissertations have had a long history in geographical higher education, being widely regarded as the pinnacle of an individual's undergraduate studies and the prime source of autonomous learning (Boud, 1981: 16). Policy concerning dissertations varies markedly between institutions, particularly with regard to whether or not dissertations are compulsory and with respect to the amount of supervision given, but assessment procedures are well rehearsed. The general view is that undergraduate dissertations are judged as 'cut-down' versions of research at graduate level, with assessment criteria as shown below:

- signs of the ability to generate a problem of interest, at best displaying originality and creative thought;
- proven ability to search literature and construct a supporting review that locates the study in a geographical background;

- ability to construct and execute a project effectively;
- ability at data collection, collation, handling and interpretation;
- ability to reach valid conclusions;
- ability to present the study to acceptable standards of written and visual presentation.

The custom in some institutions is also to assess a dissertation by an oral examination or viva. Consideration of this form of assessment, however, may best be taken as part of a wider discussion about oral presentations.

Oral presentations

The viva is probably the most familiar of individual oral presentations used in geographical higher education. It consists of an interview between the examiner or examiners and a student, and is most commonly used either in connection with dissertation assessment or as a grading tool when making borderline pass-fail or grading decisions. Whichever is the case, the viva is primarily intended to allow students to show their understanding of a subject, their powers of reasoning and, in the case of a dissertation viva, the logic behind research decisions. In skilled hands, the viva is a highly flexible form of assessment, but in less skilled hands it can intimidate the candidate. Vivas are also very time consuming and expensive to organize although, if used only for a handful of students in special circumstances, this may well not be regarded as a major problem.

Rather more problems are encountered with other forms of oral presentation, whether organized on an individual or a group basis. Teachers may well find that colleagues and students oppose assessing public speaking, particularly when first introduced, and need to be clear in their own minds about the reasons for doing so. We believe that the key justification for assessing oral contributions is that the assessment emphasizes the value that is placed upon oral communication and the skills that need to be mastered. Moreover, although the criteria by which an oral presentation should be judged may be less frequently articulated than the criteria for judging, say, an essay, the act of assessing spoken presentations is no more subjective than that of assessing written contributions. It is important, however, to realize that 'one reason why students may be uneasy about assessment is that their self-esteem is on the line. Getting a poor mark for an essay may be a relatively private experience; getting a poor mark for a speech given to an audience of one's peers can be a very public humiliation' (Jenkins and Pepper, 1988: 73).

One cannot overstate the importance of spelling out the criteria by which an oral contribution is to be judged and how such assessment relates to the overall assessment for the course. Returning to the example of Oxford Polytechnic's course on 'Geography and the Contemporary World' (see chapter 5), it may be recalled that each group or syndicate completed three oral presentations, held at the project planning stage, during fieldwork and at final conference respectively. The assessment of oral presentations is based on a standard list of criteria, covering both the worth of the group's project and the effectiveness of the presentation. At each stage, the assessment is carried out by three different parties: the teachers, the group themselves (self-assessment) and a group of student assessors (peer assessment). The assessment forms are differently worded according to who is carrying out the assessment and the stage that the course has reached, but the underlying criteria remain the same.

Figure 8.2, which is the peer assessment form used at the completion of the second, or fieldwork, phase of the inquiry, provides an example. Each group is assessed by a panel of their peers, with an assessment form completed. This is then gathered together with the self-assessment sheet collectively compiled by the presenting group and the teacher's assessment form and handed in. The three sheets are compared, the comments are collated, an overall mark is allotted and the sheets are then handed back to the presenting group. It is possible for them to negotiate if they feel that the conclusions reached or the mark given is unfair, although in practice disputes have been rare.

The idea that motivates this strategy is that assessing oral contributions can only work if building on a close partnership between teacher and student. Perhaps

---

Peer Assessment Form

This is the second of the three oral presentations. The criteria used reflect the stage that has now been reached. You must judge whether, after the end of the field-work stage, the group concerned have satisfied the following requirements.

1. Have they described a project that is relevant to the aims of this course? (If in doubt, consult the Course Guide.)

2. Did the work that they have done match their stated aims?

3. Were you clear from the presentation about how they intend to carry out the analysis and write-up stages of their project?

4. Was their presentation coherent? (Did they present their arguments clearly? Did they show a mastery of their topic? Did they answer questions adequately?)

5. Did they use visual and other supporting materials effectively?

Your suggested mark: /100

Figure 8.2   A peer assessment sheet for an oral presentation

more than any other form of assessment, the criteria used to judge oral contributions must be stated, explained and justified to ensure student confidence. If the process is seen to be open and fair, students become as willing to accept assessment in this area as they are to accept comments on an essay.

8.7 MARKING

> . . . marking is one of those embarrassing areas isn't it . . . . There isn't a lot of discussion about it . . . (yet) the more you delve into it the more you find that the whole of marking is one great minefield . . . (Gibbs et al., 1987: 19)

These words, by a geography lecturer who had just completed his first year of teaching, certainly match our experience. Few new lecturers receive any training in how to mark assessed work. In most cases, it is implicitly assumed that if you have completed an undergraduate degree yourself, you will possess the professional knowledge to handle these tasks and to discern the appropriate standards. Yet marking is a highly subjective activity. In shared courses, those who have taught on the part of a course covered by a question might mark differently from those who did not. Different markers apply different criteria, pay attention to different things and will reach different conclusions with regard to the final mark. Some are concerned about spelling and grammar; others are not. There can even be variation when marking statistical or computing practicals, given that some will give credit for the right method even when the answer is wrong and others will not (Rowntree, 1981a: 210).

Space does not allow us to provide a comprehensive guide here to *marking* (giving a quantitative description of performance on a particular test), but the following six principles are of value in improving existing practice.

1 Marking objective tests needs to have some way of correcting for guesswork. A variety of approaches and appropriate formulae are available for this purpose (e.g. Gronland, 1977).

2 Accurate marking of essays depends on well-defined criteria. Throughout this chapter, we have stressed that good assessment practices require firm formulation of criteria. Yet as markers commonly vary in their judgements about those criteria, it is essential that marking schemes be supplied to fellow assessors to indicate what to look for and reward in the student's response. For example, if an essay demands an emphasis on skills, understanding and structure, it is possible to achieve a high level of reliability by using an analytical marking scheme (Halloway, 1984: 289), as shown in table 8.4.

Table 8.4   An analytical marking scheme

Knowledge or recall of factual information	5 marks
Understanding, interpretation and application of key concepts within the context of the question	5 marks
The use of evidence and examples to support claims and conclusions	5 marks
Graphic and written communication skills	5 marks
	20 marks

3 Students also benefit from knowing the criteria by which questions will be marked. A typical listing of marking criteria (after Rowntree, 1981a: 210) for a question on the theory and mechanics of soil erosion could well include those shown below:

- *exposition* (accuracy, clarity, literary presentation);
- *grasp of literature* (understanding, interrelating different schools of thought, ability to locate the subject within the body of physical geography literature, finding sources other than on the booklist);
- *originality* (examples cited, examples constructed, appreciation of new theoretical positions and their potential application);
- *scope of topic* (conceptual difficulty, technical difficulty, relevance of material covered).

4 Whatever the temptation to avoid double marking of examinations and essays because of its time-consuming nature, it can be a valuable procedure to even out some of the discrepancies between different markers.

5 Student self-assessment should be taken into account. If student self-assessment is to have any meaning other than an exercise in feedback, then ways need to be found to incorporate its results, through negotiation and compromise, into the assessment process.

6 Thought should also be given to profiling, a method of giving a general impression of a student's abilities across a wide range of courses that has already been applied to school level geography (Graves and Naish, 1986; White, 1988). The aim of profiling is not to summarize all the component elements that are assessed in a single mark, but to represent the component elements separately. Thus, for a course in geographical research methods, a profile form can indicate degree of mastery of particular techniques, as well as overall achievement of competence in, say, computer literacy or graphicacy.

8.8 CONCLUSION

Throughout this chapter we have stressed that the teacher has more to gain from an open, honest and responsive approach to assessment than from secrecy, threat and mystification. We do not believe that there is any ideal form or even any ideal blend of assessment procedures that meet all needs and all circumstances. However, we are confident in asserting that there are few decisions that a teacher makes that have a more profound impact on the flow and atmosphere of learning in the classroom than do the choices of assessment.

In choosing an assessment procedure to meet your needs, we would suggest that you re-examine the assessment procedures that you currently use. Do they meet the objectives of your course? Do they assist or impede the flow of learning in the course? Do they assist or impede the type of teacher–student relationship that you wish to have? What do they tell students about your real priorities for their work? If you find that your assessment practices are unsatisfactory in any of these respects, then you should think about changing them. When thinking about change, we would recommend the following:

- You think of assessment as not just a measuring device but also as a means of directing and enhancing student learning and as vital channel for feedback to the student. Whatever type and timing of assessment you adopt, always give feedback to the student as promptly as possible.
- You do all possible to balance the notion of assessment as a positive source of motivation against that of assessment as a source of threat that impairs the learning experience.
- You clarify the objectives of assessment both before and after assessment is carried out, preferably allowing students to participate in the assessment process.
- You consider the wide range of different types of assessment techniques that are available. As stated at the opening of this chapter, individual departments or institutions tend to follow broad national patterns of student assessment, yet a wide range of other options are also possible. Choosing a mixture of these may well offer fairer assessment to students who might fare better at some types of assessment than others.

KEY READING

Material specifically relating to assessment in geography in higher education is limited. Several texts directed at school level, however, are well worth consulting, including Marsden (1976), Halloway (1984), Orrell and Weigand (1984) and Fitzgerald (1988). By contrast, when considering higher education generally, there is a rich and diverse literature, with current patterns of debate about assessment being reflected in journals such as *Assessment and Evaluation in Higher Education* and *Research in Higher Education*. Excellent practical guidance is given in *53 Interesting Ways to Assess your Students* (Gibbs et al., 1986). Some other sources that may be recommended are King (1981a), Harris and Bell (1986), Brown and Atkins (1988), Eble (1988), and Murphy and Torrance (1988). For specific studies of assessment in geography in higher education, King (1976c) provides suggestions on matching assessment methods to educational objectives and Unwin (1990) gives guidance on setting essay questions that require critical thinking.

9

Course Evaluation and Improvement

Study to show thyself approved.
II *Timothy*, 2:15

9.1 INTRODUCTION

We now turn from student assessment to course evaluation. In its most literal sense, evaluation is judgement of something's worth. Measurement, of course, is part of the process of carrying out an evaluation, but there are two other essential ingredients besides this. First, evaluation involves making value judgements about what constitutes 'good' or 'bad' in our courses and teaching. Second, evaluation itself has little purpose unless it is to be followed by adequate review of the findings and appropriate action where necessary.

In this chapter, we show how evaluation methods can be used for a variety of related purposes: to diagnose course problems, to identify the reasons for the success of particular courses and teaching methods, to guide course innovations and to demonstrate course effectiveness. Our aim is to explore some of the more useful evaluation methods currently available, provide practical guidance on how to implement them, report on how they have been applied in geography courses and draw out broader implications wherever appropriate. In doing so, we positively endorse the value of evaluation exercises in promoting opportunities for effective student feedback and, in turn, the health of teaching, advocating a culture which sees evaluation as beneficial rather than threatening.

The methods that we discuss in this chapter will be grouped according to the objects that can be evaluated, such as courses, teaching methods and materials, and teachers. There are many other ways of thinking about what can be evaluated. For example, the pioneering Association of American Geographers study on college evaluation (Hastings et al., 1970) identifies the primary objects of evaluation as the context, content, process and outcomes of instruction.

Table 9.1   The objects, methods and personnel of evaluation

What	Who			
	Students	Teachers	Peers	Outsiders
Lesson	D	OIJ	O	O
Module	QD	JG	I	I
Course	QD	G	I	I
Teaching method		OJT	OT	OT
Teaching material		OJT	OT	OT
Teacher	Q	J	OI	OI
Student	J	G	D	
Department	DQI	DJ		DO

J, journal; Q, questionnaire; O, observation; I, interview; D, discussion; G, grades analysis; T, testing.

Inevitably, there is a degree of overlap between the categories that we have chosen; course evaluations, for example, usually include judgements on both teaching methods and teachers. Nevertheless, we hope that our framework matches the common experience of our readers. Within each section, we describe methods that are available for evaluating a particular 'object', and we shall identify the people who are best qualified to carry out the evaluations. The relationship between the objects, methods and personnel of evaluation is summarized in table 9.1.

9.2 EVALUATING COURSES

Student questionnaires

> It's no good a teacher claiming that his or her teaching is successful if the students don't corroborate the claim. (Walford, 1979: 54)

Examining students' feelings about courses provides a useful starting point for our exploration of evaluation methods. Fox and Wilkinson (1977: 67), for instance, claim that students' feelings about a course are important, since, if they dislike it 'they are unlikely to be as well-motivated as when they are generally receptive to the ideas and approach of the course'. In some countries, direct student feedback constitutes a major component of higher education course evaluation (Flood Page, 1974): indeed, in the USA, it is frequently the only form of evaluation used (Cranton and Smith, 1986).

One way of acquiring course feedback from students is to ask them to fill in a loosely structured form of the type illustrated in figure 9.1. By this means,

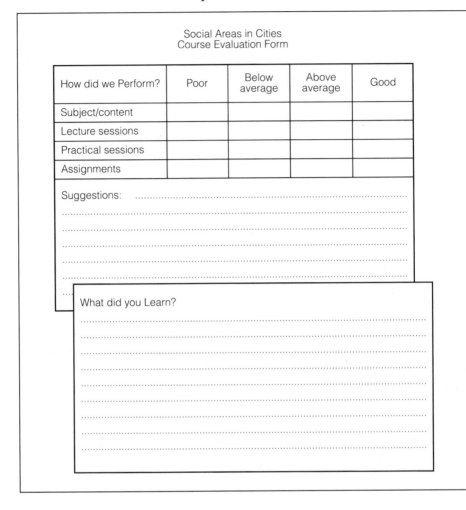

Figure 9.1   An informal student evaluation feedback form

students can be asked to comment both on the delivery of a course (i.e. the teaching performance and the course content) and on what they feel they gained from it. This type of form is useful for picking up unforeseen issues and problems. Because of its simplicity and brevity, it can be used to good effect at convenient points in a course, such as at the end of a 4-week sequence of lectures on a particular topic or after a 6-week block of practical classes. Used in this way, areas of weakness in a course can be pinpointed and rectified while the course is still being taught.

At the end of a course, a more detailed and structured questionnaire can be issued which addresses all aspects of the course, including content and structure, teacher performance and attitude, student learning gains and problems. Many such questionnaires can be purchased from educational suppliers, especially in North America, or can be designed by teachers themselves or by the college's educational methods unit (if there is one). Custom-designed questionnaires will ideally build on the results of earlier student feedback through less formal means, with Doyle (1975) providing a guide to some of the key technical issues (especially reliability, validity, generalizability and utility) that are involved in the design of effective student ratings. Some colleges store material for a comprehensive questionnaire on a word-processor, allowing tailored versions to be run off to meet the particular needs of individual courses.

However the questionnaire is produced, students are typically presented with a series of questions to which they are asked to provide a numerical rating, usually in the form of a standard 5-point scale. Where student attitudes are being elicited, it is common for questions to be phrased as statements, to which students are asked to record the extent of their agreement or disagreement (e.g. 'the teacher is enthusiastic about his or her subject' or 'the course helped me to think through contemporary issues more clearly'). Such questionnaires are commonly divided into sections dealing with particular aspects of a course, and figure 9.2 illustrates a typical example (see also Hastings et al., (1970) for examples of questionnaires designed for geography courses and Gibbs and Haigh (1983a,b) for a discussion of the principles behind their design). It is also useful to include in such questionnaires broader summary questions such as 'overall, how would you rate this course?' or 'would you recommend this course to next year's students?'

Among the advantages of using structured student questionnaires are that they are easy to administer and computerize, producing clearly tabulated results. There is the danger, however, that students are reduced to merely ticking boxes. Some commercially produced student evaluation forms, for example, restrict students to making soft pencil marks in small oval shapes ready for optical input to a computer. It is essential that this type of exercise be given a human face, that it provides students with an opportunity to reveal their own particular concerns and that it is alert to the many unpredictable consequences of teaching and learning. For this latter reason, the questionnaire should always include 'open' questions in each section, and perhaps a 'free comment' section at the end. This will be of particular value to those implementing innovative courses. The benefits of such feedback are illustrated in Jackson's (1989) account of his teaching of racism in an urban geography course.

The vast majority of course questionnaires are of the checklist variety. They attempt to assess the level of student contentment or dissatisfaction and help to identify unexpected or potential trouble spots, but they rarely probe deeply into student attitudes or examine their approaches to study. One major exception to this rule, however, is provided by the 'Approaches to Studying' and

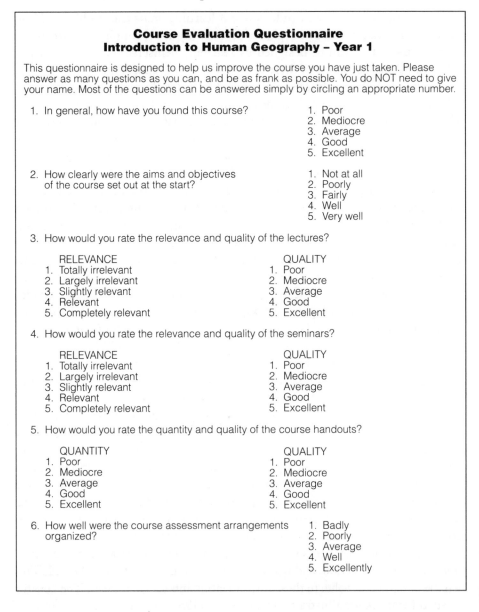

Course Evaluation Questionnaire
Introduction to Human Geography – Year 1

This questionnaire is designed to help us improve the course you have just taken. Please answer as many questions as you can, and be as frank as possible. You do NOT need to give your name. Most of the questions can be answered simply by circling an appropriate number.

1. In general, how have you found this course?

   1. Poor
   2. Mediocre
   3. Average
   4. Good
   5. Excellent

2. How clearly were the aims and objectives of the course set out at the start?

   1. Not at all
   2. Poorly
   3. Fairly
   4. Well
   5. Very well

3. How would you rate the relevance and quality of the lectures?

   RELEVANCE
   1. Totally irrelevant
   2. Largely irrelevant
   3. Slightly relevant
   4. Relevant
   5. Completely relevant

   QUALITY
   1. Poor
   2. Mediocre
   3. Average
   4. Good
   5. Excellent

4. How would you rate the relevance and quality of the seminars?

   RELEVANCE
   1. Totally irrelevant
   2. Largely irrelevant
   3. Slightly relevant
   4. Relevant
   5. Completely relevant

   QUALITY
   1. Poor
   2. Mediocre
   3. Average
   4. Good
   5. Excellent

5. How would you rate the quantity and quality of the course handouts?

   QUANTITY
   1. Poor
   2. Mediocre
   3. Average
   4. Good
   5. Excellent

   QUALITY
   1. Poor
   2. Mediocre
   3. Average
   4. Good
   5. Excellent

6. How well were the course assessment arrangements organized?

   1. Badly
   2. Poorly
   3. Average
   4. Well
   5. Excellently

Figure 9.2 A formal student evaluation questionnaire

'Perceptions of Course' questionnaires developed at the University of Lancaster (Entwistle and Ramsden, 1981). These course evaluation questionnaires, which have become standard instruments for course evaluation in several countries, are concerned with students' approaches to learning. They attempt to distinguish

7. Identify how YOU feel in relation to the following statements about this course:

	Strongly agree				Strongly disagree
The course was interesting	1	2	3	4	5
The course was intellectually stimulating	1	2	3	4	5
The course was up to date	1	2	3	4	5
The teacher was well prepared	1	2	3	4	5
The teacher was well informed	1	2	3	4	5
The teacher was enthusiastic	1	2	3	4	5
The teacher was approachable	1	2	3	4	5
The teacher used a variety of teaching methods	1	2	3	4	5
I received regular feedback on my progress	1	2	3	4	5
The objectives of the course have been achieved	1	2	3	4	5
The course has helped me to view things differently	1	2	3	4	5
The course has provided me with new skills	1	2	3	4	5
The course has provided me with new knowledge	1	2	3	4	5

8. Please identify any STRENGTHS of this course:

....

....

....

....

9. Please indicate any PROBLEMS you encountered on the course:

....

....

....

....

10. Please suggest any IMPROVEMENTS you think could be made to the course:

....

....

....

....

....

Figure 9.2 *continued*

between students who adopt a 'deep' approach as opposed to a 'surface' approach to their study. By applying the questionnaires before and after students take a course, it is possible to determine whether the teaching strategy adopted on the course has had any impact on the study approaches adopted by students.

In the Lancaster system, questionnaire scores are used to quantify particular 'scales', such as whether students are adopting a 'meaning orientation' or a 'reproducing orientation' in their study. This analysis is performed in two stages. First, scores from individual questions are combined in batches of between three and five to build 'subscales', and then scores from between three and four subscales are aggregated to form higher level scales. Therefore, for example, the meaning orientation scale (which identifies those students who intend to understand what they are studying rather than simply to reproduce it) is created from the following four subscales: deep approach, relating ideas, use of evidence and intrinsic motivation. The entire system of scales and subscales, together with the questionnaires used to derive them, is presented by Entwistle and Ramsden (1981).

Haigh (1986) provides an example of the application of these questionnaires in evaluating an innovative introductory course in physical geography. Rather than teach first year students various disparate elements of physical geography, Haigh organized his course according to the integrating concepts of general systems theory, illustrating these with themes from physical geography. His aim was to encourage students to adopt an integrative approach to their study, and to encourage them to move away from compartmentalized thinking and superficial memorization. It was to test whether these goals had been achieved that the Lancaster questionnaires were used.

The results of Haigh's evaluation were both disappointing and encouraging. Although the evaluation exercise revealed no overall increase in the meaning orientation scale, statistical analysis of the questionnaire results revealed that this general result masked a difference between the non-academic students, who retreated into memorization, and the better students who improved in their ability to think integratively.

We can now offer a number of practical suggestions for implementing student questionnaires.

- Undertake the feedback exercise for each individual course on the geography degree programme. It is important that individual teachers do not feel that their courses are being singled out for special critical attention.
- To gain some degree of comprehensive and comparable coverage of course evaluation, ask the course office to administer the exercise for all individual courses on the degree programme and to return summary results to the teachers in charge.
- Guarantee student anonymity, and thereby encourage frankness, by indicating that their names need not appear on evaluation forms. Alternatively, ask students to return their forms to the course secretary,

and ask the latter to pass on to the teacher a type-written version or a summary.

Teachers new to this type of exercise can find it deeply disturbing to read highly critical comments about their teaching. They may become angry at blunt student comment or retreat behind the defence of 'teacher knows best', but a more dangerous reaction is to choose to ignore issues raised by students. A single barbed comment might well be from the pen of a disaffected student, but a pattern of consistent critical comments has something important to say. One way around the problem of teacher sensitivity is to ask a trusted colleague, perhaps in another department, to analyse the individual forms and to present a summary of their contents, starting with points of appreciation and ending with matters that could be improved. Any personally disparaging comments can be removed.

There are several ways of ensuring that the most effective use is made of student feedback information.

- Compare student responses to your course with your own aspirations. Identify major discrepancies, and attempt to discover the reasons.
- Avoid reducing student rating scores to oversimplified numerical summaries. Many professional evaluators argue against doing this, and even more advise against making comparisons between summaries derived in this way from different course units on a degree programme. The principal use of student feedback is to identify problems with a course and put them right; the results should not normally be used to undertake spurious comparisons of courses that may differ radically. However, if this is unavoidable, ensure, as Moseley (1980) suggests in a geographical context, that the relative importance of each criterion included on the form is suitably weighted beforehand.
- Act on the basis of your findings. Without clearly signalled action, students will come to regard the evaluation as little more than a public relations exercise or a boring ritual.
- Publicize the changes made as a result of your course evaluations. For example, send a report to student representatives, display a summary on the departmental notice boards, put the details in next year's course handbook and discuss the issues at course committee meetings.
- Carry out the exercise each year, on the same courses, and compare student comments over a period of years. This will enable you to distinguish problems that apply to specific cohorts of students from those that are more fundamental in nature (Fink, 1973).

Conversations with students

One of the most sobering experiences in teaching occurs when you realize that you have taught a class for an entire year, yet know next to nothing about the progress that individual students may have made or the learning difficulties that they may have encountered during that time. If course evaluation is to be at all meaningful, then it must come to grips with this problem and try to assess the functioning of a course in terms of the students' personal experiences.

Unfortunately, the way that higher education is organized does not make it easy to monitor individual students closely. Teachers often meet a group of students only once a week, making it difficult to identify the specific learning difficulties or course-related problems of individuals. This contrasts strongly with early stages of school education, where groups of pupils are taken through the entire year by a single teacher and where the progress of each child can be monitored almost continuously.

Teachers can identify the problems that individual students are encountering on particular courses simply by listening to what they have to say (Fink, 1977). Guidelines for this form of evaluation include the following.

- Talk informally with students. Discussions need not be formal in order to unearth significant learning problems. Indeed, students are usually more forthcoming in the relaxed atmosphere of the cafeteria or bar.
- Talk to every student in the class, if class size and time permit. This will ensure that a fair proportion of potential problems are picked up, and that individual students do not feel that they are being ignored.
- Do not let the organization of your teaching or the use of particular teaching methods become a reason for avoiding informal exchanges with students. Practical classes, seminars and tutorials all provide suitable opportunities to engage in informal conversation about a course and students' views of their performance. Even when a course is largely lecture based, it is not too difficult to sidle up to students at the beginning of a lecture and ask: 'How is the course going for you . . . ?'
- Keep a paper record of students' comments and suggestions. Relate these comments to the attendance register, if one is kept. By matching periods of student absence against a student's mention of a personal or learning difficulty, remedial action can quickly be taken.

Small Group Discussions

Student opinion can also be acquired by setting time for informal but structured discussions with groups of students. One way of doing this is to hold a 'round-table' discussion, similar to a seminar, but where the topic for discussion is the course itself rather than some element of geography. The mechanics are as follows.

- Arrange a meeting with a group of about a dozen students. If a class is larger than this, split it into subgroups of four to six students and ask them to report back on key issues.
- Focus on a specific issue to do with the course and encourage students to talk frankly about it. It is often better to avoid negative or problem issues, both for your own sake and because students may be less than frank with you if you do. One method that has worked on the 'Geographical Information Systems' course at the Middlesex Polytechnic is to pose the question: 'What suggestions do you have for improving the vocational relevance of this course?' By focusing on a positive issue such as this, students are often readier to make innovative suggestions. This approach need not neglect the negative side of your course; student problems will inevitably 'leak out' during the session.
- Draw up a summary of student comments and suggestions, suitably prioritized, and present a copy to each student in the group.
- Attempt to implement at least the first few suggestions on the list as soon as possible.

An alternative approach is to meet with the entire class, and adopt the 'pyramiding' style of discussion advocated by Gibbs (1982).

- Ask each student to think through their reactions to the course, and fill in the boxes on a form such as that shown in figure 9.3.
- Ask groups of four or five students to discuss and compare their individual responses, and to arrive at a consensus in each category.
- Draw out the major responses from each group by means of a plenary discussion, compiling a set of comments in each category that are held by a majority of those in the class.

This approach ensures that individual students have time to think about their personal reactions before being immersed in group discussion. It also ensures that minority views on a course are given less attention than those held by a majority of students. Jenkins and Youngs (1983) used structured discussions of this kind in their 10-week course on film in geography, as part of a strategy of evaluating a course before, during and after it was run.

	Strengths, *good* points	Weaknesses, *bad* points
About the course		
About the teaching		
About yourself		

Figure 9.3   Student reaction sheet for classroom discussion

Course open house

The evaluation methods discussed so far are most appropriately directed at individual courses and are largely student based. We turn now to an evaluation method that is more appropriately aimed at an entire degree programme, and involves teachers as well as students.

The idea is simple. As many students and their teachers as is practicable meet together in a room for a fixed period of time and air their views, put questions to each other and exchange comments and suggestions. Although this may sound impractical, chaotic and liable only to generate hostility, these impressions are usually dispelled after the first experimental meeting. Experience suggests that these group discussions can perform several useful functions.

- They can provide early warning of course-wide problems.
- They can be particularly valuable as a prelude to undertaking a formal curriculum review, or when a course team is about to design a new course.
- They provide an opportunity for staff and students to confront issues on a face-to-face basis.

- They can induce a sense of group participation in the affairs of a course.
- They can be used to disseminate information between staff and students on course organization, procedures and objectives.

To get the best out of these meetings, the following ground rules need to be observed.

- Publicize the meetings well in advance, so that all eligible persons can attend. (One department in which the idea has been used adopted the title 'Barriers to Learning Meeting' in its publicity material.) Involve students as well as staff in the publicity drive.
- Hold the meetings in a large room, in which chairs are arranged in concentric circles. Staff should not sit together, so as to avoid a 'them and us' atmosphere.
- Bring in a neutral chairperson for the discussion. (This could be a colleague from another department, an educational consultant or a group psychologist.) The role of the chairperson is *not* to run through an agenda, but simply to keep order, to ensure that everyone can make a contribution if they wish to do so and to discourage dominant individuals from monopolizing the proceedings.
- Nominate someone to record points raised during the meeting.
- Schedule the meeting to run for about an hour or, at most, 90 minutes. The imposition of a deadline will encourage speakers to limit their oratory and prevent the event from dragging on or fizzling out at the end.
- Ask all speakers to avoid naming names when making critical statements. This will prevent the teachers present from taking defensive or entrenched positions and will avoid direct confrontations.
- Organize part of the discussion in small groups of five or six people, perhaps using the 'pyramiding' technique described in the previous section.
- Make it clear that anything, and everything, to do with the running of the course and the quality of student learning is open to comment.

This type of event must not be overdone; one or two such meetings a year are probably ample. The final requirement is a procedure for taking up the issues raised in the open house session, for identifying which of the problems discussed need to be examined further, for generating solutions to significant problems and for putting these solutions into effect. As with other diagnostic evaluation methods, action should be seen to be taken as a result of these meetings, and feedback to all staff and students must take place.

The course evaluation methods discussed in this section have ranged across a broad spectrum: non-interactive feedback from individual students, one-to-one and one-to-many discussions between students and their teachers, and many-to-many meetings of everyone associated with a course. Each of these methods involves listening to what learners have to say and, together, they can tell us a great deal about our courses. In putting them forward, we fully recognize that student evaluation causes unease, especially for those who work in systems where such evaluation is not common. We also recognize that it is commonly argued that evaluation is unnecessary, because its function is fulfilled by other mechanisms, or that students cannot evaluate a course properly since they only have narrow objectives and, as a consequence, their views on such issues as course content, level of difficulty, study methods and the like will be coloured by short-term objectives.

While taking these points seriously, we would argue that, in practice, both sets of objections are primarily defensive and contrary to experience. The widespread acceptance of student evaluation in North America would certainly suggest a large measure of support in higher education for the idea of listening to the views of those who are the immediate 'consumers'.

However, one further objection is raised, namely that student-centred course evaluations only tell us what students *think* that they have learned from a course, or how successful they *feel* that the course has been. Critics claim that the acid test is how the students actually *perform* when assessed in these courses. This criticism, which centres around what assessment results can tell us about course quality and how those results can be analysed to derive this information, needs discussion in its own right.

Using assessment information for evaluation

The nature of assessment was discussed in the previous chapter, but here we explore the view that 'assessment can be regarded as a way of testing [course] effectiveness, that is as a diagnosis of faults . . . . It is a means to an end, the end being the improvement of the curriculum' (Humphrys, 1978: 82). However, while assessment is an indicator that things may or may not be well with a course, it will probably only provide diagnostic information at the extremes. In other words, it may help to identify excellent courses and very bad courses, but will fail to say anything significant about the majority of courses in between. Examination results, in particular, will at best only provide a starting point in the evaluation of courses; they will have little to say about how to improve the curriculum and teaching (Torrance, 1986). Certainly, the following reasons would suggest that it is a mistake to rely exclusively on such information as an indicator of the success or failure of courses.

- Summative assessment is concerned with different objectives than course evaluation. While assessment concentrates on the outcomes of learning, evaluation focuses on the processes and problems of learning, and often attempts to determine how far a student's approach to study has been changed by a particular teaching strategy.

- The use of student grades as a means of evaluating a course assumes that assessment is an adequate test of the learning outcomes of a course. There is considerable evidence to suggest that examinations often only assess a small fraction of student learning, and can therefore only be rather shallow indicators of the effectiveness of courses.

- Most assessment procedures produce crude standard numerical scores, whereas evaluation exercises typically require and produce a far richer set of information.

- Although assessment might be able to indicate weak courses, it cannot indicate why such courses are underperforming. Evaluative information is needed to identify the underlying causes.

- The quality of student performance in examinations is not always an accurate reflection of the quality of the courses that they have been studying. By focusing directly on courses and teaching, evaluations provide a far more accurate picture of course quality.

Despite these limitations, assessment information should not be entirely neglected for evaluation purposes because, first, it is regularly available for virtually every course and, second, its periodic availability can provide an appropriate stimulus for teachers to explore ways in which they can improve their courses. Therefore the question is: How can we make the most effective use of assessment information for course evaluation purposes?

One readily apparent approach is to compare the results gained on the constituent course units in a degree programme. An example is reported by Moffatt (1986), who evaluated his course in computer modelling of environmental systems by comparing each student's assessment on this course with their overall degree results. The high degree of correlation between the two, over a period of 4 years, was held to indicate that the students' results in the modelling course was broadly in line with their overall ability as indicated by their final degree classification.

Geography teachers at Carleton University adopted a different approach. They hoped that student exposure to an innovative self-paced mastery course in the first year would create improved standards of learning, and that these would be reflected in improved grades awarded for subsequent courses in the second year (Fox and Wilkinson, 1977). They examined student grades to see if this was the case, and in an ensuing course review (Fox et al., 1987) they also compared the grades of students taught in the traditional way with those taught by the new approach. However, the authors urge caution in attempting such comparisons if, as in their case, there are significant differences not only in the teaching methods used, but also in the instructors, course materials, assignments, examinations and markers. We shall return to this issue a little later when we examine controlled tests of teaching methods.

Timing

Before leaving our discussion of course evaluation methods, it is important to consider a preliminary issue, namely, the question of timing. In much the same manner as for assessment (see chapter 8), an end of course timing is generally accepted as the norm, but there are also other times at which evaluation can usefully be carried out.

'Pre-course' evaluation   The 'brainstorming' technique described in chapter 5 can effectively be used to discover the amount of pre-knowledge of the subject to be covered by the course, and to elicit students' preconceptions and expectations from the course. This information can be used to modify the course content and orientation before it begins, and can also serve as a baseline against which information from later evaluations can be compared. This type of evaluation was successfully adopted on an economic geography course at the University of Chicago (Fink, 1973).

'Mid course' evaluation   An evaluation undertaken half-way through a course provides findings which can be used to improve that course to the benefit of the current cohort of students. Mid-course evaluations were used in the exercise reported by Fink (1973), and also in the film-based geography course described by Jenkins and Youngs (1983). In the latter course, a mid-course evaluation revealed that students saw little connection between the course themes and geography *per se*. As a result, the content of a subsequent class was changed, and a simulation exercise was constructed to get over this difficulty.

There is a major issue of principle here. Each group of students that takes a particular course has a distinctive ethos and its own special mix of learning styles, problems and abilities. Consequently, it may be far more sensible to use the results of a mid-course evaluation to improve the course for the current cohort of students than to use the findings from an end of course evaluation to modify the course for subsequent student groups.

'One year later' evaluation   Here students are asked to evaluate a course that they had completed a year earlier. This can be useful because it tends to pick up broader issues about course effectiveness and can identify those elements of a course, if any, which have had a lasting influence on students. This technique

can be used to monitor individual course units by interviewing final year students about their first year courses, and can also be used to evaluate an entire degree programme by interviewing students a year after they have graduated. The latter exercise can be implemented when graduates visit the institution for a degree awards ceremony or through a mailed questionnaire distributed by an alumni association. This type of evaluation is frequently able to provide information on the value of a course as a preparation for life or, more narrowly, for subsequent employment. A complementary approach, illustrated by Unwin (1986), is for academics to ask employers for their opinions of former students and to use this information to re-orient courses.

9.3 EVALUATING TEACHING

There are several ways in which teaching and teaching methods can be evaluated. We shall begin our survey with a naturalistic method – the teaching diary – before moving on to consider systematic data-gathering exercises and then rigorously controlled evaluation experiments.

The teaching diary

Most teachers emerge from a class with clear feelings about how it went. The teaching diary or journal is one way in which these reflections, comments and ratings can be recorded for diagnostic use. Several items can be recorded in a teaching diary about each class: the general context of the class (time, date, teaching methods used, subject matter covered); comments on specific teaching issues (e.g. general student group attitudes or problems raised on a particular topic); teaching problems that occurred and their possible causes; suggestions on how the class might be improved next time round.

It is tempting to use a teaching diary to record gut reactions to each class: 'That hour just dragged – none of them said anything'; 'I rather enjoyed that. I covered everything I intended to say, and they all seemed interested for the entire hour'; 'That practical exercise just doesn't work. I think I'll abandon it next year.' There are two reasons, however, why comments such as these may not be too helpful as a basis for evaluating your teaching.

First, many of your impressions might not be shared by your students. Therefore, before writing anything down, check out your perceptions of how a class went by talking it through with some of those on the 'receiving end'. For example, your 'excellent' lecture may not have had the positive impact you expected, but your 'flat' seminar or 'chaotic' workshop session might have scored an unexpected hit.

Second, the 'stream of consciousness' type of comment does little to explain what has happened in the classroom and why. It is far better to use the diary to record critical analyses of your teaching, rather than become a repository of broad unexamined value judgements. The most useful comments are those which point more clearly to causes and possible solutions to classroom problems, or that attempt to pin down why a particular approach seems to have worked.

The three principal advantages of keeping a teaching diary are its immediacy, with its contents undistorted by hindsight, its richness of data and its encouragement of a generally reflective approach towards teaching. These can be used directly as the basis for improvements in teaching, identifying, say, the amount of material included in teaching sessions, the way ideas are sequenced in a class, the most appropriate mix of teaching methods and the 'sticking points' at which students most frequently experience learning difficulties. If all else fails, and you are stuck for a remedy, follow Unwin's (1984) example and write up your reflections for a geographical or educational journal. You may be pleasantly surprised at the helpful advice that other readers are able to offer.

Systematic observation

Systematic observation of classroom behaviour can furnish valuable information on which to base improvements in teaching. It can be carried out by teachers themselves when students are engaged in activities such as simulations or practicals, or undertaken by a colleague during activities when the teacher is more centrally involved. The data produced depend on the type of observational method that is being employed. The observer, for example, may just be recording simple frequency counts (e.g. how many times students appear to be engaged in a particular desired activity) or timing activities to build up detailed 'activity budgets' for individual students or small groups of students who are working together.

An alternative method of undertaking detailed classroom observations is to use a video recorder. Video-taping has one major advantage over standard observation methods: the recording can be viewed over and over again in order to decide which activities are really going on in the classroom. As many colleges have a video-recording service on campus, and some have consultant services to help with educational analysis of tapes, this type of approach need not be as daunting as it might first appear.

Video-recording can also be employed to provide immediate feedback on teaching and learning behaviour in order to improve classroom interaction. This was attempted by Hollis and Terry (1977) when introducing small group discussion sessions into a geography practical course in the University of London. In their experiments, a selection of sessions were recorded and played back to the groups involved. This helped both the teacher and the students to clarify the previously unclear objectives of the discussion sessions, and further review of the tapes helped the teacher to establish more effective ways to begin the discussions. It was also found that playing the tapes encouraged the participants to feel a greater sense of shared responsibility for making a success of subsequent discussion sessions.

Student interviews

Interviews with students can provide complementary information to that gathered by classroom observation. Students can be interviewed at various times and for a variety of purposes. They can, for example, be interviewed before they engage in a teaching or learning activity in order to identify their expectations and attitudes. They might be interviewed again during teaching or learning activities to elicit perceptions of what they are learning. Finally, students can be interviewed after teaching has been completed in order to check on their learning experiences and to identify possible learning outcomes.

Evaluation interviews should largely consist of open-ended questions, and should not be dominated by pre-coded questions that are normally found in self-completion questionnaires. The object of the exercise, above all, is to elicit the unexpected, not to confirm the teacher's prior expectations. For this reason, and also to encourage greater frankness in student responses, it is recommended that evaluation interviews are carried out by those not directly involved in teaching the course.

Several examples of the use of student interviewing to gauge the effect of geography courses have been published in the literature. Jenkins and Youngs (1983), for instance, used student interviews alongside structured questionnaires to determine student perceptions of a geography course on film. Interviewing a sample of students is highly recommended whenever a new approach to teaching is being adopted, and is especially useful for evaluating the first-time use of new teaching materials.

Controlled tests

To many educational researchers, evaluation is essentially a form of hypothesis testing. It should not come as a surprise, therefore, to find that the entire paraphernalia of the scientific method has found its way into educational evaluation. One of the fundamental questions asked in evaluation studies is: 'How well does this particular teaching method perform its intended role?'. Converted into a testable hypothesis, this can be re-expressed in the following way: 'Teaching topic A by method B will produce outcome C in student group D.' The standard scientific approach to testing such hypotheses is to establish students' existing knowledge before teaching takes place, by means of a pre-test, and then to identify, by means of a post-test carried out after the teaching has been completed, whether the intended learning has been achieved.

This method goes beyond the rather impressionistic approach of the teaching diary or the loosely structured approach of classroom observation and student interviewing. Evaluating teaching by means of controlled tests attempts to glean 'hard' and unequivocal evidence about what happens as a result of using a particular teaching method. The general procedure for applying this approach has been developed from experimental science, and involves the principles and methods of statistically grounded quantitative research. The six steps to be taken in carrying out a formal test of a teaching method are as follows.

1 Specify the aims and objectives of the teaching.
2 Adopt teaching method(s) that you believe may best achieve these aims and objectives.
3 Design pre-test questions to determine the prior knowledge of the students, and design post-test questions to measure subsequent attainment of the objectives.
4 Carry out the teaching and implement the tests. If appropriate, monitor and record student performance during the teaching.
5 Compare the results of the two tests statistically in order to measure the extent of student learning gains. Draw suitable conclusions.
6 If the learning objectives are not attained, modify or replace the chosen teaching method(s).

Stating the learning objectives required from your teaching may not be as straightforward as it seems. Bloom et al. (1971: see also chapter 8), for example, suggest that a learning objective should not be a statement of the content matter to be covered (e.g. glacial landforms or urban ghettos), despite the frequent appearance of such statements in course syllabuses. Nor should it be a statement of what the teacher intends to do (e.g. to demonstrate the skill of using a soil auger or to provide an overview of government industrial location policy). Rather, a learning objective should focus on the way in which it is intended that the students should change in response to the teaching or learning activity. Although objectives do not necessarily have to be highly specific, they are usually more helpful if clearly and unambiguously stated and testable by the chosen evaluation procedures. Aspects of learning objectives are explored further in chapter 10 on curriculum design.

Setting up a suitable pre- and post-test presents additional problems. An acceptable test should include a reasonably large number of test items, and these should be chosen so as to probe those aspects of learning that are stated in the evaluation objectives. A number of standard tests are commercially available for 'mainstream' curricula such as mathematics and languages, but few are available for geography (see, however, Marsden, 1976).

A third problem concerns the validity of test results. Even if testing suggests that students have changed in the way intended, can this be attributed to teaching alone? For example, an evaluation of a course on natural hazards might reveal that students had grasped the mechanisms involved in situations of environmental damage from human activities, yet that understanding might have been due as much to a major television documentary on pollution that was broadcast during the trial period as to the teaching methods used. A more general threat to the validity of test findings comes from the testing itself. It is well known, for example, that the experience of doing pre-tests can sometimes help students do better on the matched post-test and can alert them to the content and expectations of the course. What this means is that in order to make a valid claim for the efficacy of your teaching, you have to ensure that all such rival explanations are eliminated.

Cooke et al. (1980) used the testing approach to determine whether their use of the Visual Response System to teach basic map skills was effective. To the usual pre-test and post-test they also added further 'post-checks' at 2 and 6 weeks after completion of their teaching. The runs of scores across the four sets of tests indicated successful acquisition of the skills taught by this particular method.

Not all teaching methods are susceptible to evaluation by formal testing. In particular, new teaching methods and materials cannot always be evaluated simply by applying pre-tests and post-tests. This is because the full range of learning effects to be achieved with these methods and materials are often not yet known. Evaluation in these circumstances therefore needs to take a different tack, aiming to identify the learning outcomes that can be achieved, rather than to measure the match between expected and actual learning gains.

9.4 EVALUATING TEACHING MATERIALS

Many geography teachers use a mixture of resources in their teaching (e.g. overhead and slide projectors, video and film, computer software), and prescribe other materials for use by students (e.g. resource-based learning materials, textbooks, programmed instruction). There are several aspects to evaluating these materials, including the decision to adopt, evaluation of materials during their use and the formative evaluation used during the design of new teaching materials. (Formative evaluation, which seeks to form or mould the object being evaluated to bring about improvements, is considered further in chapter 10.)

The process of identifying appropriate materials for adoption on a course is a perennial concern, and is one of the most common faces of evaluation, but how are educational resources best evaluated for potential use in teaching? Most educational journals support a third party evaluation industry, in that the 'reviews' or 'resources' section of such publications regularly report the views of practising teachers on textbooks, audiovisual materials, laboratory and field equipment and, more recently, educational software. Yet there are several reasons why such reviews do not always serve the needs of practising geography teachers.

- They primarily comment on content and rarely on suitability for teaching.
- They are rarely written from a classroom perspective. The contemplative review of a textbook, from the perspective of 2 or more years of classroom use, is extremely rare.
- Few reviews take a comparative perspective, despite the fact that there are usually a handful of competing resources on the market at any one time for a particular part of one's teaching, and despite the fact that teachers with little to spend on teaching materials need to select the 'best' candidate for their course needs.
- A single review by a single reviewer cannot hope to address the diverse teaching and course needs of degree level geography. Few reviews try to handle this problem by providing multi-authored, multi-perspective evaluations.
- Few, if any, reviews are provided by students.

The main conclusion to draw from this is that the only effective evaluations of prospective teaching material are ones that are carried out by the intending users and that focus directly on its suitability for their teaching. We shall now describe some techniques for carrying out such evaluations.

Evaluating individual teaching materials

A possible procedure for selecting individual teaching materials can be illustrated by looking at educational computer software. A large amount of educational software has appeared in recent years aimed at teachers of geography at various levels, and poses considerable problems as to what materials will be suitable for use in a course, how they will assist student learning and how they will affect the existing pattern of teaching.

One of the simplest ways round these problems is to run through a checklist of questions, answering each of them in order to arrive at a decision. Table 9.2 shows one such list, based on a form devised by the American educational

Table 9.2 A computer assisted learning evaluation checklist

Criteria	Quality	Importance
Subject matter content		
Definition of key concepts	1 2 3 4 5	A B C D
Discussion of underlying assumptions	1 2 3 4 5	A B C D
Validity of theories, principles, techniques, facts	1 2 3 4 5	A B C D
Guide to relevant literature	1 2 3 4 5	A B C D
Overall quality of subject matter content	1 2 3 4 5	A B C D
User documentation		
Clarity of presentation	1 2 3 4 5	A B C D
Completeness	1 2 3 4 5	A B C D
Adequacy of instructions for operating the software	1 2 3 4 5	A B C D
Documentation for different users (e.g. teachers, students)	1 2 3 4 5	A B C D
Worksheets and other teaching materials	1 2 3 4 5	A B C D
Consistency with the accompanying program	1 2 3 4 5	A B C D
Overall quality of documentation	1 2 3 4 5	A B C D
Educational support		
Ease of integration with teaching and learning styles	1 2 3 4 5	A B C D
Potential for improving grasp of principles and theories	1 2 3 4 5	A B C D
Potential for improving facility with methods and techniques	1 2 3 4 5	A B C D
Potential for improving retention and recall of knowledge	1 2 3 4 5	A B C D
Overall quality of educational support	1 2 3 4 5	A B C D
Student motivation		
Potential for capturing student interest	1 2 3 4 5	A B C D
Ability to stimulate student creativity	1 2 3 4 5	A B C D
Appropriateness for student-centred work	1 2 3 4 5	A B C D
Overall quality for student motivation	1 2 3 4 5	A B C D
Software		
Freedom from errors	1 2 3 4 5	A B C D
Ease of use	1 2 3 4 5	A B C D
Compatibility with available computer hardware	1 2 3 4 5	A B C D
Completeness of technical documentation	1 2 3 4 5	A B C D
Overall quality of software	1 2 3 4 5	A B C D
Overall evaluation	1 2 3 4 5	A B C D

Quality ratings: 1, excellent; 2, very good; 3, average; 4, poor; 5, bad. Importance ratings: A, critical; B, important; C, optional; D, inappropriate.

software clearing house CONDUIT (see also MicroSIFT, 1982; Council of Ministers of Education, 1985). Note particularly how technical subject matter and teaching issues are clearly separated in this list and how the user is encouraged to rate each attribute.

This type of evaluation can suggest various forms of action. For example, if an item of educational software is technically incompatible with existing hardware but scores well in terms of its teaching potential, then it might well be worth either purchasing appropriate computer equipment or converting the software to run on available hardware.

Comparative evaluation of teaching materials

There is much to gain from evaluating related teaching materials comparatively rather than individually. Salisbury (1981), for example, carried out a comparative review of the subject matter and teaching style of a number of introductory physical geography textbooks. In the USA, the National Council for Geographic Education has published a textbook evaluation form that can also be used for this purpose. A similar approach used for the evaluation of educational computer software is found in the CCCEM model produced by the University of Florida, which provides descriptive ratings of programs on the basis of physical, presentation, instruction and management characteristics (Micceri, 1989). It is claimed that the use of objective ratings provides a reliable and consistent evaluation of software, and avoids some of the vagaries of human judgement typical of many standard published reviews.

At first glance this might appear a somewhat trivial approach to evaluation, but we would suggest that its usefulness is partly due to its simplicity. Moreover, systematically derived summary tables can draw a teacher's attention to gaps in subject matter or educational approaches that the reading of individual books might miss. To make the most of such an evaluation, it is important not to focus exclusively on content, but to consider elements that are specifically designed to help students learn, such as self-assessed questions, data-gathering activities, reading assignments and data response exercises. Above all, it is important for each teacher to consider how easily each book can be adapted for use on their particular course and their own particular teaching style, or whether the adoption of a significant new teaching resource will itself create the need for change.

Evaluating teaching materials during their design

Evaluation methods can also be used during the design of new teaching materials to test whether they will perform satisfactorily in use (termed 'formative evaluation' above). In particular, several techniques were pioneered in the UK during the 1970s to provide 'illuminative' information during the design of new curricula (Tawney, 1976).

Whitelegg (1982), for instance, describes the evaluation of video-recordings that were used experimentally in a first year geography practical class. Besides providing information used to improve the video material, this exercise raised a number of significant methodological issues about the evaluation itself, such as how to evaluate a teaching material if it is used in a class by a different teacher from the rest of the course. Watson (1987) reports on the rigorous cycle of evaluation and testing that educational software development teams now build into their design efforts; indeed, in some items of educational software, the evaluation of the program's performance is built into the program itself.

Recent developments in intelligent educational software have taken this a step further. So-called 'intelligent tutoring systems' have been developed that are able to give a continuous evaluation of their own behaviour in relation to student performance, and adjust their instructional strategy accordingly (Sleeman and Brown, 1982; Polson and Richardson, 1987; Wenger, 1987). In such developments, evaluation is no longer a separate activity; it has become an integral part of the design and delivery of the curriculum (see chapter 10).

9.5 APPRAISING TEACHERS

This chapter has focused on evaluating teaching and improving courses, but teaching is also about teachers. Although we recognize that there are those who view teacher appraisal as a weapon that can be used against teachers by those in charge of the educational system, we believe that sensitive and sensible teacher appraisal should be a fundamental part of course improvement. There are three principal ways (Braskamp, 1980) in which this can be carried out: self-evaluation, peer appraisal and student assessment.

Self-evaluation

Self-evaluation has the considerable advantage of being non-comparative and non-competitive, and of allowing features that are unique to each teacher to come out into the open. One way that this can be achieved is by use of teaching diaries in which the teacher can record self-evaluations (see above). A more formal alternative is to produce a periodic (e.g. annual) written narrative of course objectives, teaching strategies and perceptions of student performance, which can be collated and reviewed at course or departmental level.

Critics argue that self-evaluation will be self-serving at best, and at worst will camouflage poor teachers. Although the research evidence (Braskamp, 1980) suggests that self-evaluations are generally not overfavourable to the teachers who make them, some argue for a method of self-evaluation that produces information capable of being checked for validity.

One such method is for teachers to fill in complementary versions of the course questionnaires distributed to students. The students are asked: 'Have the major objectives of the course been made clear by the teacher?' The teacher is asked: 'To what extent have you made the major objectives of you course clear to students?' Similarly, the student question 'Does the teacher encourage critical thinking and analysis?' is replaced on the teacher's form by 'To what extent have you encouraged critical thinking and analysis?' A comparative analysis of the teacher and student scores on each question will reveal discrepancies between the teacher's intentions and students' perceptions, and indicate areas where further effort is required to ensure that the course delivers what it promises.

Peer appraisal

Teaching is an unusual occupation in that the majority of workers rarely perform in the presence of their peers. Even on team-taught courses, most teachers work alone with their students throughout their entire career. When they do perform in public, as on geographical field courses, there is rarely a formal mechanism for one colleague to evaluate another's performance with a view to seeking improvements. By comparison, students who participate in regular seminars and tutorial groups are constantly subjected to evaluative criticism from their peers. What, then, can be done to encourage peer evaluation of teachers and what methods are available?

The most direct approach is for one teacher's classroom practice to be observed by a colleague, but peer evaluation can also involve the examination of a teacher's lesson plans, course handouts, coursework assignments, grading methods and evaluation arrangements. These methods are widely used in the training of school teachers and during probationary periods for new teachers. They are also used by the United Kingdom's educational inspectorate during their periodic visits to review courses or departments (Jenkins and Smith, 1990). A similar approach is taken in those North American schools which employ an educational consultant as an in-house evaluator and counsellor.

As to who should carry out a peer evaluation, we feel that while expert observers can make a significant contribution to both evaluation and improvement, observation by one's own colleagues can also be highly beneficial. An incidental benefit of being evaluated by one's colleagues is that information about non-conventional methods used by innovative teachers on a degree programme can become more widely known and practised. One of the largest problems to be overcome in peer evaluation is fear of exposure to one's colleagues. This fear can be reduced by adopting one or more of the following tactics.

- Pair off teachers with their most respected colleague, and ask each to appraise the other.
- Call in a colleague from another department to undertake the appraisal.

- Permit the teachers being appraised to set the agenda for their own appraisals.
- Build teacher appraisal initially into all new courses, and then extend it to existing courses.
- Ease teachers into the appraisal habit by getting them to teach a class with another colleague, during which each assesses the other's performance.
- Build appraisal into team-taught courses, for there may already be scope on such courses for teachers to observe their colleagues at work.
- Video-record selected classes of the teacher being appraised, and then invite the teacher and the appraiser to examine the tape together in a relaxed atmosphere.
- Teach teachers about how to give feedback to one another. A useful strategy here (outlined in chapter 8 in connection with giving feedback in student assessment) is to state the positive features first, and then present negative features as 'possible areas for improvement'.

Several options exist for teachers who remain uneasy about appraisal by their immediate colleagues. One is for the head of department to carry out the appraisal, perhaps as part of a regular cycle of staff development (Brunn, 1990). Another is for the appraisal to be undertaken by a single external assessor, either from a neighbouring department or from a geography department in another institution. Hastings et al. (1970), for example, describe interviews of geography teachers by trained staff from the Centre for Instructional Research at the University of Illinois. They found that interviews took less time than regular self-evaluation, but yielded more information than filling out a questionnaire. Finally, as Lawton (1986) indicates, the assessor's role can be carried out by external examiners, alongside their main role of scrutinizing grades awarded to students by internal departmental examiners. The latter approach could serve to forge a link between the evaluation of courses based on a study of their outcomes (i.e. student grades) and evaluations based on inputs (i.e. teacher performance).

Finally, what aspects of a teacher's performance does peer evaluation best illuminate? Braskamp (1980) suggests that evaluation by one's peers is most appropriate for judging a teacher's professional competence and the extent to which a scholarly orientation is being shown towards the subject matter being taught.

Student assessment of teachers

The idea that student views on how we teach should be a major part of evaluation exercises is not always easy for teachers of geography to accept. However, North

American practice has long been to use student opinion in the appraisal of teachers and the experience does not support the worst fears of those suspicious of such a system. Surveys show that about 80 per cent of US institutions use student evaluations for staff development purposes (Centra, 1977). Student rating of instruction is often concerned with teacher characteristics such as skill, dynamism, fairness, enthusiasm, sense of humour, openness, approachability, availability, appearance and interest (see Dowell and Neal, 1982; Kyriacou and McKelvey, 1985).

According to Braskamp (1980), the three commonest methods of collecting student information on teachers are responses to a set of alternative fixed items in survey form, written comments on open-ended questions and verbal comments in a semi-structured interview conducted by an independent third party. The choice of data collection method does not seem to matter much if an overall rating of an instructor is all that is required. However, each method varies in the amount of diagnostic and feedback information they provide, and the manner in which information is communicated back to the instructor.

We have already discussed the use of feedback forms, interviews and questionnaires in our earlier section on course evaluation; most of the principles discussed in these contexts apply equally to student assessment of teachers. Fink (1985) provides an example of the types of question that geography students can be asked on a structured questionnaire based on the IDEA course evaluation system developed at Kansas State University. This asks students to rate what they have learnt on a course. The teacher abilities about which students can be questioned are as follows:

General
    Knowledge of the subject
    Attitude towards teaching
    Ability to design courses
    Desire to continue learning about teaching

Particular abilities
    Ability to make objectives clear
    Establishes good relationships with students
    Effectively communicates course content
    Uses particular teaching techniques effectively
    Generates enthusiasm
    Provides frequent and useful feedback to the students
    Changes the teaching approach when appropriate
    Provides intellectual leadership
    Constructs good tests

Summing up, the main lessons to draw from this discussion of teacher appraisal are as follows:

- More than one method should be used to evaluate teaching ability. Pearson (1987), for example, argues that it is only when multiple and variable lines of evidence are used that different aspects of teacher quality can be identified. In his survey of new geography teachers, Fink (1985) shows how the results from self, peer and student evaluations can be compared to reveal interesting contrasts in the perception of teaching quality within a department.
- Teachers themselves must be centrally involved in the design, implementation and reporting of any evaluation which concerns their teaching or their courses. This ensures that they will not feel threatened by the process of appraisal and that they have some degree of control over both the purpose of the evaluation and the methods used. Research evidence consistently shows that the greater the involvement in evaluation by teachers, the greater is the likelihood that they will use the evaluation findings to improve their work.
- All teachers in a department or associated with a particular course should be appraised; individual teachers should not be singled out for special attention.
- Teacher appraisals that are meant primarily to improve teaching must be carefully designed to suit this purpose. They should not simply be tied in to the annual promotion round and should not be seen as a means of rewarding or penalizing teachers.
- Teacher evaluation should be undertaken regularly. Natriello (1984) provides evidence that regular evaluation is more acceptable to teachers than incidental evaluation.
- Resources should be available to help teachers improve their work on the basis of appraisal findings. This means that funds to improve teaching quality should be made available at departmental, faculty (or school) and college level.

9.6 CONCLUSION

The previous discussion of teacher appraisal points to the wider dimensions of evaluation beyond mere concern with a particular teaching method, an individual class with students or a new item of educational technology. It is also possible to go beyond teacher appraisal to towards a holistic appraisal of the total teaching system, including evaluation of the complete degree programme, the department or even the institution as a whole. While a large literature exists on this subject (e.g. Parlett, 1977; Moos, 1979; Rutherford, 1987; Kogan, 1989), its substance lies outside the terms of reference of this chapter or, indeed, this book.

We have endeavoured here to consider the evaluation of several features in the educational system: course units, individual classes, teaching methods and materials, and appraisal of the teachers themselves. We have described a number of complementary evaluation methods, and have discussed the issue of who best undertakes evaluations and when. Throughout, our main concern has been with the use of evaluation to improve how we help students to learn. In doing so, we have tried to show that evaluation need not be complex and time consuming to be useful. It is now time to draw out some general conclusions from the material that we have presented. The key ideas can be summarized in the form of a handful of precepts.

- Evaluation shows our concern, as professionals, for the highest quality in what we do for a living. It is proof to the outside world that we are accountable for our actions and it provides a seal of approval for our courses and our graduates. For these reasons and for the satisfaction that comes from doing a job properly, evaluation should be an important and integral part of our work.
- Evaluation is a multifaceted activity that can be used for various purposes. It includes qualitative as well as quantitative methods, can focus on an entire course or a single lesson and can be undertaken by a variety of different people. It can occur at regular intervals during a course or merely at the end. It can examine individual aspects of a curriculum or make controlled comparisons of two or more teaching methods. Just as there is no one way of teaching geography that is best in all circumstances, so too is there no single optimal method of evaluation. Indeed. as various people have argued (e.g. McElroy, 1984; Smith and Keep, 1988), the most satisfying course evaluations employ a variety of sources of evidence.
- Evaluation should be treated as a recurrent activity, carried out as part of a continuous process of curriculum design and improvement. Rapid change in the educational system and society generally call for courses to be regularly evaluated and continuously updated and improved. Course improvement is always possible.
- Teachers need to be centrally involved in the development and implementation of acceptable evaluation exercises. Evaluations that we ourselves instigate will be far less threatening and much more likely to lead to improvements in our teaching than those imposed from above.

We shall have only ourselves to blame if, by our indifference to evaluation, we allow it to be hijacked by those who intend using it for alternative and less acceptable purposes.

● Evaluation alone is not enough. If evaluation does not lead to change, then those who participate in the exercise will come to regard it as a time-consuming irrelevance.

● In the final analysis, the outcomes of our evaluations may not be as significant as the process of evaluating. As Cox (1976: 27) notes: 'It is not so much that we cannot think more constructively and imaginatively about our teaching, it is just that the occasion does not arise.'

● Evaluation is intimately related to all other educational activities. We should therefore regard it as an essential and integral part of curriculum design, teaching and assessment, and avoid treating it as a separate activity. Evaluation has a fundamental role to play in the design as well as the operation of teaching schemes, and it can be used to unearth problems in both teacher performance and student learning. Viewed in this light, evaluation is no more and no less than an arbiter of quality, a catalyst for continuous improvement and an essential tool for ensuring that students get the best possible deal from their learning experience.

We offer the following suggestions that you may consider for further action.

● Contact your college's educational methods unit or adviser, if it has one, and ask for copies of recommended course evaluation materials. You might also inquire if support is available for implementing your own course evaluations.

● Choose a suitable point in your courses to organize a discussion session with your students in which you ask them to identify a few things that you, the teacher, could do to improve the course, and three things that they, the students, could do individually and collectively to improve the course. Pool the suggestions, discuss them and adopt the top priorities from each list for immediate implementation.

● Invite a colleague who teaches a similar course to your own in another institution to visit you in order to discuss ways of improving both your courses.

● Set up a simple evaluation of how a new teaching method or material performs and report the results at the next course team meeting so that others can benefit from your experiments.

● If you are head of department, place the discussion of course evaluation methods on the agenda of your next course team meeting. Ask each member of the team to bring to the meeting details of an evaluation method that they would like to see implemented on the course. Implement some of these methods in the coming academic year.

KEY READING

The *Encyclopaedia of Educational Evaluation* (Anderson et al., 1975) provides a valuable overview of the concepts, methods and terminology of educational evaluation. This contains more than 140 cross-referenced articles, each of which provides a guide to further reading. Murphy and Torrance's (1987) *Evaluating Education* brings together classic material on evaluation issues and methods. Dressel (1976), Doyle (1983) and Tuckman (1985) are textbooks that supply useful overviews of the basic issues. Bloom et al. (1971) provide a comprehensive survey of evaluation methods which adopts the objectives testing tradition most highly developed in North America. A broader, but no less comprehensive, compilation of techniques is provided by Patton (1990).

For those who require a historical review of the changing emphases in modern evaluation, *Curriculum Evaluation* by Hamilton et al. (1977) can be recommended. The early 1970s switch to qualitative approaches is well illustrated by Tawney (1976). This essentially British view is complemented by the North American perspectives of Eisner (1985).

10

Designing a Geography Curriculum

The curriculum on paper is only a script: the real curriculum is acted out and lived through. Thus, in a sense we can say that the lecturer is also a kind of content, and so are the methods he or she uses, the department he or she works in and, last but not least, the assessment that is made.

G. Squires, 'The curriculum'

Every discipline includes, implicitly or explicitly, some value commitments about what is worth studying and how it should be studied.

P. L. Dressel and D. Marcus, *On Teaching and Learning in College*

10.1 INTRODUCTION

Designing and delivering an effective curriculum is the most important professional responsibility for geography teachers. In higher education, however, the curriculum is seldom publicly discussed and the geographical literature on curriculum design is limited. As Humphreys (1978, 74) suggests: 'knowledge of the professional approach to curriculum design and development amongst geography lecturers is rare.'

The starting point for our discussion of curriculum design is essentially the same as that adopted in Peter Gould's challenging essay 'The open geographic curriculum':

I want you to imagine that you have been asked to form a new Department of Geography . . . . Given the rare opportunity to write without constraint, would your curricula bear much resemblance to most of the formal courses of study to be found today? With any luck your answer will be something like, good grief no! If your answer is something else . . . there is not much hope for the future! (Gould, 1973: 253–4)

However, Gould then proceeds to examine the substantive geography that students should learn; *we* place the curriculum in a wider context, of which the geographical content is but part. The emphasis here is on the complexity and varied responsibilities that are incurred when designing a geography curriculum. While seeking to retain a focus on practical issues, we also ask questions such as those listed below (after Miller, 1987) – questions that demand discussion about the philosophical nature and purpose of geographical education.

- Why is this course being taught?
- What new knowledge, skills or attitudes do I expect my students to develop during the course?
- What levels of knowledge or skills do I expect in students when they enrol in this course?
- For students to develop the attributes listed above, with what experiences do I need to provide them during this course?
- Will all students benefit from essentially the same experiences in the course?
- If students need to be offered a range of experiences, what variation is possible, given restraints on resources?
- What resources are available for teaching this course? What materials and methods am I most skilled in using or would I like to try to use experimentally?
- Given the purposes of this course and the type of subject matter being learned, is there a logical order for the treatment of topics?
- How will I know whether this course is progressing satisfactorily?
- How will I know whether this course has been successful and whether certain changes would improve it for future groups of students?

In the first part of this chapter, therefore, we consider what is meant by the 'curriculum' and examine various definitions derived from the literature. In the second part we present a curriculum model that identifies the various elements of the curriculum and relates one to another. Having sketched this broader canvas, in the third part we then offer practical guidance on how individual teachers or groups of teachers could set about designing a geography curriculum and suggest ways in which the design process can be effectively managed. Finally, we illustrate how these principles and procedures can be applied by means of case studies of curriculum design in action.

10.2 DEFINING THE CURRICULUM

Discussion of the 'curriculum' is hindered by the term's wide variety of meanings. The standard dictionary definition, 'a course of study', gives little away. Perhaps the most constructive way of understanding what is meant by 'curriculum' is to contrast it with the more limited term 'syllabus'. A syllabus typically outlines the content of a course on paper. The syllabus specifies the course title and sketches the content areas to be covered, with perhaps the amount of time to be allotted to the different elements, and the main books to be used. Thus the focus of the syllabus is squarely on the subject matter, the aspects of the academic discipline being studied. By contrast, the curriculum goes beyond the overt content of a course to explore matters such as the aims of this portion of higher education, the nature of its teaching methods and assessment, and the changes in the students' knowledge, skills, behaviour and values that the teachers wish to occur. These are matters which we now consider.

Aims and objectives

> . . . *aims* are . . . long distance targets, and *objectives* . . .
> are seen as nearer targets more likely to be hit. (Graves, 1978: 66)

Curriculum theorists have increasingly emphasized aims and objectives, a movement which has served to move thinking away from a subject-centred view of the curriculum towards asking more fundamental questions about the purpose of education – about what we are trying to teach, and how, if at all, that can be achieved through a discipline such as geography. To Powell (1985: 308) the two critical questions are: 'what sort of society for what sort of geography; or if you prefer a more familiar version, what sort of geography for what sort of society?'

This discussion of aims directs us towards philosophical and political issues and towards identifying the educational ideology that we espouse. Scrimshaw (1983: 6) identifies an educational ideology as a 'system of beliefs that gives general direction to the educational policies and activities of those who hold these beliefs'. He distinguishes between five contemporary educational ideologies, which are shown below (Scrimshaw, 1983; summarized by Squires, 1987b: 2):

Progressivism	stresses the needs, aspirations and development of either individuals or communities;
Instrumentalism	stresses utility and relevance to the existing social and economic order, which may itself be static or changing;
Reconstructionism	emphasizes the role of education in bringing about social change;
Classical humanism	stresses the inheritance of knowledge and culture, especially for an elite;
Liberal humanism	aspires to give access to the best in cultural inheritance to everyone.

In a similar vein, Walford (1981c) has argued that many bland or high sounding descriptions of the geography curriculum are underpinned by very different ideological traditions. Decoding these statements, he identifies four such traditions in school geography: liberal humanitarian, child-centred, reconstructionist and utilitarian. The same is true of geography courses in higher education.

Teaching methods and assessment

The curriculum is further distinguished from the syllabus in that it not only asks questions about aims and objectives, but also emphasizes the importance of the teaching methods used and the way the course is assessed. These points, by now, need little elaboration. With respect to *teaching methods*, we have emphasized above that the way that a course is taught profoundly shapes what students experience. Indeed, curriculum theorists would argue that our choice of methods and skill in using in using them may be more significant to what students learn than the content we are overtly teaching. With respect to *assessment*, we pointed out earlier (chapter 8) how the way that a course is assessed also affects what students learn and how they approach their studies.

The hidden curriculum and departmental cultures

The question of the 'hidden curriculum' was also tackled in chapter 8, but it is worth noting here that an entire department can have a hidden curriculum just as an individual class can. Trow (1976) and Parlett (1977) have identified the central role of the department in shaping the wider curriculum which students experience. Parlett observes that:

> Personal experience tends to confirm that we are profoundly affected by features of our education beyond the formal realm of the curriculum: certainly memories years after are often more vivid for context (e.g. place, individuals, atmosphere) than for content [of course and texts] .... The kinds of academic impact alluded to here derive not from the focusing activities relating to teaching and learning themselves, but the context or surroundings in which they occur. (Parlett, 1977: 173)

Parlett examines how the departmental milieu shapes student experience and learning, and illustrates this by contrasting the 'cultures' of two different departments. In an environmental sciences department, 'there was a pronounced set of ideas in currency, held by both students and staff, that centred on the supposed informality existing between them. Annual field trips to remote parts to Scotland were thought particularly important in 'breaking down barriers' between teacher and students'. He contrasts this with the ideology of an experimental science programme at the Massachusetts Institute of Technology, which 'demonstrated a preoccupation with promoting independent learning . . . . [Students] were left in no doubt about how they were expected to work or what cues they should be conscious of for purposes of assessment . . . . They picked up the message that they should learn to manage on their own: [the environmental science students learned] that they could approach staff without fear of a brush-off'.

A thorough review of the geography curriculum at University College London identified that staff perceived a 'departmental traditional of individualism in research as well as teaching, only partly related to the diverse nature of the subject' (Wood, 1980: 1). First year students had picked up 'the latent hostility between physical and human geographers which they detected beneath the surface bonhomie' (Wood, 1980: 5).

Becher (1989) asks whether disciplines themselves or, rather, their practitioners have varying types of discourse or approaches to academic knowledge. In his study of academics in eleven disciplines – one of which was geography – he noted the effect of disciplinary paradigms on patterns of communication and knowledge. Although he focused on academics as researchers rather than as teachers, it can nevertheless help us to ask whether geography or its various manifestations (spatial analysis, environmental systems, humanistic geography and so on) shape the wider curriculum the student learns. For example, Pepper (1983) writes about the way in which many students who have specialized in physical geography pick up a view of science as being concerned with hard facts, and as being essentially objective and value free. Is that what we are really teaching in fluvial geomorphology or is it that many students who choose to study certain courses bring to them a set of values and attributes which shape what they take from the course? Fink's (1977) study showed how students' prior experiences and attitudes shape what they individually take from courses in historical geography, urban geography and meteorology. Thus, in a sense, each student creates an individual curriculum out of the raw material presented by a particular course.

The role of the state

Although in Western 'democracies' the state has traditionally not intruded into the curriculum, leaving matters to professional teachers and administrators, the recent trend has been for more direct intervention. In the USA, for example, an official report by the Education Commission for the States diagnosed 'an overall mismatch between the educational needs of the nation and current practice in undergraduate education' (see Chickering and Ganson, 1987). It defined a series of objectives for colleges, including 'preparing students for citizenship and social responsibility . . . improving overall rates of participation and completion' (particularly for minority students). It also criticized the curriculum in higher education for its 'premature specialization' and criticized faculties for 'not defining and requiring both breadth and depth for the education of their students'.

The Association of American Colleges is similarly critical, and diagnoses a crisis in American college education:

> As for what passes as a college curriculum, almost anything goes . . . . The undergraduate major, the subject . . . in which a student concentrates, everywhere dominates . . . [but] the major in most colleges is little more than a gathering of courses taken in one department, lacking structure and depth . . . or emphasising content in the neglect of the essential style of enquiry on which the content is based . . . . The curriculum has given way to a market place philosophy; it is a supermarket where students are shoppers and professors are merchants of learning . . . . It is as if no one cared as long as the store stayed open. (AAC, 1985: 1-3)

Thus there is increasing recognition that the college curriculum is accountable to public scrutiny, although the amount that occurs varies from country to country. There is also increased pressure to ask fundamental questions about the curriculum's aims and objectives, its coherence, its progression, and the extent to which it contributes to in-depth studies and to a general education.

One of the most significant attempts to get geography courses to answer such questions has come from the work of the Council for National Academic Awards (CNAA) in the United Kingdom. Since 1964, the CNAA has been responsible for vetting and monitoring the quality of degree programmes in the public sector of British higher education and, as such, has been the validating body for the vast majority of geography degree programmes outside the universities. Its charter requires it to analyse the quality of teaching, the resources available and the achievement of students. Its officers, and the academics who visit and inspect degree programmes, are required to ensure that 'courses must have stated aims and objectives which the curriculum, structure, teaching methods and forms of assessment are designed to fulfil' (CNAA, 1988: 55). The CNAA distinguishes between those aims and objectives which are course specific, which clearly relate to the subject matter, and those that develop the 'Council's general educational aims: the development of students' intellectual and imaginative powers; their understanding and judgment; their problem solving skills; their ability to communicate; their ability to see relationships with what they have learned and to perceive their field of study in a broader perspective' (CNAA, 1988).

Although there has been no significant research on the impact that the CNAA has had on geography courses or the geography curriculum, anecdotal evidence and our own experience suggests that its impact has been important (see also Alexander, 1979). It certainly represents a significant attempt to move academics from a subject-centred view of the curriculum, to ask more fundamental educational questions and to ensure progression and coherence in college curricula.

A focus for teachers of geography

The 'curriculum' can take on very different meanings, depending upon what is seen as the focus of formal education. Curriculum theorists have considerably widened our sense of what it is that formal education does. The curriculum, we now see, can mean any, or all, of the following:

- what was intended by teachers before the course began;
- what was 'delivered';
- what was shared and created by the interaction between staff and students, or between student and student;
- what the student(s) have 'achieved' at the end of the course;
- what the students later achieved in the job market;
- that which is remembered, is transferable and usable.

Our concern is with the curriculum in the widest sense. The care that we, as teachers, take in advising students about optional courses, future careers, individual academic and personal concerns, and, perhaps most significant, the attitudes we communicate about knowledge, learning and teaching – all these, and much more, are aspects of the curriculum over which we have control, and all contribute in no small way to what students learn.

Some aspects of curriculum theory can leave us throwing our hands up in despair, for they confront us with the inescapable fact that the wider culture and society severely limit what can be achieved by a course, department or college. They also suggest that the hidden curriculum, and students' and teachers' social class, gender, attitudes and customs all serve to limit what we as teachers can do. One way forward is to recognize these wider social influences explicitly, and then shape the 'hidden curriculum' to make it coincide more closely with the formal curriculum and what we are trying to achieve.

10.3 A CURRICULUM MODEL

Figure 10.1 presents the curriculum as an interaction between aims and objectives, methods of assessment, teaching methods and content (Graves, 1978).

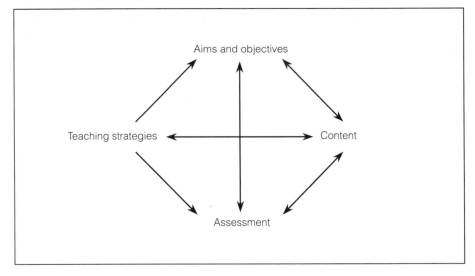

Figure 10.1   Graves' curriculum model
Source: Graves (1978)

Changing one element will affect the others and what the student learns. Suppose, for example, that the decision is made to change a course's assessment to a synoptic take-home essay instead of objective style tests. This change will almost certainly transform how students will approach the course material and what they learn without changing the overt content of the course or even necessarily the teaching strategies. Aims and objectives would be transformed regardless of whether they had ever been explicitly formulated.

This acts as a basis for a more detailed model (designed by Cowan and Harding, 1986) that recognizes the complexity of the curriculum but which centres on what teachers can do. The model (figure 10.2) shows elements which affect both one another and the curriculum that is designed and delivered. As can be seen, *aims* are the central concern. According to Cowan and Harding, nothing that takes place in the course is relevant or purposeful unless it serves to further these aims. That is why strong arrows thrust out from aims towards all the items in the perimeter. Decisions about what should be taught, by whom, to whom and with what resources are shaped by a variety of external pressures: accrediting agencies, professional standards, ideologies, government and so on. In figure 10.2, these are represented by a further set of arrows directed inwards, indicating that groups of teachers and students have little say in shaping these constraints.

The first item on the perimeter is *assessment*; the model emphasizes its close link to aims and objectives. Having defined the course objectives, Cowan and

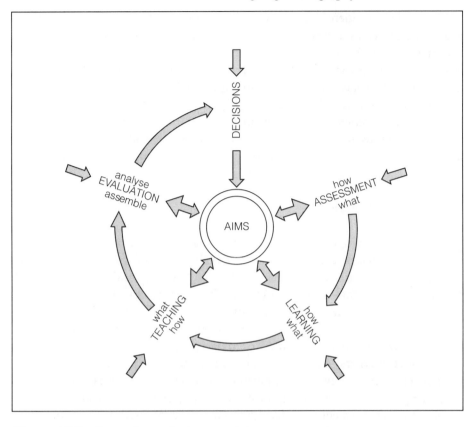

Figure 10.2 Cowan's curriculum model
Source: after Cowan and Harding (1986)

Harding argue that one should then be able to formulate a system of assessment that is compatible with these objectives. Alternatively, having started by defining a possible assessment system, one can see whether it is compatible with one's aims. The close connection established in the model between objectives and assessment is a way of ensuring that the hidden curriculum matches the official curriculum.

After dealing with assessment, one needs to consider how students learn (Hounsell, 1979). The model does not specify a particular viewpoint on this matter: it merely asks us first to consider how we think students learn before considering how teaching can facilitate that learning. *Teaching* is here defined as 'the deliberate contrivance of situations in which worthwhile learning may take place effectively and efficiently'. For our purposes, this definition provides a view of the curriculum that centres upon what we as teachers (and students) can do and recognizes teaching as encompassing a variety of strategies.

The model also identifies a close link between teaching and *evaluation*, for evaluation can communicate back to the teacher, and student, something of the effectiveness of the teaching and learning strategies used. Evidence from evaluation may indicate whether our aims are being achieved, and this can help us to decide to change aspects of assessment, learning or teaching.

Armed with this model, we have an effective systems view of the curriculum that is useful in thinking through the many issues involved in curriculum design. Our task now is to turn from a structural view of the curriculum, and to introduce an action-orientated view of how to approach the design process itself.

10.4 THE DESIGN PROCESS

There are many ways of tackling curriculum design, but an analogy which affords valuable insights is provided by the development of computer software. Commercial software is a product with a high intellectual, conceptual and technical content, that is usually produced by teams rather than by individuals and is typically destined for use by a diverse set of consumers. Complex items of software, like other manufactured products, are usually structured internally into a number of smaller modules, each carrying out a specific function and each related to others in a hierarchical fashion. Information is passed between certain modules in a carefully controlled manner, and there is usually a co-ordinating component at the topmost level that organizes the operation of the whole and presents a coherent face to the user. There are three ways in which one can manage the design of such software, which we term 'bottom-up', 'top-down' and 'middle-out' modes.

A considerable amount of modular software has been, and still is, developed in a *'bottom-up'* manner. Low level components or modules are created early on in the design process, and these are then 'bolted together' at a later stage to form higher level components, and eventually a complete functioning package. Two arguments are frequently used to support this approach. First, low level software components are often readily available, either accumulated from previous software design efforts or acquired from external sources. The use of such components, it is argued, prevents reinventing wheels and shortens the development effort. Second, a new item of software is by its very nature extremely difficult to define precisely at the outset; its shape and content only become apparent when the designers have created an initial product, seen how this operates in relation to client needs and user characteristics and then modified it so that it fits more closely what is required.

You may see similarities between the bottom-up approach to software design and traditional curriculum design methods. For example, it is not uncommon for lecture notes developed for use on one degree programme to find their way into a new one, for a practical laboratory project that has been successful in one course unit to be incorporated into another course unit or for a commercially available role-playing game to be adopted as the cornerstone of a new course. The re-use of available curriculum materials seems both sensible and cost effective. However, although the bottom-up approach can work successfully with relatively small products designed by a single person, it rapidly falls down when applied to complex products created by teams of designers.

It is now widely accepted that complex and hierarchically organized software products benefit from being designed in a *top-down* fashion. This approach involves defining the overarching design concept first, before designing individual components to fit this general concept, in terms of both their function and how they engage the user. Top-down design ensures both the consistency and the integrity of the final product. In the context of curriculum design, the top-down process would begin with the course team agreeing on a set of common goals or aims. These might include the following:

- a logical progression of content and skills from year to year, with students offered the opportunity for increasing specialization as they proceed through the degree programme;
- deferred student choice;
- inclusion of vocational skills and active learning throughout the degree programme, and not just within a separate statistics, cartography or computing course;
- assessment methods clearly linked to overall course objectives;
- working within agreed resourcing levels for all course units;
- adoption of a 'core-and-modules' framework, with modules building explicitly on the content of a clearly defined core.

Top-down design, of itself, is not enough to achieve these goals. Members of the design team must also arrive at a consensus view, and strong management is needed to ensure that objectives and standards are clearly defined and adhered to. In the software industry, as in most manufacturing contexts, the broad design goals are usually worked out by a small group of experts and then 'handed down' to lower-level personnel for implementation. The strong hierarchical management structure of most commercial organisations is purpose-built for this style of control.

However, this strict form of control over the design process leads critics to suggest that a top-down approach is inappropriate for curriculum design. They argue that it can lead to the production of a rather emasculated product if it is applied too rigidly, and that individual contributions will inevitably lack flair, inventiveness and commitment. They also argue that it easily generates dictatorial styles of course management that fail to incorporate ideas from all those involved. We would agree with this criticism if these failings were to result from adopting the top-down approach, but would argue that the approach does not of itself lead to this style of curriculum development. It is perfectly compatible for top-down design principles to be defined by contributions from *all* members of the course team and democratically agreed by them. Indeed, once a set of agreed aims is in place, the curriculum design team could bring in a manager to co-ordinate their subsequent design efforts and ensure that the agreed principles found their way down to lower levels of the curriculum design.

In general, then, a top-down approach is important in developing a shared sense of vision for a course, and for ensuring that aims are clearly defined and that these aims find their way into the entire curriculum. Perhaps the key ingredient in making a success of the approach is the formal involvement of all appropriate team members in the decision-making process at all levels of the design. Several mechanisms can be adopted to encourage participation and to elicit ideas: such as brainstorming sessions, creative play, interviewing and counselling. Principles of group dynamics can also be used to help staff to arrive at a consensus view, with a skilled 'facilitator' being brought in if members of the team need help in confronting and resolving any differences.

To the bottom-up and top-down approaches must be added the *middle-out* approach, which is felt by many to combine the best of these two approaches. According to this view, one concentrates on the middle tier of product development throughout the design process and 'shuttles' iteratively between higher and lower levels, moving upwards to ensure that strategic issues are refined and newly emergent principles are taken on board, and moving downwards to take advantage of already crafted lower level components.

Our collective experience suggests that the middle-out approach is commonly used when defining and re-designing geography degree programmes. If pressed, most of us will admit to defining our own course units in some detail early on in the course review process, and then submitting them to other members of the course team so that a common framework can emerge for all modules designed in a similar way. Subsequently, we move down to the lowest level of design, filling in the detail of individual syllabuses.

There are several advantages to the middle-out approach to curriculum design:

- individuals have control over the shaping of what they teach;
- it usually encourages greater involvement by individual teachers and generates more creative thinking;
- a variety of ideas can come forward that may be more widely and beneficially used;

- it provides a democratic framework in which all members of the team feel involved;
- it allows certain tasks (e.g. fieldwork, first year 'core' courses, skills teaching) to be devolved to small groups whose explorations can subsequently inform and reshape top level principles.

The danger with this approach is that the middle and lower tiers of the curriculum tend to receive the greatest attention – because these are the stuff of day-to-day teaching, whereas strategic issues at the upper level tend, at best, to be defined in a cursory fashion. When lip service has been paid, these principles are then largely neglected in the subsequent design work lower down the hierarchy. At worst, the middle-out approach can degenerate into a bottom-up style of design, with the result that the upper levels are ignored almost entirely and the entire design process is driven from below – in the proverbial manner of the tail wagging the dog.

Clearly, each of these three broad approaches to managing the curriculum design process has its merits. Each can be used as an appropriate and effective management tool in certain circumstances and there is no optimal style for all curricula or for all design teams.

10.5 DESIGNING THE CURRICULUM

A course team can approach the question of designing the curriculum in a variety of different ways. In this section, we discuss seven different approaches to design that are commonly employed. These are designing through aims and objectives, designing through subject matter, building on teacher motivations, designing for those with political power, designing for resource availability, refining the existing curriculum and designing for individual student needs.

Designing through aims and objectives

Starting from first principles with aims and objectives is one important approach to curriculum design. Aims are general statements which relate to the broad philosophical, and sometimes political, orientation of the course; objectives are more explicit, specifying 'what students should be able to do (or do better) as a result of working through their course' (Rowntree, 1981a: 421).

Explicitly specifying aims and objectives has advantages for the course team, since it forces them to crystallize and clarify elements that they may not have fully articulated previously. It is a particularly useful procedure when new staff are brought together to design a course or for a group of staff who have worked so long together that most of the aims are assumed and rarely discussed. For the latter, discussing aims and objectives can bring these issues back into the open and help teachers re-examine the extent to which there is basic agreement. At the same time, it should be recognized that an approach which concentrates on aims and objectives can generate considerable conflict, for it highlights the different political and educational ideologies of the participating staff. Handling that conflict, and bringing it constructively into the open, requires everyone to exercise skill and good sense. One method that can be used to good effect in such situations is to bring in an external curriculum design consultant, or a group counsellor, who can help the design team resolve their differences (e.g. see Bramley and Wood, 1982).

There are many suggestions about appropriate *aims*. Some geographers have explicitly stated that the college geography curriculum should reflect more philosophical and political viewpoints. Romey and Elberty (1980), for example, have developed a person-centred approach based on Rogers's (1969) view that 'self initiated learning which involves the whole person of the learner, (feelings, as well as intellect) is the most lasting and pervasive' (Romey and Elberty, 1980: 62). Powell (1985: 32) has argued that a 'humanist perspective' should give geography 'a renewed belief in the value of geography but a geography that emphasizes place and region, improved cooperation between human and physical camps . . . and in general a heightened regard for the teaching function'. It may be significant that those geographers who emphasize education as facilitating social change (particularly through environmental education) have been more explicit about how the college curriculum should be designed to achieve their aims (e.g. see O'Riordan, 1981; Huckle, 1983; Jenkins, 1985; Fien and Gerber, 1986; Pepper, 1987).

Much of the early work on curriculum design through *objectives* was done by behavioural psychologists who argued that learning outcomes should be observable and measurable. Particularly important here was the work of Bloom (1956) and his colleagues with their division of objectives into cognitive, affective and psychomotor categories (see chapter 8). For example, Rowntree (1974) describes a course in terms of its objectives, arguing that explicit behavioural objectives have the following advantages:

- They make it possible for teachers to communicate their intentions more clearly to colleagues and students. Where more than one lecturer is involved in teaching a course, asking questions about aims and objectives also helps to draw out aspects of the collaboration between them into open discussion.
- They provide a framework for the selection of course content and structure.

- They guide the selection of appropriate teaching and learning methods.
- They help the teacher to decide what are the most appropriate means of evaluation and assessment.

Those involved have to decide whether to take a 'reductionist' approach to objectives, attempting to specify objectives in a very prescriptive and detailed manner. (For Keller style courses, described in chapter 6, this is an essential design stage.)

The basis of behavioural schemes has been questioned in recent works. Some have also questioned the value of defining objectives too precisely, for it can lead to a reductionist approach in which we seek to define and measure the unimportant (MacDonald-Ross, 1973). Others have questioned the view of many curriculum theorists that one should start planning a course by first defining one's aims and objectives. Rowntree (1981a: 35), in a later work, notes that one reason he moved away from this position is that he came to 'realise that my course planning does not necessarily begin with objectives'. However, he adds 'this certainly does not mean I am renouncing objectives. I still believe they are extremely valuable in course development.'

In our opinion, objectives need to be stated sufficiently clearly for the teacher (or students, or external assessors) to be able to recognize whether or not they have been achieved. To do so, it is important to define as precisely as possible what it is we require students to do. Table 10.1, for example, indicates some of the caution that is needed with wording.

Table 10.1　The importance of wording

Avoid words like	Use words like
Know	List
Understand	Describe
Be familiar with	Evaluate
Become acquainted with	State
Have a good grasp of	Explain
Obtain a working knowledge of	Select

Before leaving this discussion, we must enter a few words of caution concerning aims and objectives.

- Except in specific training contexts, teachers' aims and objectives will inevitably be somewhat open ended. This should not deter a design team from attempting to pin them down, where appropriate, and should certainly not lead to supposedly 'fuzzy' goals being rejected out of hand.

- Aims and objectives will often change during a course, partly in response to student concerns.
- Students can usefully be involved in specifying course objectives – particularly in a course where students and staff negotiate a contract specifying what students will do during and as a result of taking a course. Objectives can be a good way of defining such a course.
- Objectives should not only be stated for a degree course as a whole; they should also be devised for individual sections of a course.
- Objectives should not be specified only for the geographical content of a course. Skills, values, vocational, social and cultural objectives should be equally scrutinized from this particular perspective.
- A great deal of time and effort can be spent in specifying aims and objectives to the *n*th degree. This can detract from much needed effort elsewhere, and may also result in an extremely mechanistic curriculum, from which anything that cannot be explicitly specified has been removed.

Designing through subject matter

Experience suggests that few academics start organizing their own specialist courses or a departmental curriculum by specifying aims and objectives. A member of the Nuffield group that analysed aspects of British university education in the 1970s observed that 'the impression I gained from this experience was of a predominantly subject-centred attitude to teaching and learning... This involves an approach to teaching that begins with the subject matter and seeks optimum ways of communicating it to students' (Hewton: 1987, 178). We support his criticism of the limitations of this method, but at a minimal level one has to recognize that for many teachers in higher education 'their subject or their field is in many ways their identity, even their life' (Squires, 1987a: 177). We shall continue this theme in the next section, where we discuss how to build a curriculum through staff motivations.

Even if our aims are about developing certain skills, whether these be at the level of being able to use an academic library or at the level of critical reasoning, then this requires subject matter through which to develop those skills. Many geographers would see that one of the fundamental values of a geographic education is that its diverse subject matter can enable a broad range of skills to be developed (Johnston et al., 1989). From this standpoint, the geography curriculum needs to provide opportunities to develop the various skills considered central by the course team.

What considerations, therefore, do we need to bear in mind when approaching the subject matter? A number of questions readily spring to mind:

- What are the central features of geography as an academic discipline? Many foci have been suggested for modern geography: spatial analytic, environmentalist, humanistic and so on. To which paradigmatic view, or combination of such views, does the course team subscribe?

- What are the central ideas and concepts of academic geography? Bennetts (1972: 50) has argued that 'if we wish to show our students what geography has to offer, in terms of the type of understanding it has achieved, we must identify the organising concepts and principles that summarise geographer's current thinking.' This was the route that the American High School Geography Project took in the 1960s as it sought 'to define the internal *structure* of geographic thought' (AAG, 1968: 3, emphasis added).

- What are the *intellectual* links, if any, between the various areas of the discipline: between physical and human geography; between systematic and regional specialities; between applied and theoretical foci; between analysis at local, regional and international scales?

- What is the best way of getting students to understand the internal logic and structure of the discipline? At the very least this requires an understanding of how students learn. A key influence on the school geography curriculum has been the work of Bruner (1960), who argued that 'if earlier learning is to render later learning easier, it must do so by providing a "general picture" in terms of which the relations between things encountered earlier and later are made as clear as possible' (quoted by Bennetts, 1972: 50). This is the rationale for what Bruner termed the 'spiral curriculum', which has evident implications for ensuring that the key concepts that are central to a final year compulsory course unit are first introduced in simpler more basic forms in programmes in the earlier years.

- What are the basic facts or empirical geographic material that are essential to a geographic understanding?

- What are the fundamental relations between geography and other disciplines? What other forms of knowledge and understanding can and should be developed through a geography curriculum? For example, if one shares Gould's (1973) view of the central role of mathematics as a language of academic discourse and understanding, there are clear implications for the subject matter of your geography degree programmes.

- Academically and educationally, what are the central reasons for students studying geography? Is it to acquaint them with the facts and concepts of the discipline? Is it more important that they learn the mode of enquiry of the discipline? Should there be greater emphasis on the application of the discipline and a greater readiness to jettison certain theoretical issues? Should students focus on the discipline as it is, as it will be or as it should be?

In building a curriculum through subject matter, it is important to move back and forth between quite detailed considerations (e.g. how does the advanced geomorphology course relate to the introductory physical geography course), and then move up to more general questions about the nature of the discipline. In doing this, it is useful to recognize that views about the discipline relate to wider philosophical questions about the purpose of higher education. Thus a review of the geography course at University College London showed there were contrasts, and conflicts, between those who viewed 'geography as offering primarily a generally multi-disciplinary training in the study of man–environment problems (*sic*) and those, mainly in physical and quantitative geography, who saw an important element of their teaching as developing a specialist, progressive, technical or scientific expertise' (Wood, 1980: 8). In other words, approaching curriculum design through considering subject matter should also lead one to use other approaches, in this case back to fundamental educational aims and objectives.

Building on teacher motivations

A limitation of narrowly prescriptive approaches based on aims and objectives is that they can ignore the personal needs and motivations of the staff who will teach a course. From the outset, we have counselled the need to accept the realities of academic life and recognize that teaching is only one area of the teacher's professional responsibility. We therefore stress that curriculum design should consider these issues, because staff motivations are central to the success or failure of the curriculum.

For instance, in designing a first year course, a group of staff may decide that the development of a resource-based package could be a first step towards producing a published textbook. The course may well be a better one if it capitalizes on that opportunity. In designing a curriculum, it is worth recognizing that student evaluations of courses and teachers consistently emphasize that the teachers' interest in and knowledge of their subject matter are central to the success of the course. Similarly, in choosing teaching methods, individuals know which ones they feel most comfortable with, and those which they think that they use most effectively. We should not feel guilty if we do not automatically start from questions such as: How do we think students most effectively learn? What are our aims and objectives? What are the chief epistemological directions in contemporary geography?

As an example of how teachers can find scope for developing their personal interests within their teaching, consider the undergraduate geography programme offered at an Australian university, which will remain anonymous. The details are all taken from the published departmental handbook.

In the first year of the geography programme, students are required to take two, semester-long courses: 'Introduction to Human Geography' and 'Introduction to Physical Geography'. At this level, the goal is to provide a broad coverage of the subject matter and to provide a suitable basis for future work. Nevertheless, the course descriptions suggest that, even at this stage, research interests play a significant role in shaping course content. The introductory human geography course, for example, focuses on industrial location, financial changes, trade and migration, and the influence of political systems. It also considers human adjustment, perception and the use of different environments in the Southwest Pacific. The choice of these topics clearly reflects the orientations of the two course teachers: a Marxist economic geographer whose work deals with structural changes in industry and a development geographer with interests in migration and the South Pacific. This said, however, the inclusion of regional examples drawn from outside their research interests also demonstrates a commitment to breadth of study at the introductory level.

In the second year of the course, three strands are offered: principles of geomorphology, environment and resources, and human geography. Thus, for example, geomorphology is the only branch of physical geography offered and, within geomorphology, three of the four units (coastal fluvial and cold climate landforms) are part of the research field of the person teaching the course.

In the third year, the staff teach specialized topics of most interest to them; courses have titles such as: 'Rock Weathering', 'Rural Development in South East Asia', 'Economic Geography of the Pacific Rim' and 'Coastal Morphodynamics'. Some course titles are broader ('Urban Social Geography' or 'Third World Development', for example), but the descriptions in the handbook reveal that teaching remains closely tied to the places in which the teachers conduct their research.

A curriculum of this kind clearly permits teachers to combine their research interests quite closely with their teaching assignments, especially if most of their teaching is undertaken at a post-introductory level. Such a pattern helps to sustain staff motivation for teaching, and, at the same time, provides students with clear expertise in particular subject areas. However this approach to course design has its limitations.

- Centring too closely on staff motivations may lead to an unbalanced curriculum. Recognition of staff interests might need to be counterbalanced by asking a significant number of staff to undertake 'bread and butter' teaching outside their immediate sphere of interest.

- It leads to a conservative and somewhat reactionary curriculum. Individual members of the course team may well attempt to block changes that threaten to remove or emasculate their 'pet' course unit from the curriculum.

- It can totally ignore students' background needs and interests. However fascinated a teacher might be with recent research in atmospheric physics or post-modernist criticism, first year courses are probably not the place to pursue those interests.

- Creating a close liaison between teaching and research may make the former take far lower priority than the latter, and provide a spurious rationalization for poor teaching.

Designing for those with political power

Here one starts by asking who are the 'actors' in the system – the people and interest groups concerned. These include immediate colleagues, the various internal committees through which any major course review has to pass, any external bodies that might review and validate a course, students, librarians, technicians and secretaries. For each actor, one asks what they want from the curriculum and then what power they have to block or encourage it.

There may well be no alternative to this approach if one wants to have a preferred curriculum accepted. Innovations in, say, teaching or assessment procedures that do not conform to the norms of the college may mean shaping part of the curriculum, or presenting it in a particular way, to meet the views of those with political power or collaborating with other departments or course teams to lobby for a change in the rules.

Jones (1986) reports an example of this when describing how teaching staff worked to develop a resource-based learning package for a final year core geography course that saved class-contact hours. They had to reach agreement with their institution so that they were not penalized for their efforts at reducing teaching by being assigned additional teaching duties to replace the class-contact hours that they had apparently lost. A second example comes from the University of Alabama, where the geography department was faced with the imminent loss of the laboratory status of its introductory physical geography courses (Lineback and Harlin, 1987). The course team acted immediately to meet the criticisms of the university's powerful 'core curriculum' committee, modifying the courses so that the practical work undertaken by students involved 'hands-on' experimentation – the key defining criterion of a laboratory course set down by this committee.

Designing for resource availability

Many departments have very limited control over many aspects of the curriculum. The institution may decide the overall goals and, in association with higher level authorities, allocate resources: money, staff, space and equipment. Decisions on student enrolment, the overall degree structure, timetable, acceptable methods of assessment and much more may already have been decided before the geography department can sit down to shape the curriculum. A clear task of the course team is therefore to identify these decisions and constraints.

Once the resources and the inevitable constraints have been identified, course teams are then in a position to consider what shape the curriculum can take within this framework. For example, does one structure the curriculum to ensure that the introductory course gains – and subsequently holds – students from across the college? If so, then this might mean cancelling those optional courses which attract few students, even though they may be of great interest to individual staff (Douglas, 1986), and allocating resources to organize and teach mass classes effectively (Weimer, 1987). Such constraints, as we have already emphasised in our earlier discussion of curriculum models, can have an impact throughout the system: on the educational aims, teaching, learning, assessment and evaluation that a department adopts.

Naturally, the precise nature of the constraints varies over time and from institution to institution, but what we have highlighted here is the need to ask questions imposed by this external framework, such as the following.

- How is it done here?
- In what way are we expected to specify the curriculum?
- Are we required to set out aims and objectives and specify the hours students should spend on assignments?
- Must we insist that all formal assessment be through unseen written examinations?
- Is the institution mainly concerned with whether booklists are up to date?

It may be possible to set out an overt curriculum in line with institutional requirements and then teach a different 'hidden curriculum' or it may be possible to change that which is customary. Either way, this brings one back to considering who has political power.

Refining the existing curriculum

Curriculum planning rarely starts off with a clean slate. An existing curriculum is usually in operation, with a set of agreed aims and objectives worked out some time previously. Curriculum change may be the pragmatic task of refining the current curriculum, caused by any one of innumerable causes – poor course evaluation, increasing student enrolments, major changes in resources, changes in staff, desire for innovation and improvement, major increases in intakes of mature students and demands for the provision of new sets of skills. Whatever the reason, it is inevitable that the curriculum never reaches a final optimal condition: there is simply too much change in the educational system for this to happen.

The design approach that many others use, often unwittingly, to devise the curriculum in such circumstances may be termed iterative problem-solving, (as shown in figure 10.3). In this scheme, there is a cyclical process of design and re-design. At each stage of the cycle goals are specified, a curriculum is designed and implemented to match these goals, and evaluation is carried out. This leads on to the next phase of re-design, as a deliberate strategy. Critics might call this approach 'bodging'; proponents among management theorists have elevated it to the status of a science – 'the science of muddling through' (Lindblom, 1959).

Designing for individual student needs

Most of the preceding approaches assume that a single coherent curriculum will be delivered in a comparatively undifferentiated way to large numbers of students, over a period of years. This is the *table d'hôte* approach to curriculum design. More bluntly, it represents the view that the teachers are the experts. This view of the curriculum is often accompanied by the use of lectures to impart knowledge to large groups of students, with only marginal attempts being made to

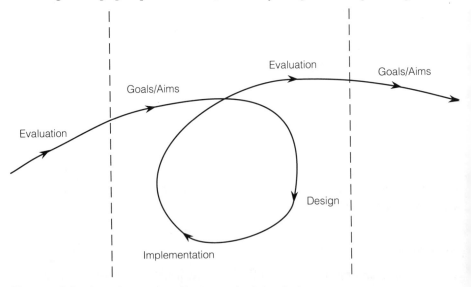

Figure 10.3　Iterative approach to curriculum design

assist individual students, perhaps by means of small group tutorials, the dispensing of personal advice in corridors or coffee bars and occasional tailored assignments.

On several occasions in this chapter, and throughout this book, we have advocated student-centred approaches to geography teaching. Examples have been described of how teaching can be tailored to individual students including self-paced mastery exercises, resource-based learning material and computer assisted learning activities. We have also considered ways in which we can determine what students know when they enter a course or course unit and what they expect from a course, and have suggested how this knowledge can be used to meet student needs better.

However, in most instances, the geographical aims and content of our courses remain the same for all students; it is largely the 'delivery' that varies in its timing, pace and sequence from student to student. The question that we invite you to consider here is this: To what extent can our attempts at individualizing the teaching process be extended to the design of the curriculum? In other words, can students be made part and parcel of the curriculum design process itself and, if so, is it possible for students to design their own personal curricula?

There are a number of ways in which students can be enabled, and not just allowed, to devise a curriculum of their own:

- by taking one or more optional modules within a more conventionally structured geography course (many geography courses now provide a 'free choice' course unit);
- by putting together a collection of course units which approximates to a personal conception of an ideal curriculum – most likely in the context of a modular degree scheme;
- by negotiating an individual curriculum with the course team, which is comparatively rare in higher education but found increasingly in technical training institutions and a normal part of many industrial training schemes (see chapter 4). (Boud, 1988, and Knowles, 1986, provide case studies and general principles of curricula in higher education that centre on individual student needs.)

This particular challenge is perhaps one of the most difficult for course teams to deal with effectively. Nevertheless, we are convinced that a carefully considered attempt to meet student needs through personalized curricula can produce major rewards for teachers and taught alike.

10.6 CURRICULUM DESIGN IN PRACTICE

In the final section of this chapter, we turn from general principles to curriculum design in action. Three detailed case studies are presented, each of which describes how a curriculum was actually designed by geographers. In the first case study we consider curriculum design at the level of an entire degree course, in the second we consider the re-design of the core elements of a graduate training course and in the third we consider curriculum design at the level of a single undergraduate course unit. Together, we hope that these illustrate some of the design principles outlined earlier in the chapter, but stress that they are not meant as blueprints or as exemplars of good practice. On the contrary, they have been chosen to reveal the frequent messiness and arbitrariness of much curriculum design, the various levels at which design takes place, the variety of approaches that are possible in any given circumstance and the difficult problems faced by curriculum designers as they struggle to design an educational product in a continually shifting environment and alongside the continuing day-to-day effort of teaching.

Case study 1

Our first case study concerns the design of an entire degree course in human geography within the Department of Geography at Queen Mary and Westfield College (QMW), University of London. The main reason for the review of QMW's human geography programme was a sudden and very large turnover of teaching staff. Within a period of 6 months, two staff left the department, four renegotiated their contracts under an early retirement scheme (which reduced their teaching obligations to one-third of the previous level), two existing staff were appointed to full-time posts and a new full-time member of staff was appointed, with intimations that a further appointment might soon materialize.

The pressure for a curriculum review had been building up for some time. First, both staff and students felt that the content of the curriculum was too idiosyncratic, in that aspects of it were insufficiently well integrated over the 3 years of the course. Second, there was concern that inadequate attention was being paid to teaching and learning strategies and styles. Third, there were broader factors contributing to the need to re-design the human geography curriculum, including the probable advent of external evaluation of teaching practice in the department, financial stringency and the imminent introduction of a new degree in Geography and Business Economics.

These pressures profoundly affected, indeed dominated, the decision to implement a curriculum review at QMW, the way that the review proceeded, the things that were excluded from the review, the things that remain to be done and the response to these omissions. The review's main – but hidden – objective became one of establishing a new curriculum suitable to the new circumstances, including the need for pedagogic improvement. The centrality of aims and the interlinked elements of the curriculum received far less consideration and had little opportunity to influence the design of the new human geography curriculum.

Once the new curriculum was in place and there was time for reflection, the gaps seemed to be major deficiencies and have necessitated an annual review of the curriculum. This, in itself, has had beneficial side-effects. It has demonstrated the desirability of diversity within the curriculum and has instituted a process in which there is a clearly structured set of indicators as to what is being done and why. Nevertheless, the urgency of the QMW review led to one feature which may not be quite so desirable, namely that it was dominated by a concern for content. In saying this, it should be noted that this concern was not simply forced onto the review team by dint of circumstances, since it also reflected the prevailing beliefs within the department. The promotion and conservation of scholarship in human geography forms the basis of the hidden curriculum at QMW and helps to explain the predominant role within the course structure of the content of conventionally defined fields of human geography. However, this objective was also seen as a means of creating a student-centred curriculum which stresses the potential of higher education: to enhance the possibilities for individuals to lead fulfilling lives; to develop their own academic interests; to offer a substantial grounding in theory, method and empirical understanding; to ensure the development of specific and transferable skills; to enhance the employability of its graduates.

The student-orientated perspective within a content-driven curriculum was reinforced by the continued existence of a diversity of teaching methods which are valued for their own sake rather than for the contribution that they can make to teaching practice within a particular course (see the third case study). Thus the teaching of the content of particular course units at QMW may be dominated by lectures, but small group teaching is facilitated through a separate tutorial programme which has a content that is influenced by the concerns of lecture, practical and project courses. The detachment of this programme allows a more critical and evaluative stance on the part of both tutor and students.

Similarly, the existence of a wide variety of assessment methods within the new curriculum ensures that, if the teaching experience is one-sided in its stress upon the lecture, then the learning experience is not. First year students, for example, receive twenty 1-hour tutorials in groups smaller than six in size; second year students have ten such tutorials and third year students have six. Likewise, fieldwork courses are run which are both specific to particular courses and general across a particular cohort of students. The amount of assessment attached to such sessions varies from course to course, but their main objective is to open another window onto the processes of teaching, learning and investigation – and so to understanding.

A major objective yet to be discussed is the provision of training for independent empirical enquiry, which reaches its culmination in the final year with each student writing a 10,000 word dissertation. There is a range of problems endemic to such a project, including the use of knowledge and techniques carried over from earlier courses and the extent of supervision offered. The perennially difficult question of teaching techniques of geographical enquiry is of particular relevance here, in that the traditional isolation of techniques facilitates the transfer of knowledge but limits the understanding of its significance in empirical research. This problem underpinned one of the major complaints voiced by the students of the previous curriculum at QMW: that insufficient attention was paid to the use of techniques in empirical research and to the role of empirical research in human geography as a scholarly discipline. The response was to concentrate much of the basic practical teaching in the first year, followed up in the second year by a more advanced course and by a tutorial programme which, in the second term, stresses the preparation for research on the final year dissertation. This must be completed by the first week of the second term in the third year and so, in the first term of the third year, tutorials are used in part to discuss the writing up of the project. In this way, not only are the crucial relationships between theory and practice in research explored throughout the three years, but the methods of supervised research are incorporated into the undergraduate programme as a whole.

Overall, the procedure adopted in making and implementing the curriculum review was one of eliciting responses from all concerned on whether a review was necessary, identifying what the aims of a new curriculum should be, and gathering suggestions on content, assessment and teaching methods. As these discussions progressed, written reports on the progress of the deliberations were fed back to the individuals who make up the department. Several meetings then negotiated the content of the curriculum and made a first attempt at establishing teaching responsibilities. Convenors were appointed for each course and made responsible for preparing detailed course outlines (including details of assessment and teaching methods) which were to be submitted to the departmental curriculum meeting. This meeting reviewed course content, but was primarily concerned with teaching methods and assessment so as to ensure a reasonable diversity across the programme as a whole. Parallel meetings involving all staff were also held on the nature and role of the tutorial programme and fieldwork in the new curriculum, and the teaching of techniques in the first year also received design attention from all staff.

The whole of the process was co-ordinated by the departmental tutor to undergraduate students – an appropriate task – but the identification of the review with this one individual led to the growing and wholly erroneous belief that the review was somehow her responsibility alone rather than the joint responsibility of all concerned. This is a crucial point, because any serious review of the curriculum will challenge not only long held and cherished beliefs and practices but will also challenge established sources of power, uncover or cause inequalities in workload and may result in most of the changed workload falling unevenly on one or two individuals.

This brings us back to the point that the review of the curriculum should be a continuous process. It should be seen as a departmental responsibility (rather than the responsibility of a particular individual), and should be 'top-down' and tightly managed. At the same time it should respect the wishes of individual teachers within the framework set by departmental discussions, and should not necessarily cover all aspects of the curriculum at once.

Case study 2

Our second case study continues the theme of revising an existing curriculum but, in contrast with the previous example, it examines what stimulated an American university geography department to revise just part of its graduate programme. In this case study, we shall explore assumptions that influenced the decision to design from the top, the procedures used in the process of revision and the outcomes.

Several circumstances prompted the decision to undertake this review. To some extent, it was part of a review process that normally occurs every few years, but the teaching staff were also aware that the broader context had gradually changed since the last review. The size of the teaching and student bodies had increased sharply and specific aspects of the programme were generating dissatisfaction. Prominent amongst the latter were a dearth of topical seminars, dissatisfaction with two compulsory courses, and confusion over the purpose of the qualifying examinations that all students take in their first semester to identify individual deficiencies and assess their suitability to be retained in the programme. Both the content and the brevity of the examination seemed to hinder achievement of the course objectives.

As for the two problem courses, the goal of the first was to move students towards articulating an individual research problem by having them develop a research proposal that they twice presented orally in a public colloquium – once as a preliminary statement and subsequently as a refined effort. The time allotted to each student was relatively short, as was the time set aside for critique. The second required course had multiple objectives: introducing new students to the department, to trends in research and to the process of doing research. To accomplish these objectives, each faculty member met with a class comprising primarily incoming graduate students and defined his or her own particular contribution. However, this format did not seem successful for accomplishing the desired goals. The department therefore decided that it was time to re-assess the structure of both the master's and the doctoral programmes, and especially to examine the core courses required of all students.

In analysing this case study, it is worthwhile noting several assumptions, common to most American graduate programmes, which influence curriculum design. There is an implicit notion that the main objective of graduate education is to prepare research scholars, although the needs of master's candidates who are seeking non-academic employment are also catered for. In our case study department, such overarching objectives were not discussed, simply understood. Second, there is an assumption that, although postgraduate programmes will be individualized, some common core is also needed to introduce all students to research issues.

Earlier in this chapter, we commented on the politics of the curriculum and who has power to influence decisions. In this instance, students as well as teaching staff were defined as relevant actors – a common practice in American graduate departments. The department head appointed a four-person curriculum committee, which included one graduate student member, to review the core programme. The committee developed a detailed questionnaire to survey the opinions of teaching staff and graduate students about each element of the programme. They tabulated responses to both closed and open-ended questions, separating out responses from teachers, doctoral students and master's students. In addition, teaching staff on the committee interviewed their colleagues and the student representative interviewed other students. Finally, the committee also surveyed the nature of the core curriculum at ten other institutions which, it felt, provided appropriate models for the department. With all these data compiled, the committee reported its findings to a meeting of the teaching staff and representatives of the graduate student body. They made recommendations for change, drawing especially on the responses to the open-ended questions in the survey.

This labour-intensive procedure produced inconclusive results. Even though students were able to express their views anonymously on the written questionnaire, their dissatisfactions were couched in milder terms than previously had been voiced and they did not advocate discontinuing requirements of the type included in the core. The consensus of students and teaching staff was that a common introductory course for graduate students was indeed needed, but that it should have more coherence. However, just what its content and style should be was not expressed nor did it emerge. Instead, the form of the new course was set by a newly hired teacher who assumed responsibility for its teaching. It became largely a review of alternative contemporary approaches to research in human geography, the format being student discussions of assigned readings.

Virtually no one disputed that the history of geographic thought should be an element of the core. On this point, the only recurring criticism voiced in the survey responses was that the course should include a greater proportion of recent material. No formal recommendations were made regarding this change, and since the course is the domain of a single teacher, mandating revision would be contrary to the institutional culture. Further, the changed nature of the other core course may have negated the need for revision of the historical course. Likewise, neither teachers nor students seriously challenged the requirement of a course in statistical analysis. A third point of agreement was that field training should be included in the core, either as an extended summer experience or as a series of local projects. Despite this agreement, no action was taken to create a field course, owing to financial constraints and lack of willingness on behalf of the teaching staff to assume responsibility for it.

Teachers expressed greater desire than students to change the remaining core requirement – the course in which students developed and presented a research plan. A number of concerns emerged. First, teaching staff thought that three courses constituted a large enough body of work for the core requirement and that a fourth course would detract from individual specialization. Second, the consensus among staff and students was that the oral presentations and public criticisms of research proposals were more stressful than constructive. Third, there was a desire to offer more topical seminars in which individuals and groups could pursue projects as a way of gaining research experience.

Changes in the department's resources made it possible to introduce a new element into the programme. Incremental growth in the size of the teaching staff, as well as a decision to incorporate geographers working in other departments on campus more fully into the programme, made available a greater array of people to teach research seminars and to see students on an individual basis. Therefore, it was feasible to eliminate the research development course that was considered unsatisfactory and to adopt a plan whereby each student worked with a committee comprising the graduate adviser and two other staff to review and guide their early progress. The notion of individual assessment was also adopted as a substitute for the unsatisfactory qualifying examination. Nowadays, those who teach the core courses meet together with the graduate adviser and a faculty member whom the student has identified as a future research adviser and collectively they evaluate progress and problems.

In summary, the procedure adopted to address the revision of this programme provided scope for all actors to express their views, although the detailed work was channelled through a committee with final decisions subject to the vote of the teaching staff. The review yielded a revised core curriculum that incorporates three rather than four required course units. One course has been substantially revised, the qualifying examination has been eliminated and a new advising system has been instituted. Nevertheless, some modifications stemmed from changes in personnel rather than following the data, and other modifications were not attempted because of resource constraints. How well the new curriculum will satisfy students and staff remains to be monitored. Teaching staff are also aware that some of what was desired is still missing and, for that reason, one is planning to teach an optional research methods course. It is also becoming evident that revisions which might have appealed to the students who reviewed the curriculum may not meet the same favour with those who have since entered the programme. Moreover, a new issue is currently emerging: should the department review the way it selects and admits students in order to achieve better compatibility between the curriculum that the teachers consider appropriate and the student body it serves?

Case study 3

Our final case study concerns the design of a single course within an undergraduate programme at the School of Geography and Planning at the Middlesex Polytechnic in the United Kingdom. This example illustrates the use of the top-down approach to designing an individual course unit. It shows curriculum development principles, use of strong management to co-ordinate design activities and ensure that deadlines are met, the employment of an assistant as a co-ordinator and to undertake production of teaching materials, and the importance of designing major curriculum components (teaching and learning methods, acquisition of student skills, geographical content and assessment methods) in parallel with one another.

The course unit considered here forms part of the foundation course taken by all first year undergraduate students. For several decades, the School had run a number of largely independent degree courses in geography and related subjects, but, as a result of a major review of undergraduate courses, it was decided that these courses would all become part of an institution-wide modular degree scheme (MDS). In this scheme, all students would take a common 'foundation' course in their first year.

The first step for the geography course team was therefore to familiarize themselves with the details of the largely unfamiliar scheme within which they would be designing their new foundation course. The MDS provides a clearly defined framework within which all courses (including geography courses) have to be designed. It establishes a number of operating parameters including the types of course that may be offered, the duration of modules, student study budgets, teaching staff allocations, and so on. The MDS also sets out major academic and educational principles that must be adopted by all constituent courses including high intakes of mature students and students from minority groups, variety and efficiency in teaching methods, deferred student choice and the provision of rapid formative feedback to students from assessed course assignments.

Having absorbed the new context, the next step was to decide on the scope and orientation of the two semester-long geography modules for the first year. Partly because of the team's interest in world problems and partly because of its belief that all MDS students should be exposed to global issues, they decided at an early stage to focus the first semester's module on world issues, while the second semester's module would build on this perspective by considering the United Kingdom in greater detail. Two teams of staff were assigned to define a curriculum for these two modules, interacting so as to ensure that they dovetailed in terms of content and that students would experience a smooth transition when moving from one to the other at the end of the first semester. The management of the design effort was undertaken by the Head of School, and the entire exercise proceeded in a top-down manner, as described earlier.

The sequence in which the initial foundation course ideas were developed and the way in which the design teams worked will be illustrated in the context of the first semester module on 'Global Environments'. Four major decisions, concerning its aims and objectives, teaching methods, geographical content and orientation and the role of theory and explanation, were made by its design team before designing it in detail.

First, they set the *aims and objectives* of the course, and in particular the role of skills in the curriculum. A course evaluation exercise had indicated that greater emphasis should be placed on developing student skills in the new programme. It had proposed that a balanced skills package should include the following broad classes of skills: general study skills, life skills, vocational skills, general technical skills and geographical skills. Building on the experience of existing practical courses, and after a number of brainstorming sessions, a list of more than a hundred potentially attainable skills was drawn up. It was clearly impossible to include them all in the time available and so several strategies were adopted.

1 A distinction was made between skills that would be actively taught (e.g. critical review of film and video material, data interpretation and role playing) and those that would simply be encouraged through student use (e.g. group discussion, reading and note-taking, and examination techniques). Only the former would be assigned class tuition time.

2 It was decided to spread the introduction of skills across two years. The 'Global Environments' would take on approximately one-third of this form of teaching, with the selection of skills for this course further limited by omitting in-depth skills training that students would be likely to obtain on other Foundation Course modules in the first year (e.g. information technology skills).

3 The distribution of skills between the two geography modules in the first year was decided on the basis of three principles: reinforcement, progression and practicality. *Reinforcement* meant that some skills (e.g. speaking in groups,

analysing data, using the computer) would be taught or used in both modules in the first year; *progression* meant that some skills would be introduced in the first unit as a basis for introducing follow-on skills in the second unit (e.g. constructing graphs of numerical data would lead to regression analysis); *practicalities* meant that the 'Global Environments' module would make greater use of film and video as learning resources, given its emphasis on world issues and its meagre fieldwork budget, whilst the 'Changing Britain' module would introduce fieldwork as a major learning method, given its more local remit.

The second major design decision concerned *teaching methods*. After much soul searching, it was agreed that the traditional pattern of teaching would give way to a pattern that lessened the role of lectures and emphasized active student learning. The weekly pattern of study for students would consist of the following activities: one 30 minute keynote lecture, a 1 hour group discussion, a 2 hour workshop, and 90 minutes of independent study. A reason for this change was that the course team wanted students to take greater responsibility for their own learning. In order to support this change, it was decided that a course reader and workshop pack would be developed for students taking the module. The second, more practical, reason was the need for more efficient use of staff time. The course evaluation exercise mentioned above had highlighted the increasing stress under which teachers were operating, owing to increasing teaching and administrative duties, and had recommended that existing courses be rationalized and teaching streamlined.

The third design decision concerned the *geographical content and orientation* of the 'Global Environments' course. While it was clearly unrealistic to cover all global problems in a single semester, the team wanted to introduce a variety of current world issues in a manner that avoided superficiality. It was therefore decided that four carefully chosen themes (global climate, hazardous environments, food and famine, and energy resources) would be selected. Each would be allocated 3 weeks for its delivery, with an introductory and summary week linking the package together. It was also decided that students would not be 'indoctrinated' with a single world view, but would be encouraged to develop their own attitudes to the environment and their own feelings about how world problems should be tackled. Since the members of the team had adopted this approach on previous courses, little of this was explicitly discussed.

The fourth decision concerned the place of *theory and explanation* on the course. It was felt that students should appreciate the combative and complementary role of theories, especially in the context of global issues and problems where cause and effect relationships are still not fully understood. Students were therefore to be exposed to several theories in each of the four themes, drawing out competing or conflicting interpretations.

| ELEMENTS / TIME | Aims and objectives | Topic scale or location | Skills, attitudes, values | Teaching strategies and content | | | Assessment and evaluation |
				LECTURE	SEMINAR	WORKSHOP	
Week 1							
Week 2							
Week 3							

Figure 10.4   Master sheet for the course team's consultations

After making these decisions, the course team turned to the task of fleshing out the themes, a process greatly assisted by the appointment of a course co-ordinator who took responsibility for the development work. While there is no room here to provide detailed discussion of how these themes developed, it is worth briefly noting a simple management technique that was introduced to co-ordinate the work of the four subgroups. At weekly meetings, the emerging ideas of the four groups were collated by the course co-ordinator and summarized by means of a master sheet (see figure 10.4). This was circulated to all teams and, following internal discussions, the subgroup leaders met with the co-ordinator to discuss possible gaps or cases of overemphasis. The co-ordinator then negotiated with the various parties involved to achieve a mix of teaching methods and skills that represented an agreed package.

The process, as in the previous case studies, was not perfect. Subsequent review procedures showed, for example, that courses were asked to take on a larger loading of skills than they could reasonably accommodate and that assessment procedures remained rooted in previous practices. Nevertheless, the new procedures enabled a group of geography teachers to put together a new course unit, together with teaching materials, in less than 6 months. A course evaluation scheme has been specially designed to assess the effectiveness of the foundation courses and its results will be used to determine how well the modules perform, and what changes are needed, in the years ahead.

10.7 CONCLUSION

In this chapter, we have looked beyond immediate classroom considerations in order to examine the complex issues encountered when designing a geography curriculum. Arising from this discussion, there are a series of points that might be considered for further action by individuals and course teams.

- Course teams need to try to make explicit their own views of the curriculum and their own interests in the curriculum that is to emerge. This includes working towards an agreement on what members regard as valuable about geography as a discipline and, particularly, what is valuable about the particular geographical specialisms that the department can offer.
- It helps to find out the knowledge, interests, abilities and values with which students start the course.
- The team has to try to decide on what knowledge, interests and abilities students should achieve as a result of the course, and what values they should examine and confront.
- Consider how the wider curriculum can be shaped in order to ensure that there is no 'hidden curriculum'.
- Recognize the constraints within which the curriculum is delivered and the political realities of the pressures on your department.
- Make frequent comparisons between the emerging detail of the course and the original aims and plans for its structure.
- Decide, at an early stage, how the process of design is to be managed and allow the problems of course team working to be a legitimate topic for discussion.
- Recognize that there is no one way to design the curriculum. Decide which, or which mixture, of the various available strategies to use.
- Agree on how the 'effectiveness' of the curriculum is to be evaluated and how this evaluation will feed back into the redesigned curriculum.

KEY READING

As emphasized in the text, there is little published on the geography curriculum in higher education other than the sources already cited in the text. Of these, we particularly recommend Gould (1973) and Pepper (1987), who consider what geography is worth teaching, Kakela (1979) and Clark and Gregory (1982) for their analysis of innovative courses, and Bramley and Wood (1982) for their frank account of the process of curriculum change in one department. Natoli and Bond's (1985) edited collection on *Geography in Internationalising the Undergraduate Curriculum* contains interesting reflections on the North American geography undergraduate curriculum.

In the wider higher education literature, there are many useful texts to help individuals and departments design the curriculum. These include Rowntree (1981a), Boyer (1987), McKeachie (1988) and Diamond (1989).

11

Towards Better Geography Teaching

11.1 INTRODUCTION

Our suspicion is that many teachers of geography in higher education perceive the most important educational problem to be that of specifying the geographical content of courses. The methods of delivering that content are taken as given and receive far less attention. We hope, however, that the alternative methods contained in this book lead you to question this position. In the earlier chapters, we presented and criticized many traditional teaching methods and tasks, such as lectures, fieldwork, practicals, seminars and tutorials, and provided our suggestions on how they might be improved. After that, we concentrated on two newer and perhaps less familiar areas – resource-based teaching and computer-assisted teaching and learning – before turning to the broader issues of assessment, evaluation and curriculum design.

The proposals that we have made for better practice are united by a single driving characteristic: rather than the traditional concern with the development and transmission of geographical knowledge, they are student centred – concerned with the development of students as geographers and as individuals. In this final chapter, we round off our discussion by sketching out ten guiding principles that underpin much of our discussion and add some final thoughts on the nature of good teaching.

The ten principles that we offer are not, in themselves, wholly original. At the time when we were trying to codify our own inventory of those principles, we came across a list of 'guiding principles' compiled by a study supported by the American Association of Higher Education, the Education Commission of the States and the Johnson Foundation (Chickering and Ganson, 1987). The first seven that we list below come from that study: we see no reason to alter them in any way other than minor changes in terminology. The remaining three (8–10 below) draw on additional dimensions that have been highlighted in this book.

11.2 TEN GUIDING PRINCIPLES OF GOOD TEACHING

1 Good practice encourages staff–student contact

Frequent staff–student contact, in and out of classes, is the most important factor in student motivation and involvement. The staff's concern helps students survive rough times and keep on working. Knowing a few members of the teaching staff well enhances students' intellectual commitment and encourages them to think about their own value and future plans.

2 Good practice encourages co-operation among students

Learning is enhanced when it is more like a team effort than a solo race. Good learning, like good work, is collaborative and social, not competitive and isolated. Working with others often increases involvement in learning. Sharing one's own ideas and responding to others' reactions improves thinking and deepens understanding.

3 Good practice encourages active learning

Learning is not a spectator sport. Students do not learn much just sitting in classes listening to teachers, memorizing pre-packaged assignments and spitting out answers. They must talk about what they are learning, write about it, relate it to past experiences and apply it to their daily lives. They must make what they learn part of themselves.

4 Good practice gives prompt feedback

Knowing what you know and do not know focuses learning. Students need appropriate feedback on performance to benefit from courses. In getting started, students need help in assessing existing knowledge and competence. In classes, students need frequent opportunities to perform and receive suggestions for improvement. At various points during college, and at the end, students need chances to reflect on what they have learned, what they still need to know and how to assess themselves.

5 Good practice emphasizes time on task

Time plus energy equals learning. There is no substitute for time on task. Learning to use one's time well is critical for students and professionals alike. Students need help in learning effective time management. Allocating realistic amounts of time means effective learning for students and effective teaching for faculty. How an institution defines time expectations for students, teachers, administrators and other professional staff can establish the basis for high performance for all.

6 Good practice communicates high expectations

Expect more and you will get it. High expectations are important for everyone – for the poorly prepared, for those unwilling to exert themselves, and for the bright and well motivated. Expecting students to perform well becomes a self-fulfilling prophecy when teachers and institutions hold high expectations of themselves and make extra efforts.

7 Good practice respects diverse talents and ways of learning

There are many different roads to learning. People bring different talents and styles of learning to college. Brilliant students in the seminar room may be all thumbs in the laboratory or art studio. Students rich in 'hands-on' experience may not do so well with theory. Students need the opportunity to show their talents and learn in ways that work for them. Then they can be pushed to learning in new ways that do not come so easily.

8 Good practice evaluates itself

Knowing how your efforts are being received by students and what they are really learning is a vital stimulus to improving teaching. Formal course evaluation may not always be necessary for this; rather, what is needed is a reflexive evaluative attitude to your teaching.

9 Good practice is clear about its aims and objectives

Educationalists state many aims and objectives and rightly so. Aims are broad desired outcomes of teaching, whereas objectives are more specific testable outcomes. Without some stated aims it is difficult to design and structure courses and, without some explicit objectives, it is hard to assess or evaluate them.

10 Good practice consults the educational literature

There is a well-researched educational literature relevant to teaching in higher education. A conscientious teacher will consult authorities such as Beard (1976), Brown and Atkins (1988) and Eble (1988). For the geographer, additional ideas and comments are to be found in the pages of the *Journal of Geography in Higher Education*. The teacher in higher education might also consult the literature for schools geography teachers in the pages of *Teaching Geography*, *Journal of Geography* and *Geographical Education* which are full of valuable ideas that can be readily adapted for use in higher education.

11.3 GOOD TEACHING

In the past, higher education has been conservative, with any changes taking place slowly and against much inertia. There is a great deal to be said for this, and we do not advocate overnight revolutionary change in teaching methods. The general message has been to make haste slowly, introducing limited, gradual changes as seem fit and appropriate. Increasingly, however, teachers in geographical higher education may well experience pressure for change from sources such as the following:

- their own development as teacher and individual;
- government action as it affects both institutions and disciplines;
- internally generated institutional change;
- changes in social expectations of higher education and in the job market for geography students; and
- the nature of the discipline itself.

Most of us struggle to accommodate the effects of these influences in what we teach and it is the great luxury of working in higher education that, by and large, we are free from external constraints on the content of our teaching. Yet, as noted in chapter 1, working in higher education forces us to take on a number of roles: in a typical day we may well have to act as teacher, researcher, administrator and manager, consultant and counsellor. How we strike the balance between these roles can vary from day to day, but we recognize that many of the external pressures identified above may well have forced, or be forcing, us to change our priorities in favour of almost any activity other than teaching. In this book we have tried to reassert the importance of teaching and, naturally, we hope that after reading it you will be sufficiently enthused to shift your personal balance a little further towards 'good' teaching.

Quite what is meant by 'good' teaching is another matter. All that we can do by way of conclusion is to say what it is not and to say something about the conditions necessary to achieve it. First, mechanistically efficient teaching is almost never good teaching. Second, thinking and reading about good teaching is not a sufficient condition for it either. Moreover, thinking and reading about good teaching is not even a necessary condition for delivering it. We have all experienced brilliant teaching from people who have never opened an educational text in their lives. However, as academics we surely believe that reflection and research should provide insights into good teaching practice. In our role as teachers of geography, we should subject what we do to the same critical scrutiny that we give to our own and other people's research. Finally, good teaching may not be all that important in gaining tenure or promotion, but it is certainly more fun and more rewarding than bad teaching. In the last analysis, it is the most direct and important way by which we can discharge our responsibilities to knowledge, to our students and, through them, to society.

About the Authors

JOHN GOLD is Senior Lecturer and Joint Head of the Centre for Geography in Higher Education at Oxford Polytechnic, where he teaches courses on urban history, futures and environmental philosophy. Formerly co-editor of the *Journal of Geography in Higher Education* (1980–6) and a founder member of its editorial board, he is now editor of *Research into Higher Education Abstracts* and on the editorial board of *Studies in Higher Education*. He has served on various professional committees concerned with geography in higher education and has published widely on urban, futures and environmental themes.

ALAN JENKINS holds a Principal Lectureship jointly in the Geography Unit and Educational Methods Unit at Oxford Polytechnic, where he is Joint Head of the Centre for Geography in Higher Education. A founding editor of the *Journal of Geography in Higher Education*, he holds a postgraduate teaching certificate from the Institute of Education in London and undertook graduate studies at the University of Wisconsin-Madison. He has held visiting positions at the University of Missouri-Columbia and at the University of Vermont. He teaches courses in political geography and the geography of China.

ROGER LEE is Senior Lecturer at Queen Mary and Westfield College, University of London. Joint editor of the *Journal of Geography in Higher Education*, and editor of *Update*, he has also served on the editorial board of *Contemporary Issues in Geography and Education* and on the Geographical Association's working parties on curriculum and syllabus development. He is currently a member of the Council of the Institute of British Geographers.

JANICE MONK is Executive Director of the Southwest Institute for Research on Women and Adjunct Professor of Geography at the University of Arizona at Tucson. She has directed various projects designed to improve undergraduate teaching and has published widely in feminist geography, including work on its curricular implications. She is editor for the USA of the *Journal of Geography in Higher Education*.

JUDITH RILEY is currently employed at the King's Fund College in London where she is engaged in management education for doctors and health service managers. Prior to that she worked at the University of Manchester and at the Open University, where she was responsible in developing courses for adults studying at a distance. She holds a first degree in geography and has a doctorate in education. She was a member of the editorial board of the *Journal of Geography in Higher Education*.

IFAN SHEPHERD is Principal Lecturer in Geography at Middlesex Polytechnic, Enfield, where he teaches courses in urban geography, geographical computing, geographical information systems and computer graphics. He is author (with D. R. F. Walker and Z. Cooper) of *Computer Assisted Learning in Geography* (1980) and served as a member of the panel of the *Computer Journal*. He has published widely on educational aspects of computing, geographical information systems and computer graphics, and is a founding member of the editorial board of the *Journal of Geography in Higher Education*.

DAVID UNWIN is Senior Lecturer in Geography at the University of Leicester where he teaches and researches in urban climatology, spatial analysis and computing. Among the posts he has held in the past are member of the editorial board of *Teaching Geography*, chairman of the Geographical Association's Educational Computing Working Group and Editor of the CATMOG series. He was co-editor of the *Journal of Geography in Higher Education* (1986-90) and now directs the Computers in Teaching Initiative Centre for Geography.

References

AAC (Association of American Colleges) (1985) *Integrity in the College Curriculum: A Report to the Academic Community*, Washington, DC, Association of American Colleges.

AAG (Association of American Geographers) (1969) *Field Training in Geography*, Washington, DC, Association of American Geographers, Technical Paper 1, Commission on College Geography.

Abercrombie, M. J. L. (1979) *Aims and Techniques of Small Group Teaching*, Guildford, Society for Research into Higher Education, 4th edn.

Abercrombie, M. J. L. and Terry, P. M. (1978) *Talking to Learn: Improving Teaching and Learning in Small Groups*, Guildford, Society for Research into Higher Education.

Adderly, K., Ashwin, C., Bradbury, P., Freeman, J., Goodlad, S., Green, J., Jenkins, D., Rae, J. and Uren, O. (1975) *Project Methods in Higher Education*, London, Society for Research into Higher Education.

Alessi, S. M. and Trollop, S. R. (1985) *Computer-based Instruction: Methods and Development*, Englewood Cliffs, NJ, Prentice-Hall.

Alexander, K. and Blanchard, D. (eds) (1985) *Educational Software: A Creator's Handbook*, Loughborough, Techmedia.

Alexander, R. (1979) What is a course?, *Journal of Further and Higher Education*, 3: 31–45.

Altman, I. (1975) *The Environment and Social Behaviour*, Monterey, CA, Brooks-Cole.

Ambron, S. and Hooper, C. (1988) *Interactive Multi-media: Visions of Multimedia for Developers, Educators and Information Providers*, Redmond, WA, Microsoft Press.

Anderson, S. B., Ball, S. and Murphy, R. T. (1975) *Encyclopedia of Educational Evaluation: Concepts and Techniques for Evaluating Education Training Programmes*, San Francisco, CA, Jossey-Bass.

Andresen, L. W. (1988) *Lecturing to large groups: a guide to doing it less . . . but better*, Occasional Publication 24, Tertiary Education Research Centre, University of New South Wales.

Anon (1984) *The design and evaluation of statistical software for microcomputers*, Applied Statistics Research Unit, University of Kent at Canterbury.

Archenold, W. F., Jenkins, E. W. and Wood-Robinson, C. (1978) *School Science Laboratories: A Handbook of Design, Maintenance and Organisation*, London, John Murray.

Ashworth, G. J. (1983) The use of data collection exercises in field courses, *Journal of Geography in Higher Education*, 7 (2): 141-9.

Backler, A. (1979) Mastery learning: a case study and implications for instruction, *Journal of Geography in Higher Education*, 3 (1): 68-75.

Batty, M., Bracken, I., Guy, C. and Spooner, R. (1985) Teaching spatial modelling using interacting computers and interactive computer graphics, *Journal of Geography in Higher Education*, 9 (2): 25-36.

Bayard-White, C. (1985) *An Introduction to Interactive Video*, London, UK National IV Centre and Centre for Educational Technology.

Beard, R. M. (1976) *Teaching and Learning in Higher Education*, Harmondsworth, Penguin, 3rd edn.

Beaumont, J. R. and Wyn Williams, S. (1983) *Project Work in the Geography Curriculum*, London, Croom Helm.

Becher, T. (1989) *Academic Tribes and Territories: Intellectual Enquiry and the Cultures of Disciplines*, Milton Keynes, Society for Research into Higher Education and Open University Press.

Beech, G. (1983) *Computer Based Learning: Practical Methods for Microcomputers*, Wilmslow, Sigma Press.

Bell, P. C. and O'Keefe, R. M. (1987) Visual interactive simulation – history, recent developments, and major issues, *Simulation*, 49: 109-116.

Bennetts, T. (1972) Objectives for the teacher, in Graves, N. (ed.), *New Movements in the Study and Teaching of Geography*, London, Temple Smith.

Beyer, J. (1988) Personal communication.

Birkhill, S. (1983) 'Designing, developing and evaluating software: the ITMA approach', in Kent, A. (ed.), *Computers in Action in the Geography Classroom*, Sheffield, Geographical Association, 20-6.

Bligh, D. A. (1972) *What's the Use of Lectures?*, Harmondsworth, Penguin.

Bligh, D. A. (1973) *Teaching Students*, Exeter, Teaching Services, University of Exeter.

Bligh, D. A. (ed.) (1986) *Teach Thinking by Discussion*, London, Society for Research into Higher Education/NFER-Nelson.

Bliss, J. and Ogborn, J. (1977) *Student Reactions to Undergraduate Science*, London, Heinemann.

Bloom, B. S. (ed.) (1956) *Taxonomy of Educational Objectives: I. Cognitive Domain*, London, Longman.

Bloom, B. S., Hastings, J. T. and Madaus, G. F. (1971) *Handbook on Formative and Summative Evaluation of Student Learning*, New York, McGraw-Hill.

Booth, V. (1984) *Communicating in Science: Writing and Speaking*, Cambridge, Cambridge University Press.

Borzack, L. (1981) *Field Study: A Source Book for Experiential Learning*, London, Sage.

Boud, D. (ed.) (1981) *Developing Student Autonomy in Learning*, London, Kogan Page.

Boud, D. (ed.) (1985) *Problem-based Learning for the Professions*, Kensington, NSW, Higher Education Research and Development Society of Australia.

Boud, D. (1986) *Implementing Student Self-Assessment*, Green Guide 5, Kensington, NSW, Higher Education Research and Development Society of Australia.

Boud, D. (1988) *Developing Student Autonomy in Learning*, London, Kogan Page, 2nd edn.

Boud, D., Dunn, J. and Hegarty-Hazel, E. (1986) *Training in laboratories*, Guildford, Society for Research into Higher Education/NFER-Nelson.

Boyd, G. and Pask, G. (1989) Why do instructional designers need conversation theory?, in Laurillard, D. (ed.), *Interactive Media*, Chichester, Ellis Horwood, 91-6.

Boyer, E. L. (1987) *College: The Undergraduate Experience in America*, New York, Harper & Row.

Bramley, W. and Wood, P. (1982) Collaboration, consultation and conflict: the process of change in a teaching department, *Journal of Geography in Higher Education*, 6 (1): 5-20.

Braskamp, L. A. (1980) The role of evaluation in faculty development, *Studies in Higher Education*, 5: 45-54.

Braun, L. (1978) Video discs: magic lamps for education? *People's Computers*, 6 (4): 14-15, 47.

Broady, M. (1986) The conduct of seminars, in Bligh, D. (ed.), *Teach Thinking by Discussion*, London, Society for Research into Higher Education/NFER-Nelson: 153-62.

Brown, B. (1989) Management strategies for meeting increased enrolments in introductory college geography courses, *Journal of Geography*, 88: 226-9.

Brown, E. H. (1969) The teaching of fieldwork and the integration of physical geography, in Cooke, R. U. and Johnson, J. H. (eds), *Trends in Geography*, Oxford, Pergamon.

Brown, G. (1978) *Lecturing and Explaining*, London, Methuen.

Brown, G. and Atkins, M. J. (1985) *Tests for Learning: Practical Guidance on the Use and Design of Tests*, Harlow, Longman.

Brown, G. and Atkins, M. (1988) *Effective Teaching in Higher Education*, London, Methuen.

Brown, J. S. and Burton, R. R. (1978) Diagnostic models for procedural bugs in basic mathematical skills, *Cognitive Science*, 2: 155-92.

Brown, J. S., Burton, R. R. and Bell, A. G. (1975) SOPHIE: a step towards a reactive learning environment, *International Journal of Man-Machine Studies*, 7: 675-96.

Bruner, J. S. (1960) *The Process of Education*, New York, Vintage Books.

Brunn, S. D. (1990) Hiring, evaluation, promotion and tenure decisions in a US geography department, *Journal of Geography in Higher Education*, 14 (2), in press.

Brunsden, D. (1987) The science of the unknown, *Geography*, 72: 193-208.

Burkhardt, H., Fraser, R. and Wells, C. (1980) *Teaching Style and Program Design*, London, Council for Educational Technology.

Burt, T. (1988) A practical exercise to demonstrate the variable source area model, *Journal of Geography in Higher Education*, 12 (2): 177-86.

Burt, T. and Butcher, D. (1986) Stimulation from simulation? a teaching model of hillslope hydrology for use on microcomputers, *Journal of Geography in Higher Education*, 10 (1): 23-39.

Byrne, C. J. (1976) Computerised question-banking systems: I – the state of the art, *British Journal of Educational Technology*, 2 (7): 44–64.

Calfee, D. and Drum, D. (1986) Research on teaching reading, in Wittrock, M. (ed.), *Handbook of Research on Teaching*, London, Collier Macmillan: 804–49.

Carter, G. and Lee, L. S. (1981) A sample of departments of electrical engineering to ascertain the aims, objectives and methods of assessing first year undergraduate laboratory work in electronic and electrical engineering, *International Journal of Electrical Engineering Education*, 18: 113–20.

Centra, J. A. (1977) The how and why of evaluating teaching, in Centra, J. A. (ed.), *Reviewing and Evaluating Teaching*, San Francisco, CA, Jossey-Bass.

Cerveney, R. S. and Balling, R. C. (1984) CONSTABLE: a simple one-dimensional climate model for climatologists in geography, *Professional Geographer*, 36: 188–96.

Chambers, J. A. and Sprecher, J. W. (1980) Computer assisted instruction: current trends and critical issues, *Communications of the Association of Computing Machinery*, 23: 332–42.

Chickering, A. W. and Gamson, E. F. (1987) *Seven Principles for Good Practice in Undergraduate Education*, Racine, WI, Johnson Foundation.

Cho, G. (1982) Experiences with a workbook for spatial data analysis, *Journal of Geography in Higher Education*, 6 (2): 133–9.

Church, M. (1988) Problem orientation in physical geography teaching, *Journal of Geography in Higher Education*, 12: 51–65.

Clark, J. and Cole, S. (1975) *Global Simulation Models*, London, John Wiley.

Clark, M. J. and Gregory, K. J. (1982) Physical geography techniques: a self-paced university course, *Journal of Geography in Higher Education*, 6: 123–31.

Clift, J. C. and Imrie, B. W. (1981) *Assessing Students, Appraising Teaching*, London, Croom Helm.

Cloke, P. (1987) Applied rural geography and planning: a simple gaming technique, *Journal of Geography in Higher Education*, 11, 35–45.

Cloke, P., Kirby, D. and Park, C. (1981) An exercise in integrated field work, *Teaching Geography*, 6 (3): 134–9.

CNAA (Council for National Academic Awards) (1983) *Open Learning*, London, Council for National Academic Awards.

CNAA (Council for National Academic Awards) (1988) *Handbook*, London, Council for National Academic Awards.

Cohen, S. A. and McVicar, M. L. A. (1976) Establishing an undergraduate research programme in physics: how it was done, *American Journal of Physics*, 44: 199–203.

Cole, J. P. (1975) *Situations in Human Geography: a Practical Approach*, Oxford, Basil Blackwell.

Coleman, A. (1978) Practical techniques for tutorial teaching, *Journal of Geography in Higher Education*, 2 (2): 95–100.

Conolly, G. (1981) The use of four selected games in a tertiary geography programme, *Journal of Geography in Higher Education*, 5: 121–32.

Cooke, N. L., Heron, T. E. and Hewald, W. L. (1980) Teaching geography in the visual response system, *Journal of Geography*, 79: 253–8

Corbridge, S. (1985) The Green Revolution Game, *Journal of Geography in Higher Education*, 9: 171-5.

Corey, K. E. (1969) The role of fieldwork in geographic research and its structure, in Association of American Geographers *Field Training in Geography*, Washington, DC, Association of American Geographers, Technical Paper 1, Commission on College Geography.

Cosgrove, D. and Daniels, S. (1989) Fieldwork as theatre: a week's performance in Venice and its region, *Journal of Geography in Higher Education*, 13 (2): 169-82.

Council of Ministers of Education (1985) *Software Evaluation*, Canada, Toronto, Council of Ministers of Education.

Cowan, J. and Harding, A. G. (1986) A logical model for curriculum development, *British Journal of Educational Technology*, 2: 103-9.

Cox, N. and Anderson, E. (1978) Teaching geographical data analysis: problems and possible solutions, *Journal of Geography in Higher Education*, 2 (2): 29-37.

Cox, R. (1976) The evaluation of teaching in higher education, in University Teaching Methods Unit, *Improving Teaching in Higher Education: A Collection of Conference Papers*, London, University Teaching Methods Unit.

Cranton, P. A. and Smith, R. A. (1986) A new look at the effect of course characteristics on student ratings of instruction, *American Educational Research Journal*, 23: 117-28

Daines, D. R. (1984) *Databases in the Classroom*, Tunbridge Wells, Castle House.

Dando, W. A. and Wiedel, J. W. (1971) A two-week field course with deferred papers: a possible solution to the problem of undergraduate fieldwork, *Journal of Geography*, 70: 289-93.

Davidson, N. and Jones, P. (1985) Mapping with micros: teaching introductory computer cartography, *Journal of Geography in Higher Education*, 9 (2): 147-55.

Dawson, J. A. and Unwin, D. J. (1984) The integration of microcomputers into British geography, *Area*, 16: 323-9.

Dawson, J. A. and Unwin, D. J. (1985) *Computer Programming for Geographers*, London, Longman.

Day, R. A. (1979) *How to Write a Scientific Paper*, Philadelphia, ISI Press.

DES (Department of Education and Science) (1973) *Safety in Laboratories*, London, HMSO.

DES (1983) *Degree Courses in the Public Sector of Higher Education*, London, HMSO.

Dethlefsen, E. and Moody, C. (1982) Simulating neighbourhood segregation, *BYTE*, 7 (7): 178-206.

Deutsch, K. W., Fritsch, B., Jaguarise, H. and Markovits, A. S. (1977) *Problems of World Modelling: Political and Social Implications*, Cambridge, MA., Ballinger.

Diamond, R. M. (1989) *Designing and Improving Courses and Curricula in Higher Education: A Systematic Approach*, San Francisco, CA, Jossey-Bass.

Disinger, J. F. (1985) Environmental education: research news, *Environmentalist*, 5: 85-8.

Douglas, I. (1986) Too many third year options, *Journal of Geography in Higher Education*, 10 (2): 191-5.

Dowell, D. Q. and Neal, J. A. (1982) A selective review of the validity of student ratings of teaching, *Journal of Higher Education*, 53: 51-62.

Doyle, K. O. (1975) *Student Evaluation of Instruction*, Lexington, MA, Lexington Books.

Doyle, K. O. (1983) *Evaluating Teaching*, Lexington, MA, Lexington Books.

Dressel, P. L. (1976) *Handbook of Academic Evaluation*, San Francisco, CA, Jossey-Bass.

Dressel, P. L. and Marcus, D. (1982) *On Teaching and Learning in College*, San Francisco, CA, Jossey-Bass.

Duke, J. (1983) *Interactive video: implications for education and training*, CET Working Paper 22, Council for Educational Technology, London.

Donleavy, P. (1986) *Studying for a Degree in the Humanities and Social Sciences*, London, Macmillan.

Durbridge, N. (1981) Student assignments: a question of design, *Journal of Geography in Higher Education*, 5 (2): 208-12.

Dyer, A. (1988) The introduction of hypermedia systems into the theoretical studies curriculum at Coventry Polytechnic Faculty of Art and Design, *CTISS File*, 7: 80-4.

Eaborn, C. (1970) A new approach to undergraduate chemistry teaching, *Chemistry in Britain*, 6: 330-3.

Eble, K. (1976) *The Craft of Teaching*, San Francisco, CA, Jossey-Bass, 4th edn.

Eble, K. (1988) *The Craft of Teaching*, San Francisco, CA, Jossey-Bass, 7th edn.

Ehrmann, S. C. (1987) Learning to design, designing to learn: a more creative role for technology, *Machine-Mediated Learning*, 2 (1-2), 9-33.

Eisner, E. W. (1975) Instructional and expressive objectives, in: Golby, M., Greenwood, J. and West, R. (eds), *Curriculum Design*, London: Croom-Helm, 351-4.

Eisner, E. W. (1985) *The Educational Imagination: on the Design and Evaluation of School Programs*, New York, Macmillan, 2nd edn.

Ellinger, R. S. and Frankland, P. (1976) Computer-assisted and lecture instruction: a comparative experiment, *Journal of Geography*, 75: 109-20.

Ellis, A. B. (1974) *The Use and Misuse of Computers in Education*, New York, McGraw-Hill.

Elsom-Cook, M. (1989) Guided discovery tutoring and bounded user modelling, in Laurillard, D. (ed.), *Interactive Media*, Chichester, Ellis Horwood: 165-78.

Elton, L. (1988) Student motivation and achievement, *Studies in Higher Education*, 13, 215-21.

Ennals, R. (1981) PROLOG can link diverse subjects with logic and fun, *Practical Computing*, 4 (3): 91-2.

Ennals, R. (1982) *Beginning PROLOG*, Chichester, Ellis Horwood.

Ennals, R. (1986) Artificial intelligence and educational computing, in Ennals, R., Gwyn, R. and Zdravchev, L. (eds), *Information Technology and Education*, Chichester, Ellis Horwood.

Entwistle, N. J. and Hounsell, D. (1975) *How Students Learn*, Lancaster, University of Lancaster Press.

Entwistle, N. J. and Ramsden, P. (1983) *Understanding Student Learning*, Beckenham, Croom Helm.

Estaville, L. E., Jr. (1988) Debate: a teaching strategy for geography, *Journal of Geography*, 87: 2-4.

Everett, K. and Jenkins, E. W. (1977) *A Safety Handbook for Science Teachers*, London, John Murray, 2nd edn.

Everson, J. (1973) Fieldwork in school geography, in Walford, R. (ed.), *New Directions in Geography Teaching*, London, Longman: 107-14.

Fairgrieve, J. (1926) *Geography in School*, London, University of London Press.

Fielden, J. and Pearson, P. K. (1978) *The Cost of Learning with Computers*, London, Council for Educational Technology.

Fien, J. and Gerber, R. (eds) (1986) *Teaching Geography for a Better World*, Edinburgh, Oliver & Boyd.

Fien, J., Herschell, R. and Hodgkinson, J. (1984) Using games and simulations in the geography classroom, in Fien, J., Gerber R. and Wilson, P. (eds), *The Geography Teacher's Guide to the Classroom*, Melbourne, Macmillan: 111-22.

Finegold, L. (1972) Open-ending a senior modern physics laboratory, *American Journal of Physics*, 40: 1383-8.

Fink, L. D. (1973) Monitoring: a method of diagnostic course evaluation, *Journal of Geography*, 72: 16-20

Fink, L. D. (1977) *Listening to the learner: an exploratory study of personal meaning in college geography courses*, Research Paper 184, Department of Geography, University of Chicago.

Fink, L. D. (1985) First year on the faculty: the quality of their teaching, *Journal of Geography in Higher Education*, 9 (2): 129-45.

Finlayson, B. (1979) Electrical conductivity: a useful technique in teaching geomorphology, *Journal of Geography in Higher Education*, 3 (2): 68-87.

Fisher, B. W. (1986) Micros and metmaps, *Weather*, 41: 196-9.

Fisher, P. F. (1989) Geographical information systems software for teaching, *Journal of Geography in Higher Education*, 13 (1): 69-80.

Fitzgerald, B. (1988) 'See Me!' or 'Darren, I think that you might have left the nomads to later', *Teaching Geography*, 13: 100-3.

Flood Page, C. (1974) *Student Evaluation of Teaching: The American Experience*, London, Society for Research into Higher Education.

Flood Page, C. (1976) *Technical Aids to Teaching in Higher Education*, London, Society for Research into Higher Education, 2nd edn.

Forer, P. C. (1984) Computers in the geography classroom, in Fien, J., Gerber, R. and Wilson, P. (eds), *The Geography Teacher's Guide to the Classroom*, Melbourne, Macmillan: 172-84.

Forer, P. C. (1987a) Encouraging failure?: lessons from an educational medium, *New Zealand Journal of Geography*, 84: 23-8.

Forer, P. C. (1987b) Symbiotic software: development and usage issues on stand-alone and networked systems, in Kent, W. A. and Lewis, R. (eds), *Computer Assisted Learning in the Humanities and Social Sciences*, Oxford, Basil Blackwell.

Fox, M. and Wilkinson, T. (1977) A self-paced instruction scheme in geography for a first-year introductory course, *Journal of Geography in Higher Education*, 1 (2): 61-70.

Fox, M., Rowsome, W. S. and Wilkinson, T. (1987) A decade of mastery learning: evolution and evaluation, *Journal of Geography in Higher Education*, 11 (1): 11-26.

Fox, P. (1984) *List of Geography Microcomputer Software*, Sheffield, Geographical Association.

Fraser, R. (1981) Design and evaluation of educational software for group presentation, in Howe, J. A. M. and Ross, P. M. (eds), *Microcomputers in Secondary Education: Issues and Techniques*, London, Kogan Page.

Friberg, J. C. (1975) *Field techniques and the training of the American geographer*, Department of Geography, Syracuse University.

Gardiner, V. and Unwin, D. J. (1986) Computers and the field class, *Journal of Geography in Higher Education*, 10 (2): 169-79.

Geo Books (1986) *A Matter of Degree: A Directory of Geography Courses, 1986/1987*, Norwich, Geo Books.

Gibbs, G. (1982) *Twenty terrible reasons for lecturing*, Standing Conference on Educational Development in Polytechnics, Bristol.

Gibbs, G. (1988) *Learning by doing: a guide to teaching and learning methods*, Further Education Unit, Birmingham.

Gibbs, G. and Haigh, M. (1983a) *Designing course evaluation questionnaires*, Educational Methods Unit, Oxford Polytechnic.

Gibbs, G. and Haigh, M. (1983b) *A compendium of course evaluation questionnaires*, Occasional Paper 17, Standing Conference on Educational Development Services in Polytechnics, Birmingham.

Gibbs, G. and Jenkins, A. (1984) Break up your lectures or Christaller sliced up, *Journal of Geography in Higher Education*, 8 (1): 27-39.

Gibbs, G., Gold, J. R. and Jenkins, A. (1987) Becoming a teacher of geography in higher education, *Journal of Geography in Higher Education*, 11 (1): 11-26.

Gibbs, G., Habeshaw, S. and Habeshaw, T. (1984) *53 interesting things to do in your lectures*, Technical and Educational Services, Bristol.

Gibbs, G., Habeshaw, S. and Habeshaw, T. (1986) *53 interesting ways to assess your students*, Technical and Educational Services, Bristol.

Gibson, L. J. (1972) Recycling an old strategy: the functions of a problem-orientated strategy, in Helburn, N. (ed.), *Challenge and Change in College Geography*, Boulder, CO, Commission on Geographical Education, Association of American Geographers.

Goddard, J. (1976) Research and teaching: speeding up the trickling down process, in Pepper, D. M. and Jenkins, A. (eds), *Proceedings of the 1975 National Conference on Geography in Higher Education*, Discussion Papers in Geography, 3, Geography Section, Oxford, Oxford Polytechnic: 38-9.

Gold, J. R. (1980) *An Introduction to Behavioural Geography*, Oxford, Oxford University Press.

Gold, J. R., Haigh, M. J. and Jenkins, A. (1990) Ways of seeing: teaching introductory human geography through a field-based simulation, unpublished manuscript, Centre for Geography in Higher Education, Oxford Polytechnic.

Goldberg, A. (1979) Educational uses of a Dynabook, *Computers in Education*, 3: 247-66.

Goldberg, A. and Robson, D. (1983) *SMALLTALK-80: The Language and its Implementation*, Reading, MA, Addison Wesley.

Goodall, B. (1977) Problems arising from the use of continuous assessment for degree classification, *Journal of Geography in Higher Education*, 1 (1): 47-52.

Goodlad, S. and Hirst, B. (1989) *Peer Tutoring: A Guide to Learning by Teaching*, London, Kogan Page.

Gould, P. (1973) The open geographic curriculum, in Chorley, R. J. (ed.), *Directions in Geography*, London, Methuen: 253–84.

Graves, N. (1978) Aims and objectives in degree curriculum design, *Journal of Geography in Higher Education*, 2 (2): 64–73.

Graves, N. (1980) *Geography in Education*, London, Heinemann, 2nd edn.

Graves, N. and Naish, M. (eds) (1986) *Profiling in Geography*, Sheffield, Geographical Association.

Gray, A. and Flowerdew, R. (1987) Reflections on reform: some implications of the ESRC's new postgraduate policy, *Journal of Geography in Higher Education*, 11 (2): 175–8.

Gray, D. E. (1970) *So You Have to Write a Technical Report*, Washington, DC, IRP Press.

Grieff, I. (1988) *Computer-supported Cooperative Work*, New York, Morgan Kaufman.

Griffith, D. (1987) Teaching spatial autocorrelation by simulation, *Journal of Geography in Higher Education*, 11: 143–53.

Gronland, N. E. (1977) *Constructing Achievement Tests*, Englewood Cliffs, NJ, Prentice-Hall, 2nd edn.

Groop, R., Dodge, S. L. and Manson, G. (1985) Microcomputer modules for undergraduate geography, *Journal of Geography*, 84: 161–4.

Habeshaw, S., Habeshaw, T. and Gibbs, G. (1984) *53 interesting things to do in your seminars and tutorials*, Technical and Educational Services, Bristol.

Haggett, P. (1965) *Locational Analysis in Human Geography*, London, Edward Arnold.

Haggett, P. (1975) *Geography: A Modern Synthesis*, New York, Harper & Row, 2nd edn.

Haigh, M. J. (1986) The evaluation of an experiment in physical geography teaching, *Journal of Geography in Higher Education*, 10 (2): 133–47.

Haigh, M. and Kilmartin, M. P. (1987) Teaching soil conservation in the laboratory using the 'bank erosion channel' flume, *Journal of Geography in Higher Education*, 11 (2): 161–7.

Haines-Young, R. H. (1983) Nutrient cycling and problem solving: a simple teaching model, *Journal of Geography in Higher Education*, 7 (2): 125–39.

Hall, D. (1976) *Geography and the Geography Teacher*, London, Allen & Unwin.

Halloway, W. (1984) Planning a school based assessment program, in Fien, J., Gerber, R. and Wilson, P. (eds), *The Geography Teacher's Guide to the Classroom*, Melbourne: Macmillan: 278–93.

Hamilton, D., Jenkins, D., King, C., Macdonald, B. and Parlett, M. (1977) *Beyond the Numbers Game: a Reader in Educational Evaluation*, London, Macmillan.

Hammond, N. (1989) Hypermedia and learning: who guides whom?, in Maurer, H. (ed.), *Computer Assisted Learning*, Berlin, Springer-Verlag.

Hammond, N. and Allinson, L. (1989) Extending hypertext for learning: an investigation of access and guidance tools, in Sutcliffe, A. and Macaulay, L. (eds) *People and Computers*, vol. 5, Cambridge, Cambridge University Press, 293–304.

Harbaugh, J. W. and Bonham-Carter, G. (1970) *Computer Simulation in Geology*, Chichester, Wiley.

Harding, R. (1988) Computer illustrated texts – I. Principles, *CTISS File*, 5: 22–4.

Harris, D. and Bell, C. (1986) *Evaluating and Assessing for Learning*, London, Kogan Page.

Harrison, C. and Luithlen, L. (1983) Fieldwork for land use students: an appraisal, *Journal of Geography in Higher Education*, 7 (1): 23–32.

Harrison, R. (1985) *Making Self-instructional Material: a Workbook*, Milton Keynes, Open University Press.

Hart, J. F. (1969) The undergraduate fieldcourse, in Association of American Geographers *Field Training in Geography*, Washington, DC, Association of American Geographers, Technical Paper 1, Commission on College Geography: 29–38.

Hart, J. F. (1979) Foreword, in Lounsbury, J. F. and Aldrich, F. T. *Introduction to Geographic Field Methods and Techniques*, Columbus, OH, Merrill.

Hastings, J. T., Wardrop, J. L. and Gooler, D. (1970) *Evaluating Geography Courses: A Model with Illustrative Applications*, Washington, DC, Association of American Geographers, Technical Paper 3, Commission on College Geography.

Heaford, J. M. (1983) *The Myth of the Learning Machine: The Theory and Practice of Computer Based Learning*, Wilmslow, Sigma Press.

Helburn, N. (1968) The educational objectives of high school geography, *Journal of Geography*, 67: 274–81.

Hershey, R. and Whitehead, C. (1989) *Desktop mapping: an evaluation of nine software packages for the Macintosh*, SERRL/LSE Working Paper 9, London School of Economics.

Hewton, E. (1977) The curricular implications of concentrated study, *Studies in Higher Education*, 2: 79–87.

Hewton, E. (1987) Teaching, learning and assessment in Becher, T. (ed.), *British Higher Education*, London, Allen & Unwin: 178–96.

Heywood, J. (1989) *Assessment in Higher Education*, Chichester, Wiley, 2nd edn.

Hindson, J. and Savin, J. (1988) *The Good Field Centre Guide*, Harlow, Longman.

Hollis, T. and Terry, P. (1977) Learning about small group teaching, *Journal of Geography in Higher Education*, 1 (1): 73–6.

Hounsell, D. (1979) Students as learners, *Journal of Geography in Higher Education*, 3 (2): 97–102.

Howard, K. and Sharp, J. A. (1983) *The Management of a Student Research Project*, Aldershot, Gower.

Howe, M. J. A. and Godfrey, J. (1978) *Student note-taking as an aid to learning*, University of Exeter Teaching Services.

Huckle, J. (ed.) (1983) *Geographical Education: Reflection and Action*, Oxford, Oxford University Press.

Hughes, A. (1976) An application of computer cartography in the teaching of cartography, *Canadian Cartographer*, 13: 139–57.

Hughes, A. (1979) *SYMAP as an aid to teaching thematic cartography*, Mapping Collection, 5, Harvard Library of Computer Graphics: 63–75.

Humphrys, G. (1978) The role of assessment in the design of a curriculum for a degree in geography, *Journal of Geography in Higher Education*, 2 (2): 74–86.

Hursch, B. A. and Borzack, L. (1979) Towards cognitive development through field studies, *Journal of Higher Education*, 50: 63–78.

Hutchings, G. E. (1962) Geographical field training, *Geography*, 47: 1–14.

Jackson, M. W. and Prosser, M. T. (1985) De-lecturing: a case study of the implementation of small group teaching, *Higher Education*, 14: 651–63.

Jackson, P. (1989) Challenging racism through geography teaching, *Journal of Geography in Higher Education*, 13: 5-14.

Jaques, D. (1984) *Learning in Groups*, London, Croom-Helm.

Jenkins, A. (1985) Peace education and the geography curriculum, in Pepper, P. and Jenkins, A. (eds), *The Geography of Peace and War*, Oxford, Basil Blackwell: 202-13.

Jenkins, A. and Gold, J. R. (1991) Effective learning: a traveller's guide, in Rogers, A., Goudie, A. S. and Viles, H. (eds), *The Student's Companion to Geography*, Oxford, Basil Blackwell, in press.

Jenkins, A. and Pepper, D. M. (1987) *Enhancing Employability and Educational Opportunity*, Birmingham, SCEDSIP.

Jenkins, A. and Pepper, D. M. (1988) Enhancing students' employability and self-expression: how to teach oral and groupwork skills in geography, *Journal of Geography in Higher Education*, 12 (1): 67-83.

Jenkins, A. and Smith, P. (1990) Quality Control in geography courses: the role and practice of Her Majesty's Inspectors in British higher education, *Journal of Geography in Higher Education*, 15 (1), in press.

Jenkins, A. and Youngs, M. J. (1983) Geographical education and film: an experimental course, *Journal of Geography in Higher Education*, 7 (1): 33-44.

Jenkins, J. (1985) *Course Development: A Manual for Editors of Distance Learning Materials*, London, International Extension College, Commonwealth Secretariat.

Johnston, R.J. and Members of IBG Working Party (1989) The role of geography in higher education, *Area*, 21: 215-19.

Jones, A. (1986) Resource-based learning: shifting the load, *Journal of Geography in Higher Education*, 10 (2): 159-68.

Jones, K. (1987) *Simulations: A Handbook for Teachers and Trainers*, London, Kogan Page, 2nd edn.

Jones, W. D. and Sauer, C. O. (1915) Outline for fieldwork in geography, *Bulletin of the American Geographical Society*, 47: 520-5.

Kakela, P. (1979) Remembering teaching, *Journal of Geography in Higher Education*, 3 (1): 5-12.

Kay, A. and Goldberg, A. (1977) Personal dynamic media, *Computer*, 10: 31-41.

Kay, D., Kay, N. and McDonald, A. (1982) Teaching catchment hydrology: two dynamic models for classroom use, *Teaching Geography*, 7: 118-24.

Kay, J., Lublin, J., Poiner, G. and Prosser, M. (1989) Not even well begun: women in computing courses, *Higher Education*, 18: 511-27.

Keene, P. (1982) The examination of exposures of Pleistocene sediments in the field: a self-paced exercise, *Journal of Geography in Higher Education*, 6 (2): 109-21.

Keene, P. (1987) *Thematic Trails*, Oxford, Oxford Polytechnic Press.

Keene, P. (1988) Teaching physical geographers to talk, *Journal of Geography in Higher Education*, 12 (2): 85-94.

Keller, F. S. and Sherman, J. C. (1974) *The Keller Plan Handbook: Essays on a Personalised System of Instruction*, Menlo Park, CA, Benjamin.

Kemper, R. V. (1981) Comments on teaching urban anthropology, *Urban Anthropology*, 10: 363-8.

Kent, A. (ed.) (1987) *Computers in Action in the Geography Classroom*, Sheffield, Geographical Assocation.

Kenzer, M. S. (ed.) (1989) *On Becoming a Professional Geographer*, Columbus, OH, Merrill.

Kern, E. L. and Carpenter, J. R. (1986) Effect of field activities on student learning, *Journal of Geological Education*, 34: 180-3.

Kiewra, K. (1985) Learning from a lecture: an investigation of note-taking, review and attendance at a lecture, *Human Learning*, 4: 73-7.

King, C. A. M. and McCullagh, M. J. (1971) A simulation model of a complex recurved spit, *Journal of Geology*, 79: 22-37.

King, R. L. (1976) Assessment in geography: approaches to the formulation of objectives, *Studies in Higher Education*, 1: 223-32.

King, R. L. (1979) More on assessment, *Journal of Geography in Higher Education*, 3 (1): 102-6.

King, R. L. (1981a) How shall they be judged?: notes and sources on assessment, *Journal of Geography in Higher Education*, 5 (1): 61-72.

King, R. L. (1981b) To play or not to play: an introduction to games and simulations in geography teaching, *Journal of Geography in Higher Education*, 5 (2): 111-12.

Kirkby, M. and Naden, P. (1988) The use of simulation models in teaching geomorphology and hydrology, *Journal of Geography in Higher Education*, 12 (1): 31-49.

Kirkby, M. J., Naden, P. S., Burt, T. P. and Butcher, D. P. (1987) *Computer Simulations in Physical Geography*, Chichester, Wiley.

Kirkpatrick, C. (1987) Implementing computer-mediated writing: some early lessons, *Machine-Mediated Learning*, 2 (1-2): 35-45.

Knight, D. B. (1979) Role playing, decision making and perception of place: the use of discussion groups for an introductory cultural geography course, *Journal of Geography in Higher Education*, 3 (1): 38-44.

Knowles, M. S. (1986) *Using Learning Contracts*, San Francisco, CA, Jossey Bass.

Knowles, M. S. and Associates (1984) *Androgyny in Action: Applying Modern Principles to Adult Learning*, San Francisco, CA, Jossey-Bass.

Kogan, M. (ed.) (1989) *Evaluating Higher Education*, London, Kogan Page.

Kolb, D. A. (1976) *Learning Style Inventory: Technical Manual*, Boston, MA, McBer.

Kyriacou, C. and McKelvey, J. (1985) An exploration of individual differences in 'effective' teaching, *Educational Review*, 37: 13-17.

Lambert, S. and Ropiequet, S. (eds) (1983) *CD ROM: The New Papyrus*, Redmond, WA, Microsoft Press.

Laurillard, D. (1978) Evaluation of student learning in CAL, *Computers and Education*, 2, 259-65.

Laurillard, D. (1984) The problems and possibilities of interactive video, in O'Shea, T. and Jones, A. (eds), *New Technology for Distance Education*, vol. 1, Brighton, Harvester Press.

Laurillard, D. (1987) Computers and the emancipation of students – giving control to the learner, *Instructional Science*, 16: 3-18.

Laurillard, D. (1988) Evaluating the contribution of information technology to students' learning, in: Miall, D. S. (ed.), *Evaluating Information Technology in the Arts and Humanities*, Bath, CTISS: 6-12.

Laurillard, D. (ed.) (1989) *Interactive Media: Working Methods and Practical Applications*, Chichester, Ellis Horwood.

Lawton, R. (1986) The role of the external examiner, *Journal of Geography in Higher Education*, 10 (1): 41-51.

Lee, M. P. and Soper, J. B. (1987) Using spreadsheets to teach statistics in geography, *Journal of Geography in Higher Education*, 11 (1): 27-33.

Levin, J. A. (1987) Computers as media for communication: learning and development in a whole earth context, in Forman, G. and Pufall, P. B. (eds), *Constructivism in the Computer Age*, Hillsdale, NJ, Lawrence Erlbaum.

Levine, D. U. (1985) *Improving Student Performance through Mastery Learning Programmes*, San Francisco, CA, Jossey-Bass.

Lewis, L. T. (1979) All-purpose learning games for computer-assisted instruction, *Journal of Geography*, 78: 237-44.

Lewis, P. F. (1969) On field trips in geography, in Association of American Geographers, *Field Training in Geography*, Washington, DC, Association of American Geographers, Technical Paper 1, Commission on College Geography.

Limbard, A. (1982) Development of a multi-experience approach in introductory soil and vegetation geography courses, *Journal of Geography*, 81: 101-5.

Lindblom, C. E. (1959) The science of muddling through, *Public Administration Review*, 19: 79-99.

Lineback, N. G. and Harlin, J. M. (1987) *Physical Geography Lab Manual: A New Experimental Approach*, Dubuque, IA, Kendall Hunt.

Lonergan, N. and Andresen, L. W. (1988) Field-based education: some theoretical considerations, *Higher Education Research and Development*, 7: 63-77.

Lopushinsky, T. and Besaw, L. (1986) Field experiences for non-science students, *Journal of College Science Teaching*, September: 21-4.

Lounsbury, J. F. and Aldrich, F. T. (1979) *Introduction to Geographic Field Methods and Techniques*, Columbus, OH, Merrill.

Lowman, J. (1984) *Mastering the Techniques of Teaching*, San Francisco, CA, Jossey-Bass.

Macdonald-Ross, M. (1973) Behavioural objectives – a critical review, *Instructional Science*, 2: 1-52.

Mackinnon, A. C. (1984) Demonstrating the use of spatial optimising techniques by means of a freight distribution game, *Journal of Geography in Higher Education*, 8 (2): 151-7.

Maguire, D. J. (1989) The Domesday interactive videodisc system in geography teaching, *Journal of Geography in Higher Education*, 13 (1): 55-68.

Maizels, J. K., Hodge, M., Kelly, N., Milton, I. H., Murray, G., Robertson, I. and Smart, D. (1984) A teacher/student commentary on field test of Manning's roughness coefficient, *Journal of Geography in Higher Education*, 8 (2): 137-50.

Malone, T. W. (1981) Towards a theory of intrinsically motivating instruction, *Cognitive Science*, 4: 339-69.

Marble, D. F. and Anderson, B. M. (1972) *LANDUSE: A Computer Program for Laboratory Use in Economic Geography Courses*, Washington, DC, Association of American Geographers, Technical Paper 8, Commission on College Geography.

Marsden, W. E. (1976) *Evaluating the Geography Curriculum*, Edinburgh, Oliver & Boyd.

Mason, J. L. (1980) Annotated bibliography of field trip research, *School Sciences and Mathematics*, 80: 155-66.

Mather, P. M. (1989) Image processing on small computers, *Journal of Geography in Higher Education*, 13 (1): 81-3.

McAleese, R. (1990) Concepts as hypertext nodes: the ability to learn while navigating through hypertext nets, in Jonasson, D. (ed.), *NATO Advanced Workshop on Hypertext*, Berlin, Springer-Verlag.

McCormick, S. and Bratt, P. (1988) Some issues related to the design and development of an interactive video disc, *Computer Education*, 12: 257-60.

McCullach, M. J. and King, C. A. M. (1970) *SPITSYM: FORTRAN program for spit simulation*, Computer Contribution 50, State Geological Survey, Lawrence, KA.

McElroy, B. (1984) Evaluating your geography courses, in Fien, J., Gerber R. and Wilson, P. (eds), *The Geography Teachers Guide to the Classroom*, Melbourne, Macmillan: 294-305.

McKay, I. A. and Parson, H. E. (1986) *The Successful Field Trip*, Dubuque, IA, Kendall Hunt.

McKeachie, W. J. (1986) *Teaching Trips: A Guidebook for the Beginning College Teacher*, Lexington, MA, D. C. Heath, 2nd edn.

McKenzie, G. D., Utgard, R. O. and Lisowski, M. (1986) The importance of field trips: a geological example, *Journal of College Science Teaching*, September: 17-21.

McNee, R. B. (1987) Metropolitan adventure: exploring the hidden city, *Journal of Geography*, 86: 92-9.

Megarry, J. (1988) Hypertext and compact discs – the challenge of multi-media learning, *British Journal of Educational Technology*, 19: 172-83.

Ments, M. van (1989) *The Effective Use of Role-play: A Handbook for Teachers and Trainers*, London, Kogan Page, revised edition.

Micceri, T. (1989) Must computer courseware evaluation be totally subjective?, *British Journal of Educational Technology*, 20: 120-8.

MICROSIFT (1982) *Evaluators' Guide*, Eugene, OR, International Council for Computers in Education.

Midgeley, H. (1985) *Microcomputers in Geography Teaching*, London, Hutchinson.

Mikesell, M. (1978) Tradition and innovation in cultural geography, *Annals of the Association of American Geographers*, 68: 1-16.

Miller, A. H. (1987) *Course Design for University Lecturers*, London, Kogan Page.

Miller, C. M. L. and Parlett, M. (1974) *Up to the Mark*, London, Society for Research into Higher Education.

Milton, O. (1978) Classroom testing, in Milton, O. and Associates, *On College Teaching: A Guide to Contemporary Practices*, San Francisco, CA, Jossey-Bass: 101-24.

Moffatt, I. (1986) Teaching environmental systems modelling using computer simulation, *Journal of Geography in Higher Education*, 10 (1): 53-60.

Monk, J. J. (1971) Preparing tests to measure course objectives, *Journal of Geography*, 70: 157–62.

Monk, J. J. (1978) Women in geographic games, *Journal of Geography*, 77: 190–1.

Monk, J. J. and Alexander, C. S. (1973) Developing skills in a physical geography laboratory, *Journal of Geography*, 72: 18–24.

Moos, R. H. (1979) *Evaluating Educational Environments*, San Francisco, CA, Jossey-Bass.

Morgan, A. (1983) Theoretical aspects of project based learning in higher education, *British Journal of Educational Technology*, 14: 66–78.

Morgan, M. A. (1967) Hardware models in geography, in Chorley, R. J. and Haggett, P. (eds), *Models in Geography*, London, Methuen: 727–74.

Moseley, M. J. (1980) Valuing and evaluating university teaching, *Journal of Geography in Higher Education*, 4 (2): 30–7.

Mullins, C. J. (1980) *The Complete Writing Guide*, Englewood Cliffs, NJ, Prentice-Hall.

Murphy, R. and Torrance, H. (eds), (1987) *Evaluating Education: Issues and Methods*, London, Harper & Row.

Murphy, R. and Torrance, H. (eds), (1988) *The Changing Face of Educational Assessment*, Milton Keynes, Open University Press.

Natoli, S. J. and Bond, A. R. (eds), (1985) *Geography in Internationalising the Undergraduate Curriculum*, Washington, DC, Association of American Geographers, Resource Publication in Geography 1.

Natriello, G. (1984) Teachers' perceptions of the frequency of evaluation and assessments of their effort and effectiveness, *American Educational Research Journal*, 21: 579–95.

Newsom, M. (1978) Rivers – we must catch up, *Teaching Geography*, 2: 72–73.

Nievergelt, J. (1980) A pragmatic introduction to courseware design, *Computer*, 13 (9): 7–21.

Nightingale, P. (1986) *Improving student writing*, Kensington, NSW, Higher Education Research and Development Society of Australia, Green Guide 4.

Nightingale, P. (1991) Speaking of student writing, *Journal of Geography in Higher Education*, 14 (1), in press.

Novak, J. D. (1976) Understanding the learning process and effectiveness of teaching methods in the classroom, laboratory and field, *Science Education*, 60: 493–512.

Nowell, D. E. (1988) Postgraduate studies in North American and British geography: a comparative view, *Journal of Geography in Higher Education*, 12: 95–105.

Open University (1977) *Man and Environment*, Course D204, Unit 2, Approaches to the Study of Man and Environment, Milton Keynes, Open University Press.

Open University (1985) *Changing Britain: Changing Worlds*, Milton Keynes, Open University Press.

O'Riordan, T. (1981) Environmentalism and education, *Journal of Geography in Higher Education*, 5: 3–18

Orrell, K. and Weigand, P. (eds), (1984) *Evaluation and Assessment in Geography*, Sheffield, Geographical Association.

O'Shea, T. (1982) Intelligent systems in education, in Michie, D. (ed.), *Introductory Readings in Expert Systems*, London, Gordon & Breach.

O'Shea, T. and Self, J. (1983) *Learning and Teaching with Computers: Artificial Intelligence in Education*, Brighton, Harvester Press.

Panton, K. and Dilsaver, L. (1989) Americans in Britain: geographic education and foreign field trips, *Journal of Geography in Higher Education*, 13: 45-54.

Papert, S. (1980) *Mindstorms: Children, Computers and Powerful Ideas*, New York, Basic Books.

Parkinson, R. and Reid, I. (1987) A physical model for shallow groundwater studies and the simulation of land drain performance, *Journal of Geography in Higher Education*, 11: 125-32

Parlett, M. (1977) The department as a learning milieu, *Studies in Higher Education*, 2: 173-81.

Pask, G. and Boyd, G. (1989) Conversation theory as a basis for instructional design, in Laurillard, D. (ed.), *Interactive Media*, Chichester, Ellis Horwood: 97-115.

Patton, M. Q. (1990) *Qualitative Evaluation and Research Methods*, London, Sage.

Payne, C. and Fetherston, R. (1983) Fieldwork in the classroom: how to make and use a stream table, *Teaching Geography*, 8: 162-4.

Peacock, D. (1981) A simulation exercise on scientific research for use in undergraduate teaching, *Journal of Geography in Higher Education*, 5: 139-43.

Pearce, T. (1987) Teaching and learning through direct experience, in Bailey P. and Binns, J. A. (eds), *A Case for Geography: A Response to the Secretary of State for Education from Members of the Geographical Association*, Sheffield, Geographical Association: 34-7.

Pearson, K. D. (1987) Teacher evaluation with multiple and variable lines of evidence, *American Journal of Educational Research*, 24: 311-17.

Pepper, D. M. (1980) Thinking again about tutorials, *Journal of Geography in Higher Education*, 4 (2): 92-5.

Pepper, D. M. (1983) Bringing physical and human geographers together: why is it so difficult? in Cannon, T., Forbes M. and Mackie, J. (eds), *Society and Nature*, London, Union of Socialist Geographers: 19-31.

Pepper, D. M. (1985) *Are there natural limits to what human societies can achieve?*, Study Guide, Unit 1, Module 2605, Oxford Polytechnic.

Pepper, D. M. (1987) Physical and human interaction: an educational perspective from British higher education, *Progress in Human Geography*, 11: 379-404.

Phillips, E. M. and Pugh, D. S. (1987) *How to Get a PhD: Managing the Peaks and Troughs of Research*, Milton Keynes, Open University Press.

Polson, M. C. and Richardson, J. J. (eds) (1987) *Foundations of Intelligent Tutoring Systems*, Hillsdale, NJ, Lawrence Erlbaum.

Powell, J. (1985) Geography, culture and liberal education, in Johnston, R. J. (ed.), *The Future of Geography*, London, Methuen, 307-25.

Powell, J. P. (1974) Small group teaching methods in higher education, *Educational Research*, 16: 163-71.

Raper, J. R. and Green, N. P. A. (1989a) *GIST: an object-oriented approach to a GIS tutor*, SERRL Working Report 9, Birkbeck College, University of London.

Rees, P. H. (1987) Teaching computing skills to geography students, *Journal of Geography in Higher Education*, 11: 99-111.

Reeve, D. (1985) Computing in the geography degree: limitations and objectives, *Journal of Geography in Higher Education*, 9: 37-44.

Renouf, J. (1989) An alternative PhD, *Area*, 21: 87-94.

Richmond, B. (1985) *A User's Guide to STELLA*, Lyme, NH, High-Peformance Systems Inc.

Ridgway, J. (1989) Of course ICAI is impossible . . . worse though, it might be seditious, in Laurillard, L. (ed.), *Interactive Media*, Chichester, Ellis Horwood: 28-48.

Riegeluth, C. M., Bunderson, C. V. and Merrill, M. D. (1978) What is the design science of instruction?, *Journal of Instructional Development*, 1 (2): 1-11.

Riley, D. (1989) Learning about systems: by making models, in Lewis, C. H. (ed.), *Proceedings, CAL89: Human Factors in Computing Systems*: 29-36.

Riley, D. (1990) *Design for active learning with Hypercard*, King's College, University of London.

Rivizzigno, V. L. (1980) Overcoming the fear of using the computer and basic statistical methods, *Journal of Geography*, 79: 263-8.

Roberts, N. (1983) *An Introduction to Computer Simulation*, Reading MA, Addison Wesley.

Rogers, C. R. (1969) *Freedom to Learn: A View of What Education Might Become*, Columbus, OH, Merrill.

Romey, B. and Elberty, B. (1980) A person-centred approach to geography, *Journal of Geography in Higher Education*, 4 (1): 61-71.

Rosser, S. V. (1989) Teaching techniques to attract women to science: applications of feminist theories and methodologies, *Women's Studies International Forum*, 12: 363-77.

Rowntree, D. (1974) *Educational Technology in Curriculum Development*, London, Harper & Row.

Rowntree, D. (1981a) *Developing Courses for Students*, London, McGraw-Hill.

Rowntree, D. (1981b) *Teaching through Self Instruction*, London, Kogan Page, 2nd edn.

Ruddick, J. (1978) Interaction in small group work, *Studies in Higher Education*, 3: 37-43.

Rutherford, R. J. D. (1987) Indicators of performance: some practical suggestions, *Assessment and Evaluation in Higher Education*, 12: 67-75.

Salisbury, N. E. (1969) The field seminar in geography, in Association of American Geographers, *Field Training in Geography*, Washington, DC, Association of American Geographers, Technical Paper 1, Commission on College Geography: 41-9.

Salisbury, N. E. (1981) Introductory textbooks in physical geography: an American perspective, *Journal of Geography in Higher Education*, 5: 181-96.

Sauer, C. O. (1956) The education of a geographer, *Annals of the Association of American Geographers*, 46: 287-99.

Sauer, C. O. (1976) The seminar as exploration, *Journal of Geography*, 75: 77-81.

Savage, G. (1964) *The Planning and Equipment of School Science Blocks*, London, John Murray.

Scrimshaw, P. (1983) *Educational Ideologies*, Unit 2, E 204, Purpose and planning in the curriculum, Milton Keynes, Open University Press.

Seamon, D. (1979) Phenomenology, geography and geographical education, *Journal of Geography in Higher Education*, 3 (2): 40-50.

SERC (Science and Engineering Reseach Council) (1982) *Research student and supervisor: a discussion document on good supervisory practice*, Science and Engineering Research Council, Swindon.

Shaw, G. and Wheeler, D. (1985) *Statistical Techniques in Geographical Analysis*, Chichester, Wiley.

Shepherd, I. D. H. (1983) The agony and the ecstasy: reflections on the microcomputer and geography teaching, in Kent, A. (ed.), *Computers in Action in the Geography Classroom*, Sheffield, Geographical Association: 51-64.

Shepherd, I. D. H. (1984) The electronic reading list: handling bibliographic references on a computer, *Journal of Geography in Higher Education*, 8 (2): 159-76.

Shepherd, I. D. H. (1985) Teaching geography with the computer: possibilities and problems, *Journal of Geography in Higher Education*, 9 (1): 3-23.

Shepherd, I. D. H., Walker, D. R. F. and Cooper, Z. (1980) *Computer Assisted Learning in Geography*, London, Council for Educational Technology.

Shotton, M. (1989) *Computer Addiction?: A Study of Computer Dependency*, Basingstoke, Taylor & Francis.

Silk, J. A. (1979a) *Statistical Concepts in Geography*, London, Allen & Unwin.

Silk, J. A. (1979b) The use of classroom experiments and the computer to illustrate statistical concepts, *Journal of Geography in Higher Education*, 3 (1): 13-25.

Silk, J. A. and Bowlby, S. (1981) The use of project work in undergraduate geography teaching, *Journal of Geography in Higher Education*, 5 (2): 155-62.

Silvert, W. (1984) Teaching ecological modelling with electronic spreadsheets, *Collegiate Microcomputer*, 2: 129-33.

Sleeman, D. and Brown, J. S. (eds) (1982) *Intelligent Tutoring Systems*, London, Academic Press.

Smith, D. and Keep, R. (1988) Eternal triangulation: case studies in the evaluation of educational software by classsroom-based teacher groups, *Computers and Education*, 12: 151-156.

Smith, P. R. (1987) Outdoor education and its educational objectives, *Geography*, 72: 209-21.

Snyder, B. R. (1971) *The Hidden Curriculum*, New York, Knopf.

Spencer, D. and Hebden, R. (1982) *Teaching and Learning Geography in Higher Education: An Annotated Bibliography*, Norwich, Geo Books.

Squires, G. (1976) *Breadth and Depth: A Study of Curricula*, London, Nuffield Foundation.

Squires, G. (1987a) The curriculum, in Becher, T. (ed.), *British Higher Education*, London, Allen & Unwin, 155-77.

Squires, G. (1987b) *The Curriculum Beyond School*, London, Hodder & Stoughton.

Stark, R. (1986) Demonstrating sociology: computers in the classroom, in McGee, R. (ed.), *Teaching the Mass Class*, Washington, DC, American Sociological Association: 130-41.

Stein, M. L. (1977) *How to Write Better Compositions, Term Papers and Reports*, New York, Cornerstone Library.

Steinberg, E. R. (1984) *Teaching Computers to Teach*, Hillsdale, NJ, Lawrence Erlbaum.

Stephens, J. D. and Wittick, R. I. (1975) Simulation of urban residential segregation, *Professional Geographer*, 27: 340-6.

Stoddard, R. H (1982) *Field Techniques and Research Methods in Geography*, Dubuque, IA, Kendall Hunt.

Stoddart, D. (1986) *On Geography and its History*, Oxford, Basil Blackwell.

Stonier, T. and Conlin, C. (1985) *The Three Cs: Children, Computers, and Communication*, Chichester, Wiley.

Stratton, N. (undated) *Social sciences CMAs guidance on improving questions*, Paper 12, Student Assessment Research Group, Institute of Educational Technology, Open University.

Sumner, G. (1984a) Video kills the lecturing star: new technologies and the teaching of meteorology, *Journal of Geography in Higher Education*, 8 (2): 115-24.

Sumner, G. (1984b) Lightning never strikes twice!, *Area*, 16: 109-14.

Swinnerton-Dyer, P. (1982) *Report of the Working Party on Postgraduate Education*, London, HMSO, Cmnd 9537.

Tawney, D. (ed.) (1976) *Curriculum Evaluation Today: Trends and Implications*, London, Macmillan.

Thomas, S. M. (1978) Some notes on the status and nature of field method courses at colleges and universities in the United States and Canada, *Professional Geographer*, 30: 407-12.

Thornton, J. W. (ed.) (1972) *The Laboratory: A Place to Investigate*, Washington, DC, Commission on Undergraduate Education in Biological Sciences, American Institute of Biology.

Torrance, H. (1986) What can examinations contribute to school evaluation?, *Educational Review*, 38: 31-43.

Tranter, P. J. (1988) *Enhancing the value of field trips in tertiary education*, Working Paper 1988/2, Department of Geography and Oceanography, Australian Defence Force Academy, Canberra.

Trow, M. (1976) The American academic department as a context for learning, *Studies in Higher Education*, 1: 11-22.

Tuckman, B. W. (1985) *Evaluating Instructional Programs*, Boston, MA, Allyn & Bacon, 2nd edn.

Tyler, R. W., Gagne, R. M. and Scriven, M. (1967) *Perspectives of Curriculum Evaluation*, Chicago, Il, Rand McNally, American Educational Research Association Monograph Series on Curriculum Evaluation.

Unwin, D. J. (1980) Make your practicals open-ended, *Journal of Geography in Higher Education*, 4 (2): 39-42.

Unwin, D. J. (1981) *Introductory Spatial Analysis*, London, Methuen.

Unwin, D. J. (1984) Things I do badly: tutorials, *Journal of Geography in Higher Education*, 8 (2): 189-92.

Unwin, D. J. and Maguire, D. (1989) CTI Centre for Geography at the University of Leicester, *CTISS File*, 8: 22-5.

Unwin, T. (1986) Attitudes towards geographers in the graduate labour market, *Journal of Geography in Higher Education*, 10 (2): 149-57.

Unwin, T. (1990) 2.1 or not 2.1? The assessment of undergraduate essays, *Journal of Geography in Higher Education*, 14 (1): 31-8.

UTMU (University of London Teaching Methods Unit) (1976) *Improving Teaching in Higher Education*, London, UTMU.

Walford, R. (1979) Listening to the learner, *Journal of Geography in Higher Education*, 3 (1): 54-9.

Walford, R. (1981a) *Games and Simulations in Geography Teaching*, Sheffield, Geographical Association.

Walford, R. (1981b) Geography games and simulations: learning through experience, *Journal of Geography in Higher Education*, 5: 113-19.

Walford, R. (1981c) Language, ideologies and geography teaching, in Walford, R. (ed.), *Signposts for Geography Teaching*, London, Longman, 215-22.

Walker, D. R. F. (1988) The interactive video for geography project, *CTISS File*, 7: 64-7.

Walton, R. E. and Balestri, D. (1987) Writing as a design discipline: exploring the relationship between composition and programming, *Machine-Mediated Learning*, 2 (1/2): 47-65.

Ward, C. (1980) *Designing a Scheme of Assessment*, Cheltenham, Stanley Thornes.

Watson, D. (ed.) (1984) *Exploring Geography with Microcomputers*, London, Council for Educational Technology.

Watson, D. (ed.) (1987) *Developing CAL: Computers in the Curriculum*, London, Harper.

Webb, G. (1980) Student participation in tutorials, *Journal of Geography in Higher Education*, 3 (1): 38-44.

Webb, G. (1987) Using spreadsheet software as an aid in the administration of marks and grades, *Programmed Learning and Educational Technology*, 24 (2): 151-5.

Webb, M. and Hassall, D. (1988) Opportunities for computer based modelling and simulation in secondary education, in Lovis, F. and Tagg, E. D. (eds), *Computers in Education*, Amsterdam, Elsevier: 271-7.

Wedekind, J. P. E. (1982) Computer aided model building and CAL, *Computers and Education*, 6: 145-51.

Wehry, E. L. (1970) Open-ended experiments for undergraduate analytical chemistry, *Journal of Chemical Education*, 47: 843-4.

Weimer, M. G. (ed.) (1987) *Teaching Large Classes Well*, San Francisco, CA, Jossey-Bass.

Weizenbaum, J. (1976) *Computer Power and Human Reason*, San Francisco, CA, Freeman.

Wenger, E. (1987) *Artificial Intelligence and Tutoring Systems: Computational and Cognitive Approaches to the Communication of Knowledge*, Hillsdale, NJ, Lawrence Erlbaum.

Weyer, S. A. and Borning, A. H. (1985) A prototype electronic encyclopaedia, *ACM Transactions on Office Information Systems*, 31: 63-88.

Wheeler, J. O. (1985) Creating local field trips: seeing geographical principles through empirical ideas, *Journal of Geography*, 84: 217-19.

White, M. (1988) Developing assessment in years 4 and 5, *Teaching Geography*, 13: 108-13.

Whitelegg, J. (1982) The use of self-produced video material in first-year undergraduate practical classes, *Journal of Geography in Higher Education*, 6: 21-8.

Whiting, J. (1988) New perspectives on open and distance learning for adult audiences, in Harris, D. (ed.), *World Yearbook of Education: Education for the New Technologies*, London, Kogan Page.

Williams, N. and Holt, P. (1989) *Computers and Writing*, Oxford, Basil Blackwell.

Wood, P. (1980) *The undergraduate teaching review, 1978–1980*, Occasional Paper 37, Department of Geography, University College London.

Wood, R. K. and Stephens, K. G. (1978) An educator's guide to videodisc technology, *People's Computers*, 6 (4): 12–13.

Woods, D. (1985) Problem-based learning and problem-solving, in Boud, D. (ed.), *Problem-based Learning for the Professions*, Sydney, Higher Education Research and Development Society of Australia: 19–42.

Wooldridge, S. W. (1945) The Geographer as Scientist, in Wooldridge, S. W. *The Geographer as Scientist*, New York, Greenwood Press, reprinted in 1969.

Wooldridge, S. W. (1955) The status of geography and the role of fieldwork, *Geography*, 40: 73–83.

Woolf, B. and McDonald, D. D. (1984) Building a computer tutor: design issues, *Computer*, 19 (9): 61–73.

Yankelovitch, N., Meyeowirz, N. and Van Dam, A. (1985) Reading and writing the electronic book, *IEEE Computer*, 18 (10): 15–30.

Yorke, D. M. (1981) *Patterns of Teaching*, London, Centre for Educational Technology.

Zollman, D. and Fuller, R. (1982) The puzzle of the Tacoma Narrows Bridge collapse: an interactive videodisc program for physics instruction, *Creative Computing*, 8 (10): 100–9.

Index

Related Titles: List of IBG Special Publications

Also published by Basil Blackwell for the IBG